CW01082733

Other Borders

OTHER BORDERS

History, Mobility and Migration of Rudari *Families between Romania and Italy*

Sabrina Tosi Cambini

Translated by
Angela Whitehouse and Sabrina Tosi Cambini

berghahn
NEW YORK • OXFORD
www.berghahnbooks.com

Published in 2024 by
Berghahn Books
www.berghahnbooks.com

English-language edition
© 2024 Sabrina Tosi Cambini

Italian-language edition
© 2021 Mimesis Edizioni / Eterotopie

Originally published in Italian as
Altri Confini: Storia, mobilità e migrazioni di una rete di famiglie rudari
tra la Romania e l'Italia

Library of Congress Cataloging-in-Publication Data

Names: Tosi Cambini, Sabrina, author, translator. | Whitehouse, Angela,
translator.
Title: Other borders : history, mobility and migration of Rudari families
between Romania and Italy / Sabrina Tosi Cambini ; translated by Angela
Whitehouse and Sabrina Tosi Cambini.
Other titles: Altri confin. English
Description: English-language edition. | New York : Berghahn Books, 2024. |
"Originally published in Italian as Altri Confini: Storia, mobilità e
migrazioni di una rete di famiglie rudari tra la Romania e l'Italia." |
Includes bibliographical references and index.
Identifiers: LCCN 2023021701 (print) | LCCN 2023021702 (ebook) | ISBN
9781805391838 (hardback) | ISBN 9781805391845 (ebook)
Subjects: LCSH: Romanies--Italy--History. | Romanians--Italy--History. |
Ethnology--Romania. | Romania--Emigration and immigration--History. |
Italy--Emigration and immigration--History.
Classification: LCC DX233 .T67 2023 (print) | LCC DX233 (ebook) | DDC
305.891/497045--dc23/eng/20230627
LC record available at https://lccn.loc.gov/2023021701
LC ebook record available at https://lccn.loc.gov/2023021702

British Library Cataloguing in Publication Data
A catalogue record for this book is available from the British Library

ISBN 978-1-80539-183-8 hardback
ISBN 978-1-80539-399-3 epub
ISBN 978-1-80539-184-5 web pdf

https://doi.org/10.3167/ 9781805391838

In memory of Lorenzo, Gelu and Christian

CONTENTS

Figures, Graphs, Maps and Tables

Figures

Graphs

Maps

Tables

ACKNOWLEDGEMENTS

I sincerely thank all the *rudari* families that I met in Florence and in the villages of Romania. My deepest gratitude goes to the Stînga, Anghel and Banciu families. Among them, I offer my heartfelt gratitude to Vasi, my 'Romanian sister', a woman with a great capacity to move between (her) different worlds and to face the events of life with a profound sense of dignity.

My sincere thanks go to the Giovanni Michelucci Foundation for its stimulating and interdisciplinary environment, and the trust that its directors have always placed in my research.

I had the privilege of receiving feedback and encouragement from Bruno Riccio, Stelu Şerban, Pier Giorgio Solinas, Giuseppe Beluschi Fabeni, Nadia Breda, Mosè Carrara Sutour, and my colleagues and friends of the Italian Association of Applied Anthropology (SIAA).

I am in debt to Viorel Achim, Ştefan Dorondel, and Sabina Ispas for their starting suggestions; to Avram Cezar for the bibliographic materials at the 'C.S. Nicolăescu-Plopşor', and to Nicolae Panea and Ovidiu Drăghici of the University of Craiova. I have also benefited from research grants at the University of Verona, under the direction of Leonardo Piasere.

I want to thank Angela Whitehouse, a close friend of Lorenzo and Donato's mother, who generously contributed to the translation of the Italian work; and Caterina Cirri for her skill in creating the maps of the families' mobility.

Special thanks go to Donato, my husband.

This book is dedicated to Lorenzo, a man who championed the struggles of many homeless people and had deep feelings and values, who has left a great human and political void; to Gelu, proud to be *rudar*, who has crossed different worlds; and to Christian, who always teased me about my Romanian, whose kids I have seen born and now growing up.

FOREWORD

This volume is the result of a deep and collaborative multisituated ethnography and deals with the life experiences of a network of *Rudari Lingurari* families which arrived in Italy in the 2000s, from southern Romania. The network of families extended into other European migration countries (Spain, France, Great Britain). Tosi Cambini adopts a gaze that she defines as 'pendular', having followed the events of the family in Italy and in Romania (but also in Bulgaria and in England), their building occupation, local political negotiations, homing and mobility processes. The author also takes into account the complex relationship between the historical dimension and the ethnographic dimension, by intertwining their kinship and mobility histories with the History of Romania.

The existence of a significant number of minority groups in South East European countries other than those listed as national minorities has attracted the attention of social scientists. 'Small is beautiful', says Christian Promitzer in relation to these minority groups, proposing to theorise their collective identity under the umbrella of the concept of 'hidden minorities' (Promitzer 2009). Examples of this kind include Bulgarian speakers in Romania (so-called 'Serbs'), Wallachians in Bulgaria and Serbia, *Rudari* in Bulgaria and *Boyash/Băieși* in Serbia and Croatia, all Romanian-speaking populations (Mladenov 1993; 2007; Sikimić 2005; Sorescu-Marinković 2008), the Aromanians scattered in almost all the countries of South East Europe (Kahl 2002), or the Gagauz, Orthodox Turks and Tatars living in the Western Black Sea from the Republic of Moldova to Bulgaria (Holsapple 2022). Their identity is based on the language spoken, clearly different from the official language of the country in which they live. Religion, too, is an issue that differentiates these populations in the cases of Muslim Pomaks in Bulgaria (Ghodsee 2010) or Roman Catholic Csangos in Romania (Davis 2019).

Among these groups, *Rudarii/Băieșii*[1] occupy a special place for their unusual geographical mobility covering, since the period of the 1900s through successive migration waves, an area that includes eastern and southern Europe, but also managing then to reach regions far from their place of origin, such as the United States and Latin America (Marushiakova and Popov 2021; Salo 2021). The study of *Rudari* started in the second half of the nineteenth century and took a significant interest in the exoticism of their daily lives as well as their striking isolation in a conglomeration of traditional peasant societies, themselves living in relative isolation. The language spoken by them, an archaic Romanian, as well as the specialisation in making wooden handcrafts, which forced them to live an isolated life near the forests, was the subject of exhaustive descriptions from ethnographers and linguists, first Hungarians and Croats, then Romanians (Sorescu-Marinković, Kahl, Sikimić, 2021: 15). The interest of ethnographers and linguists was preserved in the interwar period and even in the socialist period, especially in the countries of the former Yugoslavia, growing exponentially after 1990 (ibid.: 18).

The increase in the number of papers on *Rudari* after 1990 turned the research interest also to the current situation of the *Rudar* population. The exoticism that marked the initial research perspectives became less attractive and raised questions such as their ethnic identity (Benglesdorf 2009) or the contribution of the spoken language to the consolidation of their identity and thus the *Rudari* transformation into a minority that would benefit from government policies in the states where they live (Sorescu-Marinković 2021; Kahl and Nechiti 2019). No less challenging are the works based on anthropological fieldwork, in which processes such as migration, mobility or their involvement in political life or in networks of economic clientelism and patronage are brought into the foreground. Magdalena Slavkova, for example, addresses the migration of *Rudari* from Bulgaria on the basis of long-standing anthropological fieldwork in north eastern Bulgaria, where Tosi Cambini has been with some *Rudari* searching for their relatives (Slavkova 2010). Bulgaria's entry into the European Union in 2007, preceded by a series of pre-accession steps, created multiple opportunities for Bulgarian citizens, including Romanian-speaking *Rudari*, to migrate to countries such as Greece, Italy and Spain. Without being a process necessarily connected to the previous stages of the migration of the *Rudari* (they came from Romania in the first half of the twentieth century and practised nomadism in search of timber resources even after the regulation of their sedentarisation by the Bulgarian socialist regime), the *Rudari* invigorate, in the 2000s, the same traditional patterns of kinship and family relations, household and group subjectivity.

Another topic that highlights the adaptability of *Rudar* populations is that of local political life. Designing a system based on the rules and institutions of liberal democracy in the former socialist countries has placed people in unprecedented situations. The *Rudari*, at least those from Bulgaria, reacted with involvement in a system of political clientele, which at first glance is an undoubted index of deep corruption (Şerban 2007). Still, constructing and making this kind of clientele network function is easy, as the *Rudari* social organisation is based on horizontal family ties. This comes from their traditional spatial mobility and social adaptability, which shaped a very pragmatic value orientation.

The plasticity of the social life of the *Rudari* is even more evident in the social and economic field. In Dragomireşti, a rural settlement in central Romania, the restitution of forests led to the vertical assembly of a clientele system, also empowered by the presence of *Rudari*, through which the forests were logged without permissions. Mainly responsible for this situation, however, was the State, which after 1990 led to deep social dissatisfaction, caused by neoliberal policies reorganising forest funds and restoring property (Dorondel 2008; 2016).

I highlight these issues, which actually occupy a modest place in the bibliography of the works about *Rudari*, precisely because Sabrina Tosi Cambini's book reveals and is based on them. The group of *Rudari* gathered in the early 2000s in the abandoned 'Luzzi' hospital close to Florence, a group with which Tosi Cambini began her field research, is one of the plethora of groups that emigrated from Bulgaria, the countries of the former Yugoslavia and Romania in massive waves of migration to work. And here, as in the home countries, the *Rudari* were placed on the margins of society, trying in a 'mobile' way to gain social and economic integration. Their paths crossed with the housing struggle movements, and with the support of these other groups they occupied a large public property, turning it into a kind of *Rudari* part of a Romanian village, although the occupants included other marginals – migrants from North Africa, Roma from the former Yugoslavia and even a few Italians. *Rudari* also kept in touch with their extended families in Romania, the place where they came from. In fact, in a different way from Romanians, *Rudari*'s migration usually takes place in family groups based on the nuclear family. Finally, they manage the money earned from their (occasional) jobs by investing it in the construction of modest houses and households in their places of origin. Expelled from the Luzzi after 2010, some of them returned to their home in Romania; others were displaced in some houses in Tuscany; others moved to some countries in Western Europe. Significant, at least for the group returning home, is the integration of the experience from Italy into their long history of mobility and adaptability. Tosi Cambini follows these processes by moving her field research to the Romanian villages of the *Rudari* encountered at the Luzzi hospital and highlights the subjectivity and an ethic of the possible future coming from inhabiting a familiar territory (Appadurai 2013), through which they reconstruct long-standing family histories, kinship networks and mobilities.

Stelu Şerban is a sociologist at the Institute for South East European Studies, Bucharest, with an interest in postsocialist transformations in South East Europe, everyday life in rural societies, ethnicity and political ecology. He is the author of *Elites: Parties and Political Spectrum in Interwar Romania*, and of *A New Ecological Order: Development and the Tranformation of Nature in Eastern Europe* (edited with S. Dorondel).

Note

1. For a long time the *Rudarii*/Băieşii were included in the category of Roma population, despite their self-identification as a different population, which does not even speak the Romani language, their mother tongue being an archaic Romanian strongly influenced by the Romanian languages from the areas of origin of different groups of *Rudari*. Recent research based both on the oral history of the *Rudari*, on the linguistic analysis of their spoken language, and on the social history of the regions where they lived for longer durations leads to the conclusion that the main factor which generated the identity of the *Rudari* was the specialisation of the extraction of ores, especially the auriferous ones in the Transylvanian mines. Hence the two main names by which *Rudarii* are known: in the south of Romania, from *ruda* (mine in Slavic); *Băieşi*, in Transylvania, from the *baia* (mine in Romanian in Transylvania). The reformation of mining by the Habsburg government at the end of the eighteenth century excluded the *Rudarii*/Băieşii from among the miners (Calotă 1995; Tosi Cambini in this volume). After this date, they specialised heavily on wood processing, migrating to the geographical areas where access to forest wood was easier. Costescu argues pertinently that the *Rudari* practiced in parallel the extraction of gold and wood processing (2013). They retained the latter occupation until the 1960s, when the laws of the countries in which they lived, mostly socialist countries, banned nomadism.

INTRODUCTION

Liviu is going to England to my uncle's next week, to see how the situation is there; in America there are my first cousins who have made their fortunes. On my dad's side there are 21 first cousins and lots on my mum's side too, that's why we marry among ourselves, because we are so many, so we are all related.

—Mihai, February 2014

This work presents a long-term ethnography of an extensive network of Romanian *rudari* families, who have immigrated prevalently to Italy since the early 2000s.

I started to learn about the world of this composite minority, and particularly of the families whose lives permeate this text, in 2008. From the situation of an urban squat, back to their villages of origin, passing through the stories of migration and places where they lived *here* (in Italy), *there* (in Romania) and spread around the family network (Britain, Spain, Germany, France, Norway), my ethnography has developed with the ageing, growing up and birth – but also, regrettably, the death – of the people I will be describing. It is interwoven with interests that are more specifically linked with these families' cultural intimacy and history as part of History as a whole, sometimes concentrating more on 'home making', the forms of migration, families' composition and recomposition, and sometimes on coping strategies in the face of the enormous difficulties of living in a rich, exclusive, Western European city, Florence.

In addition, interlinked with the various study phases and in the field, my research has on several occasions had a change in application, which marked the first opportunity for development, linked to my work at the Giovanni Michelucci Foundation. I gradually became acquainted with almost all the families that I will be describing, as part of a big occupation of a publicly owned building complex that, until 1998, had been open and providing health-related services, situated on a hillside just outside Florence. The first meetings in this former hospital, at the end of 2008, with some Italian people and families coming from Morocco and Romania, a year and a few months after the start of the occupation, aroused a strong interest on my part, as a researcher and as a person, living at that time on the other side of the hill, but in the same municipality, Sesto Fiorentino.

I had been to see the occupation without any justification, stealthily, just to find out about a situation that I had read of in the press and from people in some Florentine social centres and movements, who had put me in contact with the occupant to whom they referred, Camilla. She had begun a process of linking with the territory of which the former Luzzi hospital, as 'bare' ownership, is still a part. When I went to see her, after explaining to her over a coffee, which she offered me in her occupied house, that I was an anthropologist, she told me enthusiastically, 'At last, someone has come!'

After the following March, an opportunity for fieldwork at the Luzzi appeared. The Tuscan regional government had asked the Michelucci Foundation to look into the case of the occupation as part of the project *Housing frontline: modelli di inclusione abitativa e sociale attraverso processi di autocostruzione e autorecupero*[1] (housing and social inclusion models through self-building and self-recovery processes).

I was responsible for the ethnographic part of this work, in a first, prolonged phase as a researcher and coordinator of a team that was to carry out a series of ethnographic interviews for the purpose of creating a social framework of the inhabitants. On that occasion I designed a database (to which I refer in several parts of the volume), to collect and process information referring to each of the occupying families, who had been given a reference number for identification. In that period, I always went there and my presence covered the whole day, from morning to late evening. By doing this I established my first relationships, which grew deeper and deeper, with many Romanian families and with the Italian inhabitants.

I immediately realised that the Romanians belonged to minorities and I understood that almost all of them were *rudari*. I remember that shortly after I had begun to frequent the former Luzzi, I went to meet Constantin, the person who the Romanian occupants indicated as a sort of 'head' of the occupation. I fully understood this figure only later, in Romania, when I realised that his function could be assimilated to the historical figure, present among the *rudari*, of the *vătaf* (see chapter 1).

In one of our early conversations, at one point I put my intuition to the test and asked Constantin what their mother tongue was. He replied, '*il romeno*' (Romanian). Then I asked him how they were considered in Romania. He looked at me, waited a moment and said to me, '*noi siamo rudari* [we are *rudari*], means, as in your country ... you are Italians, but you are Tuscans'.

Little by little the internal networks became clearer to me, but it took a lot of time and space for someone who does not belong to them before they finally lost the apparently tangled form that the extended and trans-national families possess.[2]

In the summer of 2009, I decided to make my first trip to Romania. I had said to the families of the Luzzi that I would go and see them: 'Really? Will you come to Romania?' they asked me.

When I reached Constanța, I realised that I only had Italian mobile phone numbers ... and they did not work. So, I went to Sibu Mare without knowing exactly where to go: at the time I hadn't thought, I could not have understood then, that it would have been enough to walk into the town and I would surely meet someone in the street who would recognise me. So, somewhat naively, I went to the Town Hall and introduced myself as an Italian researcher and asked if they could accompany me to the families I knew, telling them some surnames. I recall the glances that the employees exchanged with each other, a mixture of incredulity and suspicion.

The first person they took me to see was Constantin's brother. He was a person, to tell the truth, who I had not had much to do with in the previous months during my fieldwork at the former Luzzi and who, in fact, received me rather suspiciously, above all because I was being accompanied by a municipal clerk. It was clear that he was wondering whether I had precise reasons for coming to Sibu Mare.

Fortunately, I managed to get free of the clerk almost immediately and soon after, I found a family that I knew well: as I approached a house along the road, the children recognised me and ran toward me; it was the house of Lucian and Mălina. They welcomed me and offered me something to eat and drink, and went immediately to call their closest relatives who had been with them at the Luzzi and lived in Romania, just a few metres away – Lucian's sister and her husband, Ionica and Virgil. This couple invited me to dinner the following day and Şerban, the oldest son, gave me his Romanian mobile phone number so I could call him. I phoned him the next day, as agreed, and he asked me straight away if I would really come; he seemed very pleased. When I arrived, there to meet me was a 'piece' of their large nuclear family, comprising the parents and their eleven children. The house was the old one, which no longer exists, built by Virgil with his own hands. A *rudărească* house, made of earth and straw, of *adobe*. They had installed the electricity with an improvised system and in this way they could get the fridge, sent from Italy, to work. For the meal there were only fizzy drinks, which I drank out of respect and in exchange for their hospitality without saying that I couldn't manage such quantities. So, the next day, which was Ferragosto, a public holiday, I spent the whole day with a blanket on a beach sunbed at Mamaia, a well-known, bustling tourist resort in the city of Constanţa, and I left the following day.

This dinner proved to be a founding moment, the beginning of a friendship; now it is also a remembrance of Virgil, who has left us.

Of all the Italians – from those for whom they worked, to those who lived in the occupied houses – who, over the years had said that they would go and visit them in Romania, in fact I was the only one who had kept my promise, and the tale of this first visit of mine was told for many years. 'So, Sabrina, you really came?!', almost as though they could hardly believe that I was there, in 2009 at Sibu Mare, because such behaviour toward them was not in line with their expectations of the relationships they had with Italian people. Their amazement was immediately followed by strong appreciation: in the consistency between my words and deeds, they read respect and appreciation, which from that moment have always been reciprocated.

I had thus opened a new field of research: from the urban context of precarious living (occupations, unauthorised settlements etc.) to the mobility and the migratory processes of a large network of *rudari* families, which would be intertwined with the genealogical reconstruction of the cultural 'patterns' and historical events in Romania.

Between Italy and Romania

In the way that I have written the text, I have tried to link in time and space some of the issues that make sense in the families' present lives – lives that often come up against problems of an economic nature and concerning health, with sudden or too swift changes, and with nostalgia and solitude. A fundamental feature that emerged from the start is family bonds, which I have seen over all these years as constantly central to their social organisation, both in Romania and in the migrations. If we just think of the emic explanation of the term *rudari* – 'rudari because we are all related',[3] they told me – we can immediately realise that the path of kinship had to be tackled and followed in order to reach the heart of these groups of families. Part of the work is therefore dedicated to understanding which features make the people in our reference family network feel they are part of a specific *we* – the elaboration of a feeling of union among them, which produces a boundary and which enables a distinction to be made between oneself and the others, a boundary maintained through endogamic marriages.

We are clearly in the minefield of what are defined as processes of 'ethnicisation', deeply pervaded with changes and the result of complex contextual dynamics. The intention, however, as we shall see, is not so much to dwell on questions concerning the *rudari* in general, as to show in practice the intertwining of self-attributions and hetero-attributions, referring to our family groups, in precise space and time contexts.

In Romania the *rudari* are considered *gypsies*, but they do not consider themselves as such, and still less as Roma. Often with migration into Western European countries, in the new contexts they are not recognised as *gypsies* and can therefore introduce themselves as *romeni (Romanians)*, and be seen as such. *Par contre*, the connotation of *gypsies* regains value in the (rare) cases in which they practise begging.[4] Thus, it is fundamental to understand the inner meaning of '*rudari*' in relation to specific groups, the categorisation made by the society in which they are living, the consequences in the contexts of the origin of the discriminations associated with the connotation of *gypsies*, but also how they themselves sometimes 'play' this identity attribution, turning it in their favour. Likened to the Roma minority, both in Romania and in other Balkan countries, they find it difficult to escape this, even for researchers.

Therefore, I will try to reflect on the processes that have led to the establishment of the family groups we refer to as a *we* and how this has been maintained, in reference not so much to the generic category of *rudari*, used by society, by the institutions and by scholars themselves, but to the inner depth of relationships with those specific groups. How this *we* becomes a resource in the migrations in order not to *get lost* as individuals and family nuclei.[5] How this *we* in Romanian villages is translated into relationships with the Roma, and interpreted by the Romanian majority, configuring the relations among these different groups also in terms of space. Which opportunities emerge or are denied as the result of the relationships, there in Romania, and here in Florence, where the word '*rudari*' does not exist, but in which they follow a destiny like that of the migrants who come from similar situations of great socio-economic difficulty. I will speak of the *rudari* as *gypsies* where it makes sense in the specific context, meaning this denomination as the result of a long history that in our case, today, in Romania, we find in the configuration of relations between the various groups of inhabitants of the villages (*rudari*, Roma and 'Romanian Romanians' as 'my' families would call them), in the general perception of the *rudari* as *gypsies* by mainstream society and in their relations with the institutions.[6] I shall speak of them therefore, from a 'gypsiological' perspective (that critically explores the relationship between *gypsies* and *non-gypsies*) and never as Roma.

It is a paradigmatic case that allows us to investigate the meaning of the present in an ethnonym, in the light of the past and in different life contexts. For minority groups, the question of how the majority 'creates' them, 'thinks' of them and the treatment it reserves for them, just as how they themselves 'create' themselves and 'think' of themselves, are fundamental processes for the real lives of the people involved, for whom they open, close or transform real possibilities.

If the local dimension, as Appadurai (2013) also suggests, is revealed as the repertoire of the 'conditions of possibilities' based on which individuals and groups experience themselves and establish their future, we should also ask ourselves about how the two migratory localities – that of the city of immigration and that of the village of emigration (where the experiences of the other migrants also converge) – interact and enter the process of a new thinkability, practicability and therefore mobility of things concerning our own lives, the ones that we consider important and how to fulfil them, between constrictions, imagination and aspirations.

Mobility is embedded in the history of this large network of Romanian *rudari* families, strictly linked to their social and economic organisation, and the rise of the network itself. Furthermore, the socio-spatial morphogenesis of the villages of origin (that I found in the present) is the 'product' of the mobility (by choice, induced or forced) of the families during their history. The volume is divided into two parts: the first ('History and Mobility') delves into the micro-history of this group of *rudari lingurari*,[7] mapping the spatial and geographical mobility of the families – characterised by border-crossing, deportations and forced transfers – since the end of the nineteenth century, and intertwining it with the genealogical space and with their social and economic organisation. All this allows us to understand the present of cultural and relational frames, and mobility (chosen, induced or forced) as the principal ground of the flexibility through which they face economic and social situations, the perception and management of time and space of their life. The second part, 'The Time of Migrations: Home, Mobility and Transnationalism', focuses on the families' mobility today. Adopting a 'moving gaze' that I define as 'pendular', I have explored the migration paths of the families in various countries, their experiences related to the occupations of uninhabited buildings (in Italy), the homing processes (both in Italy and Romania), the movement of objects, ideas and imaginaries, the movement/displacement in time of the sense of presence and being at home, and the meaning of the movement/displacement among the different generations of the families' members. The *rudari* family-cultural intimacy joins the forms of mobility and the marriage patterns, which shape the transnational configurations that life histories reveal, together with the aspirations of people and the transformations faced in their lives and in their multiple life contexts.

The interweaving of micro and macro, the continual intersecting of cultural elements and social configurations, are proposed throughout the text for a prismatic interpretation of the dynamics that intervene in mobility and migratory processes. *What does* migration do to the people we are referring to? To those who leave, and to those who remain? What do they *feel*? How and on what basis do they *transform* their lives?

What I am presenting is a dense, suffering mobility, in which the protagonists find an anchorage in cultural intimacy, which enables them to face the multiple social insecurities, to which, in the present historical context, the majority of the population is increasingly exposed. In this sense their lives also speak of ours, in a reflexive circularity that places them and us in a *common history*.

Methodological Note

The Romanian *rudari* families in my research come from south east Romania, in particular from the Region of Muntenia, *Judeţul* (district of) Călăraşi, and from the Region of Dobruja, *Judeţul* Constanţa. The context is rural; there are several villages,[8] situated on the Lower Danube (*Dunărea de Jos*) and near the artificial canals leading from the great river to the Black Sea, built during the communist regime and the dictatorship of Nicolae Ceauşescu (in the vicinity of the city of Medgidia, approximately 40 km from the city of Constanţa). This territorial provenance is the product of a social and historical process, which I reconstruct throughout the text. It represents the spatial dislocation of relations within the families in the network, linked to the socio-spatial morphogenesis of the villages.

When I explained to the families about the research that I wanted to continue with them, as well as the work done at the former Luzzi, they immediately translated my intention, within their network, as the fact that I would write 'a book on the *rudari*'. This book, then, I promised to Gelu's family, I will dedicate to him, who one evening at their house, during the occupation of the former hospital, said to me, 'You must come and stay with us, so you can learn our language and understand many things'.

From 2009 to 2020 I went through many phases of field research and study, so that my ties with the *rudari* slackened and tightened several times, becoming enriched and more complicated with interpersonal relationships – as a friend and then 'sister', 'niece', 'aunt' – becoming intertwined also with the activities associated with the matter of the former Luzzi and those of the *Movimento di Lotta per la Casa* (Movement for the Fight for Housing) – and above all the flow of life events, daily and extraordinary, joyous and sorrowful, involving them and me.

My research in the Italian context was more prolonged; the thread with Romania has always been kept, with periods in which it was easier to cultivate the ethnographic field in the country of origin.[9]

My acquaintance with these families for many years has given me the opportunity to see over time different kinds of changes in their biographies and in various contexts. Then the fact that I was *acasă în România* (at home in Romania), accompanying different people in the family in time (the eldest daughter and the children, the mother, the eldest daughter and her husband, the eldest son, at the time their house was being built, or alone with the grandmother etc.), enabled me to understand relational balances and social situations involving knowledge and skills that I had to develop, sometimes making mistakes in my behaviour, which were moments rich in ethnographic learning.[10]

The creation of a database in 2009 based on information gathered during the occupation of the former Luzzi between March and July of that year, the subsequent experience of negotiation and the deeper knowledge of my families, enables me to provide a longitudinal summary overview of some spheres of the migratory experience of this network of families.[11]

During the ethnographic fieldwork various interviews were also recorded: in August 2011, five in Romania and two in Bulgaria; sixteen in Florence in the months of January and February 2015; and three in Romania between March and April of the same year.[12]

Linguistic Note

The Romanian dialect spoken by the *rudari* is identified by linguists as 'archaic' Romanian, dating back to the dialects spoken in south west Transylvania in the fourteenth and fifteenth centuries, south east of Crişana and to the north east of the Banato, subsequently influenced by travel and in particular by the Romanian Valacchia dialects (Calotă 1995).

While I was in Oltenia, in 2015, thanks to Nicolae Panea of the University of Craiova, I was able to contact at the same university, Ovidiu Drăghici, a linguist and student of Ion Calotă, who had done plenty of research on the *rudar* dialect (Calotă 1974; 1995; 1996).

Asked to listen to some recorded interviews, Drăghici immediately identified the specific phonetism of this dialect, represented by the phenomenon of palatalisation. This characteristic is very noticeable among the elderly or among young people who have undergone only a short period of schooling. People in Romania who have attended classes up to professional diploma level usually speak Romanian with a less palatalised sonority.

Also from a terminological point of view, while familiar with the dialectal words used by the elders, younger people tend to lose them as they grow up.

Below are some of the terms and expressions of the *rudar* dialect used by the families, with the corresponding Romanian terms next to them and the English translation in brackets:

Anghețată – Înghețată (ice cream)

Bardă – topor (little axe or bill hook). *Bardă* exists also in Romanian but seems not to be used for that type of tool.

Cartoafe – cartofi (potatoes)

Cherpedean – cleste (pliers)

Copáie – albie. *Copaie* literally means 'trough' in Romanian. It indicates a wooden receptacle, bigger than a tub, *albie*, of an elongated shape, used once used both to make bread, and among the *rudari* to cradle a baby.

Ciușcă – ardei iute (chilli pepper, from the Bulgarian *chushka*)

Cuțit de linguri (special knife to carve spoons used by the *rudari lingurari*)

Dadă (used as a mark of respect toward an older person of the female gender, e.g. *Dádă* Rada). In Romanian the term is indicated as a regional word used by peasants.

Fa – ma (used in expressions such as 'fa fata ce faci?', 'what are you doing, my girl?')

Fe (used to address someone very colloquially, like 'Oh')

Halvațele – drojdie (leavening, but *halvațele* is actually the yeast made in *rudari* fashion)

Logodeala – logodnă (engagement)

Nădragi – pantaloni (trousers)

Nána/Nene (used as a mark of respect toward an older person of the male gender, e.g. Nene Radu).

Paar – Pahar (glass)

Pîne – pîine (bread)

Stergár – prosop (towel)

Suite în pat – urcă în pat (climb onto the bed)

Toala/toale – haine/rufe (clothes)

Treapă – rupt/cârpă (rag)

Zar – zahăr (sugar)

Further Information

The Italian edition of the volume was published in 2021 by Mimesis (Milan, Italy); this English original version contains several changes and updates.

The English translation of the text, including citations from the foreign-language sources listed in the bibliography, is by Angela Whitehouse and me.

Pseudonyms are used (or the initials of names) for the *rudari* people involved in the research, and also for the Romanian localities of origin, which in the parts of a more historical character are marked with an asterisk.

The interviews and conversations are transcribed accurately, reproducing any inaccuracies on the part of the interlocutor.

Lastly, the maps in the first part of the text were made with the graphic support of Caterina Cirri.

Notes

1. Experience brought together in Marcetti et al. (2011).
2. We can envisage this process subdivided into three phases: the first, in which I met the families; the second, when I discovered that these are 'tips of the iceberg' of transnational nuclei and networks that are 'tangled' and with no precise limits. Then later, over time, I started to create some order, gradually identifying behavioural patterns that go beyond linguistic classifications and show that the 'family' is built from daily practices (which are a fundamental part of this study). The verbal actions, in the form of conversations, to explain to me for example, who is the brother of whom, which initially confused me, acquire their own meaning in their being discursive practices of a constant building of kinship, and not a mere description. The aforementioned 'tanglement' is a sort of intermediate phase from which – thanks to a prolonged ethnographic experience – patterns emerge, creating interpretative categories of the kinship network.
3. The word *rud/ă* in Romanian means 'relative', and it is from this that my interlocutors derive the term '*rudari*'. In the literature, however, the most commonly accepted interpretation is that it derives from *ruda* (metal), a word of Slav origin. Already in the nineteenth century, in fact, authors associated the *bajeşi* with those who extracted gold in the mines and the *rudari* with the gold prospectors in rivers and streams (Fotino 1859), and therefore the names themselves derive from regional expressions, like the Romanian *baie* (mine) and the Slav *ruda* (metal). Groups of *rudari* have spread through the Balkans, and their names vary according to the different regions: in Muntenia they are called, above all, *rudari*; in Transylvania *bajeşi*; in Oltenia *rudari* and *bajeşi*; in Hungary *beás* e *bojaš*; in Moldova, *lingurari* is more frequently used; in Bulgaria *kopanari* and *rudari*, but then divided into *lingurari* and *ursari*; in Croatia *koritari* and *bajaš*; in Serbia *karavlaši*, but sometimes also *lingurari* and in certain areas *banjaš*. These are almost always names of trades, but the groups outside Romania insist that they are Romanian, to the point that they sometimes called themselves

simply *rumuni* (in Serbia) or *vlaši* or *vlahi*, and in Bosnia they are the *karavlaši*, all expressions that mean 'Romanians'.

4. See Teodorescu (2020).
5. I refer to Italian anthropologist Ernesto de Martino – 'two antithetical terrors inform the age we live in: that of 'losing the world' and that of 'being lost in the world'' (de Martino 2002: 475). This is extremely significant in rendering how the experience of passing from one world to another, and of going beyond the confines of the known world, can be terrifying in terms of sense and meanings. See also chapter 14.
6. 'Historical destiny, that is, if we consider the present, the political situation within a larger social whole, shapes the aspect of such a group. This is as much an identity for others as it is an identity for oneself. For all groups designated with the term "Gypsies" (or any other equivalent appellation), however different from each other, it is in this dimension – a dimension that, just as much as cultural traits and embodied culture, participates in the definition of identity – that the stereotypes and prejudices imposed on them by the societies they have gone through or to which they belong, are introduced. This is how the collective level comes to impose itself on that of the single community and even on that of the individual' (Williams 2011: 9).
7. As highlighted above, considered *gypsies* in Romania and, with different names, in the Balkans but not in Italy and in other migration contexts, I'm going to discuss also their movement between these ethnic borders. *Lingurari* means makers of spoons, from *lingure* in Romanian, spoon, and that in a broader sense indicates, indeed, the makers of tools for the home. The micro-history of the families intersects the great History of the *Cadrilater* between the First and the Second World War, the shifting of the Romanian-Bulgarian borders and the population exchange, the arrival of communism, the abandonment of the *lingurari* craft, the end of the regime, the increase in poverty and the departure.
8. In the text I will frequently use the corresponding Romanian word *sat* (singular).
9. I carried out research in Romania in the following periods: mid-August to early September 2016; 21 July to 12 September 2015; 17 March to 7 April 2015; 14 to 29 August 2014; 10 to 22 August 2012; August 2011; October 2010; 28 October to 14 November 2009; 12 to 25 August 2009.
10. As narrated in chapter 12, dedicated to the house in Romania.
11. When providing quantitative data, the families' identification numbers (ID) to which the information refers will be given. The tables drawn up will therefore provide an overall view of the 2009–2019 decade, above all concerning working and living conditions. The Filemaker programme was used for the preparation of the database.
12. The interviews in 2015 were organised thanks to the opportunity I was given by my participation in that year, as a research fellow, in the *MigRom* project – *The Immigration of Romanian Roma to Western Europe: Causes, Effects, and Future Engagement Strategies*, http://migrom.humanities.manchester.ac.uk/. For the majority of the interviews I was accompanied by Mara Stînga, who transcribed the texts, together with Angela Petre. The translations were done by the latter and me, with Alexandra Anghel's support. The interviews were conducted with people I had known for many years, who agreed to be interviewed precisely due to the relationship of trust that had been built up over time. Mara, Angela and Alexandra's collaboration is also to be understood in this sense.

PART I

History and Mobility

Chapter 1

THE NINE SISTERS

My mother, Maria, is the seventh.
Vana, Iana, Constanda, Floarea, Rada, Pena, Maria,
Paulina, Ghina: nine, nine sisters.
                    —Gheorghe, Sibu Mare*, August 2011[1]

This chapter has two objectives: the first is to take an overall look at the micro-history discussed in the next part, and also to engage with the long period of slavery in Romania that directly concerns the *rudari* and the *lingurari*. The second is to account for the main elements that emerge from the genealogy reconstructed, starting from the 'nine sisters', keeping it anchored to the mobility of families (free, induced or forced mobility depending on the periods). I will therefore focus on the genealogical space connected with the territorial space where, over time, people's lives move in one direction or another.

The second chapter follows a more detailed path, for a prismatic reconstruction of family groups and their socio-spatial configurations that we see today in Romania.

History and Micro-History

I give below an overview of both the spatio-temporal and political coordinates revealing the micro-history and mobility of families and the interpretations inherent to the processes of construction and maintenance of the 'borders' of a given socio-cultural group, that of 'our' network of families.

With respect to the latter, unravelling the tangle of events from the end of the nineteenth century until the time of communism has led to a series of hypotheses, gradually modified and refined. Thanks in particular to the ethnographic knowledge that has deepened over the years, I have developed those possibilities of understanding not only the relationships in the present between the family groups, but also those of the past. The contribution of the people was fundamental, not only, as I have said, for the hospitality and openness shown to me, but also for the genealogical reconstruction of previous generations and the attention with which they welcomed my requests for clarification. I refer, for example, to the fact that they introduced me, as a friend, to Gogu of Vadrea,* a *rudar* who from the end of the 1990s to the middle of the first decade of the 2000s had drawn up many requests on behalf of families to the authorities (we will see, later, how and for what reasons); and they accompanied me to Popina in Bulgaria and introduced me to the older members of the families.

In order not to get lost, therefore, I will now give a picture of the families' micro-history and social organisation.

> The ethnologists often forget to include, in the community way of life that they compose, the historical depth that would allow us to understand that the situations appearing in the present are the result of a particular chain of events, and above all that, being so closely linked to a historical moment, are not eternal. (Williams 2011: 2)

It is a genealogical history and a European history that are intertwined and whose stages I reconstruct from the end of the nineteenth century, with some hypotheses about the arrival in Bulgaria.

In those years, we are in the region of Southern Dobruja, called *Cadrilater* (Quadrilateral), which corresponds to two 'provinces': Durostor and Caliacra. Although, with the collapse of the Ottoman Empire and the 1878 Berlin Peace Congress, Romania acquired Northern Dobruja (and therefore an outlet on the Black Sea), it was with the Peace Treaty of Bucharest in 1913, at the end of the Second Balkan War, that Southern Dobruja became part of Romania. The latter entered the Great War against the Austro-Hungarian Empire in 1916 and, in the same year, with the Battle of Tutrakan, temporarily lost the government of the region. At the end of the First World War, the borders between Romania and Bulgaria were again ratified and with the Treaty of Neuilly-Sur-Seine, Southern Dobruja returned to Romania once and for all. For over twenty years, until 1940, the territory of Durostor and Caliacra was, therefore, Romanian.

In this changing scenario, our *rudari lingurari* moved to southern Romania (Dobruja and southern Muntenia) and, depending on the permeability of the borders at the various historical moments, they may or may not, with more or less difficulty, have crossed the course of the lower Danube or circulated freely in the Dobruja. They usually moved with the arrival of good weather, to sell their wooden artefacts from one country to another, while in winter they lived at the edge of the villages, near or in the woods, near the waterways, where they procured soft wood, from poplar and willow, for the artisanal production of kitchen utensils and spindles.

In 1940 the Russians occupied these territories too, and, with the Craiova Agreement, Romania ceded to Bulgaria the two provinces that form Southern Dobruja, where about 100,000 Romanians, including *rudari* resided.

As is well known, the Treaty allowed the exchange of populations (*schimbul de populație*) between the two parts of Dobruja.[2]

The 'Bulgarians' in the identity placement of our families who define themselves as '*rudari-lingurari-bulgarii*' or '*rudari-bulgarii-lingurari*' arises precisely from the intertwining between the variability of the borders, free or forced mobility and the decision to stop, stay or cross.

Some of the families experienced other dramatic moments during the Second World War: in 1940 the Soviet occupation of Bessarabia left behind civilian deaths and destruction of villages in the border areas and, therefore, also in Dobruja. Some were involved in the deportations, too, which began in July 1942. Romania, entering the war alongside Nazi Germany, also espoused its cruel approaches and, in particular, that of Robert Ritter, with the figure of General Ion Antonescu, who across the Dniester had over 50,000 *Țsigani* deported to Transnistria, at least 36,000 of whom died in extermination camps.[3]

During the two wars, moreover, some of our groups of *rudari* were subjected to forced displacements, while with the start of the communist government and the tightening of its policies, they were subjected, although not all in the same way, to two other processes. The first – for those who had acquired small plots of land thanks to the agrarian reform of the 1940s – was the confiscation of their property for collectivisation. The second was progressive sedentarisation, with 'enlistment' in the CAP (*Cooperative Agricole de producție*) and simultaneous intensification of checks in relation to their profession of *lingurari*.

We find them, therefore, at the end of all these movements, free, induced or forced, and also in 1989, the year of the Romanian revolution, settled in some villages of the district (*Județul*) of Călărași in Muntenia and the district of Constanța in Dobruja.

The *Rudari* as a Minority Formed of Networks of Families with an Endogamic Tendency

Regarding the 'Classifications'

It is useful – for those aspects inherent to our discussion – to look at how *rudari* and *lingurari* are included in the classifications of *robi* (slaves) according to various summaries.[4]

The *slaves-gypsies* synonymy, in fact, gave rise to a sort of overlap between the classification according to the tasks/trades during slavery and the ethnic or cultural belonging of the *gypsy* groups; the subsequent translation made, then, from the synonym *slaves-gypsies* to that of *slaves-roma* certainly emphasised the problems that this overlap had generated in 'fixing' the *gypsies* in certain categories and placing them all under the *Roma* 'umbrella'.

Mihail Kogălniceanu in his *Esquisse* of 1837 (1976), following the discussion of the Civil Code of Moldova (*Regolamentul Organic*)[5] concerning slaves, inserts the *rudari* and the *lingurari* among the four classes of the '*Cigains de la couronne*' (of the prince or, also, of the State). *Rudari* and *aurari*, which he matches together, represent one: they are 'the only ones who have the right to seek gold in the rivers and in the sand of the mountains', recording that 'today their profession is no longer so lucrative' (ibid.: 362–63). The *lingurari* constitute another separate trade: manufacturers of wooden spoons and pots, but also charcoal burners, they pay an annual tax to the government of between 20 and 30 piastres (equivalent to 7–10 francs), like the *ursari*.[6] According to Kogălniceanu the *lingurari* 'are the most civilised of the four classes; and they begin to build fixed dwellings' (ibid.). Following the description of *lâessi* – 'people without a confession and without any fixed profession' (ibid.) – the author states that none of the four classes of *cigains* has a fixed abode:

> in the summer they camp in tents, in the winter they settle in huts underground [*bordeie*], which they dig in the forests, always however in the vicinity of some village, to obtain work or have the possibility of putting into practice their propensity for theft. (ibid.: 363)

With respect to the organisation of the four classes, it is said that there were the *sălaşe*, that is, groups of 10–15 families 'under the jurisdiction of a man they themselves choose', whose power, however, changed between the groups. In our reference groups, the *vătaf* seems to have had a negotiating role with the government, mainly regarding the taxes due, and no function comparable to that of a real internal 'judge' (of whom there is no trace either in the present time of my interlocutors or in their narratives). Respected and usually richer than the others, a *vătaf* could be a hasty solver of an internal conflict, sometimes a 'good counsellor' – as defined by a *rudar* in Stahl's research (1991: 65).[7]

The other slaves belong to monasteries or boyars and are divided into *lâessi* and *vâtrassi* [*vătrasi*].

Popp Serboianu (1930), referring to the same Code of Moldova, recalls article 67 on the per capita tax of the *gypsies* of the State, established as 50 lei for the *aurari* and as 30 lei for all the other *gypsies* without distinction, while article 95 regulates the statistics that had to be recorded every seven years of the families of *gypsies* of the State, and establishes that the *aurari* can carry out their job only through a specific authorisation from the government. Starting from art. 117, also

> the Gypsies of the State were divided into 'Vatrachii' (tribes) [... who] collected the taxes of the Gypsies and paid the tax to the 'Vornicie' every quarter. The 'vataf' received a leu for each Gypsy, per year, and while he had this function, he did not pay any kind of tax. (1930: 50)

With regard to the period of the *Regolamento* (1830s), Popp Serboianu proposed that the *gypsies* should be divided into three classes: the first, the *laïechi* (*lâessi*) 'forming corporations, according to their different conditions: gold prospectors, *Ursari* (bear trainers), manufacturers of wooden spoons, charcoal burners, tinsmiths' (ibid.). The gold prospectors and the *ursari* belonged solely to the State, to which they paid an annual tax. The second class consisted of *vatrachi*, domestic servants; the third class, of *netotsi*, were considered by the author to be semi-wild. Therefore, according to this classification, as far as we are concerned, the *rudari* and the *aurari* do not appear to overlap, and the woodworkers could also be owned by someone other than the prince, an aspect that was also confirmed by Chelcea (1943) and others later. In any case, we know that the prince could donate his slaves to monasteries and boyars and among these there could also be *rudari* and *lingurari*, which brings us back to the question of categorisation and the risks of overlapping between trades, living conditions and groups of families.

C. Şerban, in an article in 1959, analyses the case of *ţigani rudari* gold seekers (in line with Kogălniceanu's overlap between *rudari* and *aurari*) at the Monastery of Cozia, in Oltenia (in line with what Popp Serboianu tells us about the groups owned by the prince/State), whose presence is documented in the archives from the beginning of the seventeenth century to the end of the eighteenth. The author tells us that these

> rudari were constituted in *sălaşe* and divided into *vătăşii*. In each *vătăşie* the gypsies were grouped by families and close relatives. For example, next to the man is his wife, their married children, as well as the man's brothers all married. (1959: 133)

This organisation is traceable among our *rudari*, in the present with the practice of virilocality and in the relatively recent past with the existence of the *vătaf*. The *gypsies* worked to collect gold only for part of the year, with favourable weather, from spring to autumn. During the winter, due to the cold and the frozen rivers, they were forced to interrupt their activity and, therefore, 'found employment on other properties, in other words, "they have stopped to winter" as declared in an 18th century document' (ibid.: 138). From a legal point of view, taking up the *Travels of Macarius, Patriarch of Antioch 1853–1858* by Cioranu (1950), Şerban tells us that before becoming slaves of the monastery, thus becoming *mănăstireşti*, the *rudari gypsies* had been both slaves of the prince (*domneşti*) and domestic servant *gypsies* (*ţigani din vatră*) (ibid.: 141). Over time they tried to improve their condition, fighting against feudal oppression: they refused to pay the tax at the Monastery of Cozia, they fled from its lands and hid with the *rudari* in *baltă*,[8] and with the prince's *rudari gypsies*, 'who among all the categories of *gypsies* seemed to enjoy the best of conditions' (ibid.). In this sense, the author cites various examples from archival sources in the seventeenth and eighteenth centuries. During the Austrian presence in Oltenia (1718–1739), many *rudari* fled to Muntenia, as in the period of the Russo-Turkish War in 1769–1774. In addition to fleeing, they made continuous complaints before the court, asking to leave the jurisdiction of the monastery and toward the end of the eighteenth century became the property of the prince.

Popp Serboianu, who published in 1930, presents us with a classification of *gypsies* 'updated' to that time, divided between *laïechi* and *vatrachi*. The former would include a number of corporations starting from the trade they practised, including the 'Rudari or Blidari or Lingurari, they manufacture drinking troughs, pitchforks for the fields, spools and spindles, wooden plates, knives, brooms' and 'have meagre shelters in the mountains. They are honest, they keep their word, and they are very humble in their attitude' (ibid.: 54). This is an example of a sharp division – between nomads and permanent residents, and between occupational groups – whose schematism has long remained like a sort of background in the approach to *gypsies* in Romania, since it was difficult during the communist regime to carry out research on minorities. A possible fluid reading of groups and transformations, more exquisitely emic, on the one hand, and more connected to wide-ranging processes, on the other, began to be part of the research work on the *rudari* from the second half of the 2000s.

'Rudari Lingurari' and 'Rudari Bulgarii'

A careful reconstruction of cases during slavery, such as Şerban's research, can reveal, through archival materials, the flexibility of these groups of *rudari* in relating to their trades, to the opportunities that could be opened, and to negotiating their labour. As well as the changes in the names of the same group of families, linked to the type of property rather than to their profession, it also tells us something about the smaller social unit formed by the extended virilocal family, which we find today, and where – for at least sixty years – the segments of the new family nuclei, after a period of virilocality, practise neolocality, going to live on their own.[9] This is an aspect that – after the end of communism and the beginning of migration – becomes particularly important, touching a central node represented by the house and its construction.

This possibility of grasping the character of fluidity in the history of these groups makes it possible to disengage the ethnographic work, which takes place in a certain situation in the present, from the pitfalls of categorisations and bring out how they think of themselves not only as being *Rudari*, but above all as specific groups of *rudari* families.

There is still little field research on the *rudari* in Romania, although there has certainly been a renewed interest since 2000.[10] Multiple aspects have been analysed: the presence or absence of rituals (Neagota and Benga 2016); issues related to migration and housing (Teodorescu 2020); the possible recognition of *rudari* contribution to the Romanian 'intangible cultural heritage' (Sorescu-Marinković 2018); ethnicity from a critical point of view in relation to political practices in a territory (Şerban 2007; Alexa-Morcov 2013); and as a case study on access to natural resources and land restitution (Dorondel 2007; 2008). Usually, the groups of *rudari* living in certain localities, on which the studies focus, are introduced through a general look at the elements of the debate that have been established (the so-called *wood itinerancy*) or are still under discussion (aspects of social organisation and the age-old question of origin). Bengelstorf (2009), whose current research probably represents the most organised ethnographic survey (at least among the published works I know), gives an account of the positions in literature with respect to 'ethnic' belonging, and notes, albeit briefly, some reciprocal relational 'postures' between groups of *rudari* in his village and those of other villages that have different 'traditional' trades.

With regard, therefore, to the current studies on/with the *rudari*, my research work aims to contribute to this knowledge, also investigating the processes that led to the establishment of a network of families in a certain context – the one where the researcher finds them in the present in Romania – the formation of the family network itself and the practices that contribute to maintaining it as a unit, since this 'maintenance action' continues to make sense in the present, both in Romanian life contexts and in those of the migrations.

In the course of the ethnography among the *rudari* to whom I refer, from the outset, in the context of immigration, the importance of family ties and their configuration has proved to be one of the main keys to understanding the unfolding of people's lives; the attention of the research, therefore, in certain periods, has been focused on the reconstruction of the 'micro' dimension of this network, that is, of the networks of kinship (if we can indicate with 'micro' that represented by the relationships of the family nucleus, and the 'macro' one related to the social categories and to the structural aspects of the territories in which they live). In dealing with genealogical reconstruction, there had also been precise underlying stresses, emerging from the statements of my *rudari*, real nodes that asked me: why 'Bulgarians'? Why the strong reference to the 'nine sisters' from whom everyone apparently descends? Why do they say 'we got a little mixed up'? And then, again, because if those belonging to the maternal line and to the paternal one are considered relatives in the same way and virilocality prevails, Ionica says of her husband Virgil's relatives 'are they Virgil's relatives and not mine'? And finally, the statement 'we marry between cousins' and the definition of themselves as *rudari* since 'we are all relatives', of which marriage practices were they the translation?

The rebuilt family network, although complete only in some segments, from the end of the nineteenth century to today, sees five generational levels, in addition to the oldest – which I have called level 0 – of which we have, at least for now, little data, because of family memories that have been lost long ago. The horizontal line of the 'nine sisters' (level 1) covers a long period, of which we know the date of birth of the first (1904) and the sixth (1925), separated by twenty years, but this is not surprising since the age of the mother at the birth of the first child could also be very low (15/16 years) and that in the middle, in that timeline, there was also the First World War. There are, throughout the genealogy, other cases of very large families, also due to the conversion to Pentecostalism of some of them (to give just one of the possible examples: Vasile has ten children and there are 27 years between the first and the last).

What follows is the synthesis of the reconstruction – of which we will see more details in the next chapter – with respect to the social organisation of our families, based on a system of bilateral kinship, which follows the use of virilocality and preserves its borders through the endogamic tendency. As Williams states, endogamy is not to be considered a rule but a tendency and 'it is not the group that contains a tendency to endogamy, but it is the tendency to endogamy that founds the group' (1984: 339).[11] And this is what happens for our network of families, the result of a micro-history of *rudari lingurari* families, which find themselves, at a precise moment, putting in place an exogamous strategy, becoming 'allies' with another group of *rudari* non *lingurari*, the so-called *rudari* – taking up the emic terminology, known as – 'Bulgarians'. An exogamy that concerns different groups of the larger set of *Rudari*.[12]

History is also responsible: with the changes of boundaries, the endogamic tendency 'solidifies' the *rudari lingurari–rudari bulgarii* network of families, maintaining its boundaries, and this is how we see it today, spatially located in the Romanian villages that are part of my research. Endogamic tendency – exogamous need – endogamic tendency reinforced by the fact that family branches remain divided between the two parts of the Danube, due to the complex events linked to the Treaty of Craiova.

For clarity I show these steps visually in figure 1.1.

The end of the 1800s certainly presented some shadows; what could be understood about this period from the sources that we are sure are reliable? First of all, the *rudari lingurari*, to whom the 'nine sisters' belong, once past the Danube, came into contact with other *rudari* who had already lived in the Silistra area for at least two decades – those 'Bulgarian *rudari*', of whom our *rudari* tell us today.

Our interlocutors from both Vadrea* and Sibu Mare* and Badra*, in rebuilding with me level 0 of the genealogy (the generation before the nine sisters), the first (that of the nine sisters) and the second (children of the nine sisters), indicate with the term ' *rudar* ' or 'Romanian' those belonging to the *rudari lingurari*, for whom – and this is very important – they use the first person plural; while they indicate with '*bulgar*' those who come from families of the '*rudari bulgarii*' (those with whom they have, in fact, 'mixed'). These belonged to other *rudari groups* and were not *lingurari*; they were wood workers but were in the service of *boieri*

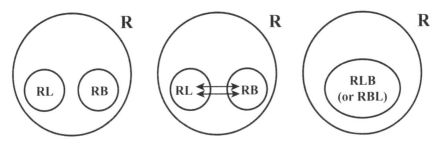

R = Rudari
RL = Rudari Lingurari
RB = Rudari Bulgari
RLB = Rudari Lingurari Bulgari (or RBL = Rudari Bulgari Lingurari)

Figure 1.1. Network of families' formation process. © Sabrina Tosi Cambini.

(to be understood with a broader meaning than the original one: that is as owners of rural land and real estate), and had a *vătaf* (named Ilie) as a reference person, who was in charge of economic agreements with the 'owners'. The *rudari lingurari*, on the other hand, moved around to sell their products, stopping in individual countries until they finished their goods, changed *baltă* (swamp, wetland) or *pădure* (forest) according to the conditions they managed to negotiate with the *pădurar* (guardian of the forest). It would seem that they did not have a *vătaf* to refer to (at least in that period) and could move away or stay as a single family nucleus. Gheorghina (future mother of the nine sisters), 'Romanian' or belonging to the *rudari lingurari*, contracted an exogamous marriage (i.e. outside the *lingurari*) families, with a '*bulgar*' (*rudar bulgar*). We know from the stories that Gheorghina and her husband did not stay in the service of the *boieri*, but moved to the southern part of the Danube, producing and selling *linguri*. This could indicate that the exogamous marriage contracted by Gheorghina had been 'reabsorbed' by the group, not fulfilling the practice of virilocality (it is no coincidence that Gheorghina's husband is not even mentioned in the stories, except to say that he was '*bulgar*'). This is similar to what happened in the marriage, some decades later, between Ionica and Viorel, the latter belonging to other *rudari* family groups – coming from Ciucurova and of Moldovan origin ('Dad was Moldovan', their children told me several times at various intervals). In this case, too, virilocality has not been respected and Viorel's family disappears from their discourse as from their kinship[13] – just as Viorel's cousins, whom I met in Vadrea,* are not considered relatives (they are not their 'own' cousins but their father's).

If in Gheorghina's marriage, exogamy is compensated by the absence of virilocality, the exogamous need arises more clearly, however, with Gheorghina's direct descendants (level 1 of the genealogy), who are only female: the 'nine sisters'. Some of them, in fact, would marry, in turn, 'Bulgarian *rudari*' (related to each other), starting in fact to compromise the endogamous seal of those branches of *lingurari*, and who, with those unions, began to be brought into the families of the other family networks, those of the 'Bulgarians' precisely, and with the concomitant and equally progressive loss of the itinerant craft of *lingurari*. On the other hand, a linear process of this type did not take place, but we observe the formation of a group, a network of families – some more mobile, linked to the trade of *lingurari*, others more 'stationary', mainly in service – who would re-establish the endogamous tendency, maintaining it over time until today.

At level 1 of the genealogy, as proof of exogamy, we have multiple marriages: the 'exchange' of two sisters of the nine *rudari lingurari* sisters, married to two Bulgarian *rudari* brothers (double marriage, see figure 1.2, level 1)

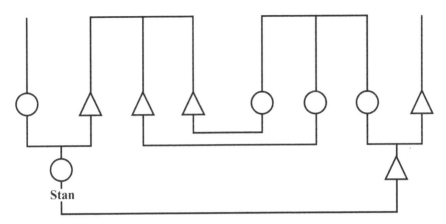

Figure 1.2. Level 1: marriage of a group of brothers with a group of sisters; level 2: marriage between 'cousins of cousins'. © Sabrina Tosi Cambini.

In figure 1.2, always in the wake of the exogamy, a further marriage was also added. It belonged to level 2 of the genealogy, defined by Solinas as marriage between 'cousins of cousins' (1998).[14] This type of marriage, which is part of the area of affinal relinkages or *rechainement d'alliance*[15] allows, as Solinas indicates (1998), marriage to the first available non-relative. Although only some of the marriages have been observed at this genealogical level, this strategy does not seem quantitatively significant, but it is important for our reasoning, as a record of passages of marriage practices. In the figure I have specifically inserted the name of Stan because it links us to the following levels of the genealogy:[16] my goal, in fact, is to make the endogamy-exogamy-endogamy passages visible, showing their traces throughout the genealogy. We go, therefore, from an endogamy (that of the respective groups of *rudari*) to a 'zone' of turbulence (with the exogamic strategy), which is also traced on the second generational level, but which fades in the next generation, with a very clear endogamous tendency in the fourth generation, in which marriage between third cousins is the most practised (figure 1.3).

Following marriage strategies and settlement-economic strategies, we see that, among the 'nine sisters', those whose husbands' 'Bulgarian' origin we know with certainty tend to remain in a much more limited territorial area, which belongs to Silistra.

Those sisters, on the other hand, of whom we know with certainty that they married a *rudar lingurar*, with the annexation of southern Dobruja, moved beyond and along the Danube (in the area of Silistra, in Muntenia in the area of Călăraşi and in northern Dobruja in the area of Tulcea). We also find some traces of their movements 'that can be fixed' through dates of birth (see map 2.3 below).

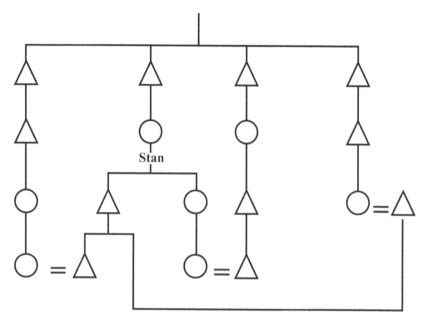

Figure 1.3. Marriages between third cousins (generational level 4). © Sabrina Tosi Cambini.

It is in those decades, therefore, that the 'mixing' of which my interlocutors speak took place: that is, mixing between branches of families of '*rudari lingurari*' and those of '*rudari bulgarii*'. In this moment of 'genealogical turbulence' there is also a corresponding double settlement tendency, between mobility and a sedentary lifestyle (one part of the families is more mobile, the other more stable), which corresponds to their profession. Two contemporary trends, therefore, one of which is characterised by unions between *lingurari* (who maintain mobility), and the other, by unions between *lingurari* and Bulgarians; through these tendencies, families are 'linked' to each other by the 'nine sisters', recognised in fact as common 'forebears'.

With the Treaty of Craiova in 1940 and, above all, with the consequent *schimbul de populație* (population exchange) the sisters' family nuclei, except certainly that of Rada (the fifth), the *rudari lingurari* relatives and some of the Bulgarian *rudari* relatives passed into Romania, but crossing the new borders in different ways and leaving relatives beyond the new borders, in Bulgaria especially in the area of Silistra, which – from this period onwards – on our maps is represented by the locality of Popina.[17]

Several family nuclei from the Silistra area were forcibly displaced (*strămutat*) and taken to several villages, then from there moved again. Other families were induced to pass through Romania to settle in some of the villages where other families were forcibly taken; these villages were more suitable for woodworking (we will see this in detail in the next chapter, see map 2.3). Those more mobile families – who at the time of the establishment of the border were already moving between Southern Dobruja and Northern Dobruja – went to, or in fact, remained in Romania (leaving relatives across the border).

In Romania, between the two wars, where possible, the families in the network tried to move closer to each other, to maintain also a spatial proximity. In Sibust,* Badra,* in Mânăstirea and descending from Brâila in the Ostrov area, places near which we find forests and water, there are parts of the family nuclei. Some are moved by the authorities several times: this is the case of the families who were taken to Marsilieni, now in the municipality of Albești. The movements continued immediately after the end of the war (free and forced) and were resumed in the 1950s (again, free and forced) to find places for the 'coagulation' of family groups: Pelinu, Pelicanu and later Vadrea.* Throughout level 2 of the genealogy we record marriages and births in the area of Ostrov, Pelinu and Pelicanu.

Level 3 of the genealogy also covers a temporal space that reflects the distance between the births of brothers of the previous horizontal lines (therefore, in this case, the distance between the nine sisters, that between births of their children and their children's children). On this horizontal line we find, therefore, people of whom we have certain data on their birth (the descendants, in fact, of the nine sisters and relatives of their *lingurari* and Bulgarian) husbands ranging from the 1950s to 1996 (year of birth of the granddaughter – daughter of the son – of the last sister Ghina, who is ten years younger than her older brother). Marriage unions at this level allow us to see the endogamic tendency connected to the spatial configurations of our groups of families – the result of all the previous movements and those of the 1960s under Ceaușescu – taking place between members of the family network who live in the villages of Sibu Mare,* Vadrea,* Badra*/Sibust* and Burdu.*

The next level, level 4, which involves members of the genealogy directly or indirectly involved in migration processes, shows us that endogamous marriages, mainly through unions between third-degree cousins (figure 1.3), are maintained both in Romania and in the emigrations.

Notes

1. Pseudonyms are used for the Romanian localities of origin, which in the case of a more historical character are marked with an asterisk.
2. See Basciani (2001; 2009). To date, the question of the properties of the families involved in this exchange has not been resolved: there is, in fact, a section of the Archive at the Romanian government containing the files of the families who were,

at the time, registered in the exchange, with procedures for the recognition of compensation still pending.

3. On the deportation see Achim (2004a; 2007); Achim and Iordachi (2004).

4. The intention is not to review the classifications, but to start from the problem that derives from the overlaps between occupational, ethnic/cultural groups and specific groups or family groups. I will cite, therefore, only some authors who allow us to contextualise the theme. For an in-depth study on slavery, see Piasere (2005), the monographic issue of *Études Tsiganes*; *L'esclavage des Rroms*, 29, 2007 and Petcuṭ (2015). This is useful, for the purposes of our discussion, to broaden our outlook on these situations by building a fluid panorama in which to place our *rudari*.

5. See Achim (2004b).

6. With respect to the condition of slavery and the *gypsies* a notable exception 'was the separate nomadic groups patronised by the prince. The letters of safe passage, passports, and safe conducts they carried with them allowed them to move about freely and independently. As late as 1802, a charter (*hrisov*) established by a prince with the *vătaf*, or court judge for Gypsy cases, stated that the very numerous ("from time immemorial") *Lingurari* and *Ursari* were fiscally useful to the Crown and that their privileges were to be respected … For the nomadic groups alone, collective interior mobility was normal and accepted by all those in power' (Asséo et al. 2017: 29).

7. Chelcea (1943) attributes to the figure of the *vătaf* greater authority in internal conflicts, than it has been possible to detect among our *rudari*. In any case, nothing comparable to the internal conflict resolution procedure called *kris* ('court', 'council', 'assembly') – present among Roma groups – in which the *krisnitoria* (and variations of the term) embody the community and guarantee its rules; in this regard, see the essays contained in the *American Journal of Comparative Law*, 1997, 45, 2, 'Symposium on Gypsy Law'.

8. Swampy area in the woods (wetland), where they lived part of the year when they practised the craft of *lingurari*.

9. We cannot say, in reality, if and how the 'detachment' of the family segments took place even in the time of slavery; it was certainly more difficult if the groups were slaves of a monastery or a boyard, but among the *Rudari* and the *Lingurari* who could circulate freely, as they were owned by the prince, we cannot rule out the possibility that the units could be detached and recomposed according to the goals and routes they chose to follow. On the other hand, the narratives of our *rudari* at the time of their mobility tell us of a type of flexible organisation, also mobile, which we could define as being like an 'accordion', in which families became closer and then spread, and then were closer again.

10. The current main field studies in Romania that go beyond or criticise the issue of the 'origin' of the *Rudari* are cited, adding Şerban 2007 and Dorondel 2007 since their reference territory is the Quadrilateral. On the question of the ethnic 'self-identification' and 'hetero-identification', the doctoral thesis of Costescu 2015 should also be noted. As regards the studies on the *Rudari* in other Balkan countries, see in particular those by Slavkova on the migration of the Bulgarian *Rudari* in Western Europe (including 2017; 2010a; 2010b) and the recent one by Kahl and Nechiti (2019), on two groups of *Boyash* in Hungary, especially from a linguistic point of view.

11. It will be noted that I often prefer to use the term 'network of families' rather than 'group' because in my opinion, conceptually it better evokes, for our *rudari*, the 'branching and spatialisation' of kinship relations, both in the mobility of the past, when they travelled from village to village or from forest to forest, and in the present time with the migrations.

12. Stahl reports, as an explanation provided by the *rudari* themselves with respect to endogamous marriage, the statement '*nu se corceşte*' or 'we do not want to be bastardised' – the author specifying that the verb used has a pejorative meaning and is used, above all, for animals (1991: 64). The reference is to *Gypsies* of the village: 'everyone seeks his race [*rasa lui*]' (ibid.). Ionica also told me that the *Gypsies* 'are another race'. If there is the recognition of *rudari* belonging to a wider community, that of the *Rudari*, where specific groups of *rudari* are interacting, a perception of the differences between them also emerges, as noted – although *en passant* – Bengelstorf (2009), and as I noted at present in Sibu Mare*; differences that can be connected to different trades and relationships with the territory, but above all to the fact of conceiving themselves as part of different groups of families or different family networks.

13. Kinship is continually built and rebuilt through daily discourse. It's a daily job of weaving.

14. See also Piasere (2015: 95–98).

15. These expressions denote marriage between members of two groups of blood relatives, previously linked by another marriage, but which do not have direct links of consanguinity or affinity between them.

16. We know that the groups can also resort to this strategy in order not to incur prohibitions on the part of ecclesiastical authorities. In practice, it is a matter of 'circumventing' the so-called negative impediments of the Church, including the so-called blood or acquired kinship (blood relatives and the like). This may have also been true for the families in our network. Beyond the Romanian law of 1948 that establishes its control by the State, and apart from the persecution of the clergy, the Orthodox Church does not disappear from the lives of Romanians, with all the differences from context to context. Just as it does not disappear from the life of many families of our *rudari*, who in celebrating the *nuntă* (marriage), when this happens, in the past as now (if they are not Pentecostals) also envisage the performance of the Orthodox rite in the village church. We can hypothesise that this factor has also contributed to the maintenance of an exogamous strategy such as this. The dates of birth we know for certain, for the second genealogical level range from 1924 to 1960. Stan was born about halfway through this time, in 1944; his wife was born in 1949 and she told me that her parents had baptised her at nine years old: 'we were all Orthodox', she told me, now that her family is Pentecostal. The years of that marriage, moreover, are those of sedentarisation (mid-1960s) and, therefore, of the obligation to formalise unions by law, within a group for which the first sexual relationship between a man and a woman corresponds to marriage (both Chelchea in his research and later Stahl record a considerable number of 'concubinages', as I myself have done in the present). The forms of marriage and the changes that have taken place are discussed see below.

17. It is the only place for which I have certain data after 1940 and which I visited during the search, thanks to the 'expedition' organised *ad hoc* with the members of two *rudari* families to find their relatives' house (that of the first cousin with her husband).

Chapter 2

GENEALOGICAL, HISTORICAL, GEOGRAPHICAL SPACE

'Yes, we are *rudari*, do you know why? Because we marry among cousins.'

'Keep quiet!' her friend tugs her.

Lidia's sister laughs. 'Don't worry', she says, 'she is Sabrina, she understands. Don't you, Sabrina?'

'Yes, of course. I do understand.'

The friend stops. She looks at the two women as though they were talking rubbish.

'Come here, stupid', Lidia says to her in Italian and then adds, turning toward me: 'Sorry, she has just arrived; she doesn't know anything.'

'*Rudari* … Where did you hear this word?! It's not written anywhere! We learn it from our parents'. Rodica looks at Ionica with a questioning expression. 'Don't worry', Ionica tells her, 'she's my friend.'

The first conversation took place in 2010 in Piazza San Marco in Florence, a historical piazza where demonstrations would traditionally begin. At that moment, about fifty people had gathered in occupied buildings, and among them were the protagonists of the dialogue with me. The spring sun warmed the square and the procession was getting organised.

During the second conversation, two years later, we were in Ionica's rented house in a street in the inner suburbs of Florence. We were sitting at the kitchen table, rather squashed against the wall, having dinner.[1] The passages reported and the hesitation or fear that arose among the people who, at the time, did not know me, contain a deep emic sense, which I have come to fully understand over time, with the combination of narratives about themselves – as *rudari* – that have been 'donated' to me over the years and comparing them with those left to other researchers, even after decades.

Anyone preparing to carry out research among the *rudari* in Romania cannot fail to refer to some key texts, which for decades have represented the only studies of a certain consistency, due in part to the impossibility of publishing on 'ethnic' minorities during the communist dictatorship.[2] The reference author par excellence is Ion Chelcea, to whom reference is often made for one of the central questions he addressed, namely what is the origin of *rudari*? Few, however, have focused on the fact (with the exception, in particular, of Şerban (2007) and Neagota and Benga (2016)) that this concern of the Romanian ethnologist, which frequently returns in his writings, was linked to the political situation in which Chelcea carried out his most important research. In September 1940, Charles II appointed Ion Antonescu as head of government; the latter immediately proclaimed himself *Conducător* in parallel with the roles of Mussolini (Duce) and Hitler (Führer). In the same way as the two dictators, Antonescu started a systematic racial persecution in Romania, with the consequent deportations.[3] For this reason, one can clearly intuit the ideological instances behind the 'identity' question – which will become visible again, under completely different guises, with the fall of Ceauşescu – that revolve around the pivot of whether they are 'originally' Roma or not.

This reference to deportations to Transnistria – an atrocious episode in European history – deliberately appears at the beginning of this chapter because the intention is to immediately change the direction of the investigation perspective, moving from a narrow view, which risks leaving our subjects in a 'shadow cone', to a broader one that explores their family events – their history, mobility and migration – on the double emic and ethical track.

Once we have emerged from a 'generalist' view (the *Rudari*), of the a-temporal and a-spatial type, and leaving aside the question *cine sunt Rudari?* (who are the *Rudari?*), we can begin to follow 'our' specific *rudari* in the space of their mobility – which I have called: by choice, induced or forced – from the end of the nineteenth century to today. This investigative approach allows us to weave the threads of the families' micro-history with those of the History of Romania, focusing on the south of the country, along the part of the Lower Danube, between the south eastern Muntenia, the *Cadrilater* and Northern Dobruja. At the same time, the memory of the interlocutors is placed in a dialogue with the studies of the researchers (including myself) and the written sources, restoring to the present of 'we *rudari*' a layer of history and humanity.

The research material, of a different nature, is treated as if each (oral or written) document represented a piece of a mosaic, which despite leaving some areas still uncovered, gives us a dynamic image over time and which reaches completion in the current movement in the social and spatial configuration of families in Romania, in Italy (though not only) and between one country and the other.

The fluidity of the narratives collected during the ethnographic fieldwork (through informal conversations and interviews) is counterbalanced by data contained in institutional and archival documents, and by instances from the scientific literature, both with respect to necessary historical settings and – in a comparative key – with respect to data and information collected in other studies conducted among groups of *rudari*.

Therefore, this part presents a *social* and *mental* geography of the families, through a composite research methodology, which links oral history, genealogies, archival documents and documents produced by a *rudari* 'representative'.

The 'map' that emerges from it, multiple and very dense, holds together a given portion of physical territory specifically lived in, crossed, assigned emic and ethical meanings, and the genealogical space, in an indissoluble intertwining.

The network of our families is composed of spatially localised family groups, whose territorial location is the result of the interweaving of internal and external factors: the residence model of the new couple based on virilocality; the circulation of information on work-economic opportunities (element of continuity in the social organisation of the *rudari* known to us, from the times when they went to *baltă* to the new contexts of emigration); and the historical-political dynamics (the very complicated ones of the borders between states, those subsequent to the end of the Second World War and the beginning of the communist regime, and those linked to the policies of sedentarisation).

To unravel the tangle of family histories, I have also followed people's names through oral testimonies and written documents, but it is important to keep in mind that these names change from country to country, and according to family use. From a formal point of view, it should be remembered that in Romania at the time of registration of a marriage, the bride takes the surname of her husband, completely erasing that of her family of origin. This means that women's surnames begin to change at some point in their family history. Another fact, always formal, and which is important for the possible granting of compensation linked to the exchange of populations – for any real estate left in Bulgaria or for having been displaced – is the Slavisation of surnames and first names, which I encountered during the research. Finally, for the first generations of genealogy, I found that male siblings may have acquired different surnames or that in the act of formal registration the name was swapped with the surname.

Map 2.1a. Framing of the research area within the larger territory of the two countries (Romania and Bulgaria), with the indication of the places using grey, black and white pointers. As with all other maps, the colour grey indicates the Romanian locations, and black indicates the Bulgarian ones (even when they are Romanian); while the cities with the white pointer are useful for orientation when reading the map. © Sabrina Tosi Cambini.

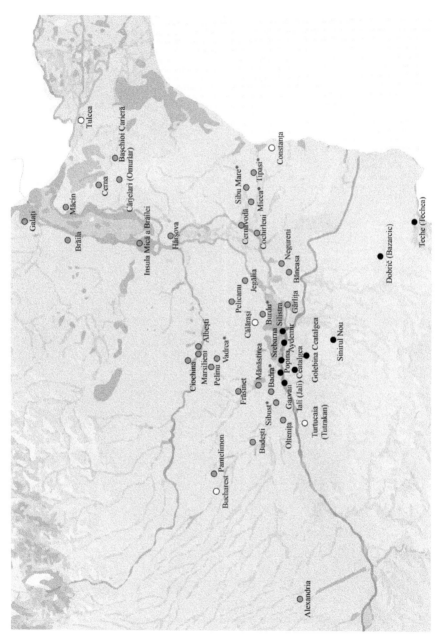

Map 2.1b. Detail of the research area. The asterisk that accompanies some names of the locations indicates the use of a pseudonym, necessary to guarantee the anonymity of the people in the research. © Sabrina Tosi Cambini.

As for the internal use of names in families, we can find more than one for a person (this is certainly true for the last generation that was born and raised in Romania and that began to emigrate from the age of majority, while it seems to fail – at least for the data collected – in the generation that was born and/or raised in the country of immigration). Often one is preferred at the community level (sometimes, a 'nickname'), while another is preferred in the family. Equally often, this 'family' name may not correspond to the name in the registry.

Keeping in mind the overviews provided in the previous chapter, in this, the 'time' of the families has been divided following the scans of the historical events of South-Eastern Europe, thus showing, also in the choice of this architecture, the need to highlight the microhistories belonging to the History.

From 1878 to 1913

From my first encounters in Romania, in Sibu Mare*, over ten years ago, with *rudari* born in the 1960s and previously, the definition given to me with respect to the naming of their group contained a tripartition: *rudari, lingurari, bulgarii*.[4] Then, as we have seen, came the explanatory 'Bulgarians' because the 'nine sisters', from whom they would all descend, came from Bulgaria.

Concerning the 'nine sisters', oral history confirms that they spoke Romanian and had Romanian names, and it could not be otherwise, since the *Rudari* scattered throughout the Balkans originally came from Romania, and in Bulgaria they represent a Romanian minority, sometimes defined as a subgroup of *Vlachs*, however considered *Gypsies* and now included in the category of Roma.[5]

Exploring the history of Dobruja, so I had the idea that this 'Bulgarians' used by our *rudari* was 'only', from the fact that – with the multiple border movements of this region between the two nations and the mobility of the families *rudari lingurari*, who sold their products from country to country – in 1940 following the Treaty of Craiova, some had passed from Bulgaria to Romania (that of the current borders) or had remained in Bulgaria, only because 'coincidentally' they were in the lands of one or the other bank of the Danube at the time the border was established between the two States. It wasn't quite like that.

At the end of the 1878 Berlin Peace Congress, Romania obtained Northern Dobruja, until then the possession of the Ottoman Empire (figure 2.1), while Southern Dobruja was included within the borders of Bulgaria.

Where were our *rudari* in that period and in the following years until Southern Dobruja became Romanian?

As map 2.2 shows (the result of several different sources, both oral and written, such as identity cards and marriage certificates), they are located in two areas in particular. The first includes an area just below the Danube and along it, in the district of Durostor. The second, on the other hand, is a little further down, closer to the Black Sea, and touches the cities of Dobrič (Bazarcic in Romanian) and Teche (Techea).

> The Viennese Felix Philipp Kanitz, travelling through Bulgaria in 1875, [regretted] that the maps of that country were inaccurate and unreliable and reported, as far as the territories near the Danube were concerned, imagined locations without marking the existing ones instead, and agreed with Professor Kiepert, who proclaimed Bulgaria the least known country in Eastern Europe … Kanitz corrected the meritorious maps of Lejean, less exact than those of the Nile, and could therefore define Bulgaria 'a perfectly unknown land'; the Danube was more unknown than the Nile and less was known of the people on its lower course, Professor Hyrtl insisted, than was known about the South Sea Islands. (Magris 2011: 397).

A land, that of Southern Drobruja, which in the eighteen sixties welcomed Tartars and Circassians, where there was a sort of mixture of Balkan and Caucasian populations.

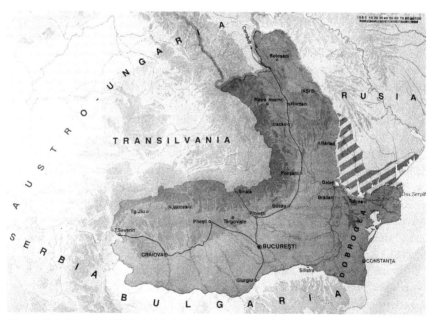

Figure 2.1. Romania 1878–1913. © Sabrina Tosi Cambini.

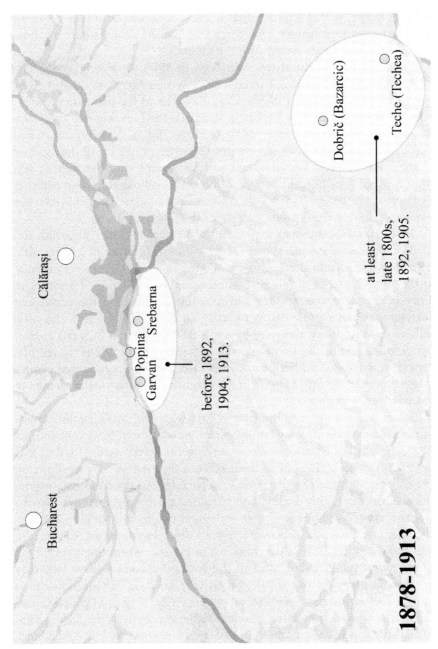

Map 2.2. Territorial location between the end of the nineteenth century and 1913 ©
Sabrina Tosi Cambini.

In this melting pot of people, in that harmonious landscape where the woods breathe, with a Danube that is about to reach its mouth 'foaming with struggles and history'[6] we meet our *rudari*, connoisseurs of those woods and those lands mixed with the waters.

Vana, the first of the sisters, was born in 1904, according to the historical memory of two of our interlocutors in Sibu Mare*, as confirmed by Angelina – granddaughter of Vana and daughter of the fifth sister Rada – who we visited in 2011 in Popina in Bulgaria, then seventy-two years old. According to the testimonies of these three *rudari*, Vana's parents had already been in Bulgaria for some years. Given the young age of the mothers at the birth of their first children, we can assume that the mother was present in the area at least since the 1880s. In Angelina's stories, in addition to Popina, the names of two other places appear – Srebarna and Garvan (which we find in the documents also for the following years).

About Bazarcic (see map 2.2), Gogu of Vadrea* tells us – also with ties of descent from the nine sisters – his *strabunicul*, father of his grandfather (Bîtu), was from there. Gogu was born in 1952 in Pelinu (Romania, at the time a district of Ialomiţa, subsequently of Călăraşi), his father in 1924 in Srebarna (present-day Bulgaria but at the time Romania) and therefore we can assume that his great-grandfather was born in the years following 1880: it can therefore be said that they were in Bulgaria at least between the end of the 1870s and the beginning of the 1880s. In the historical memory of our interlocutors there are few references to that period, fragments that can still help us understand more, in particular thanks to the relatives in Popina.

In fact, when we were in Bulgaria in 2011 with Angelina (daughter of one of the nine sisters), retracing family stories, *fratele* Gheorghe (son of another of the nine sisters, Maria, and therefore Angelina's first cousin), told us that her grandmother – Gherghina, the mother of the nine sisters – was born 'on the other side of the Danube' that is in Romania in the Muntenia region, but she had married in Popina and remained there. Angelina says that she was the last of five siblings – three males and two females in all – and that she was now alone, the others are now all dead. Her husband, Godea, 74, still has a brother and a sister who live in Popina, where there are, in all, seven *rudari* families, but most of the younger members 'have left, they are one on one side, one on the other, very far away', that is, they have emigrated, leaving the 'old at home' – adds Godea – 'we old people are all ailing, they have left us alone'. Godea's father was born in the Silistra area, his mother was born in Badrea* in Romania and there were five daughters, one of whom after the Treaty of 1940 returned to Romanian territory.

Aurel clearly tells me in Florence: 'we got a bit mixed up with them', where *them* indicates '*rudari* who were in Bulgaria'. It should be borne in mind that the area of the Lower Danube has an affinity between the two banks, beyond political borders. In the territory of Silistra, in addition to that of Tuturcaia, for example, the Ottoman Authorities had allowed the development of Romanian schools, on the other hand the Principalities were not politically autonomous from the Empire, with a border that separated them from Dobruja – traced by the course of the Danube – which in the nineteenth century was not difficult to cross:

> The Danube, as an ancient political frontier, could not interrupt existing relations on its two banks, especially if Romanians lived there. But the area I am referring to now includes a large Bulgarian population. An architecture based on huts developed on both sides of the Danube. If we saw them on a map, the statistical data concerning the huts would prove the presence of a common area from an architectural point of view. The long exchanges of populations, the Bulgarians from the north Danube and the Romanians from the south can be an explanation. We cannot ignore the fact that proximity and similar environmental conditions have played an essential role in understanding similarities, which do not take into account political or ethnic boundaries. (Stahl 2007: 184)

The hypothesis is that a group of *rudari lingurari* families, who moved in the area of the Lower Danube of Muntenia – especially in the area of Călăraşi –, crossed the great river, starting to gravitate in some areas of Southern Dobruja (remember: first Turkish, then Bulgarian, then Romanian, finally again Bulgarian), where the nine sisters were born gradually over the years, of which the first five (Vana, Iana, Costanda, Floarea and Rada) married in the territory of Silistra, staying there until 1940 or until they died. The sixth – Pena, born in Aydemir in 1925 – married Ion (born in 1916), also from the territory of *Judeţul* of Durostor, whose family however in those years, thanks to the absence of a border between Southern Dobruja and Northern Dobruja (since all were Romanian) moved between the areas of *baltă* along the wing of Northern Dobruja, in the territory of Tulcea, up to the area of Ostrov.

From the testimonies and reconstructions of the nearest descendants,[7] it emerges that the husbands of at least three of the sisters (Vana, Costanda and Rada) were from *rudari* families who had passed the Danube before them, 'Bulgarian *rudari*'. While the family of Ion (husband of Pena), in turn linked by marriages with the families of Gogu of Bazarcic and Techea, whose *strabunicul* Bîtu was related to the father of the nine sisters (cousin, but if first or second degree remains uncertain), arrived in the same years and therefore presumably together. Bîtu with his family moved between the district of Caliacra and the district of Durostor, to then prefer the area of Silistra, returning to the marshy areas of the woods and waters near the Danube, the *lingurari*'s favourite environments of the Lower Danube.

So, going back to that 'Bulgarians' that our *rudari* use, it originates not only from moving between the borders, crossing the great river, or moving in the territory of Dobruja (between South and North when there was no border), leaving some relatives on one side (Romania) and others on the other (Bulgaria), but also from a deep genealogical trail, which keeps alive the link with Bulgaria born through the union, through multiple marriages (as we saw in the previous chapter), with a group of '*rudari bulgarii*'.

The latter, says Godea, Angelina's husband, were certainly *rudari* (including, of course, his parents) 'but not *lingurari* because they did not work wood to make spoons, but they worked wood for the *boieri*.'

If to this picture, we add also the practice of virilocality, we understand how the nine sisters, in the history handed down within the generations, represent a founding point that corresponds, for these families of *rudari lingurari*, to the birth of a new alliance, through exogamous marriages, with families of '*rudari bulgarii*', from which the family network originated, and whose border will be maintained thanks to the endogamous tendency. While, in fact, some of the sisters entered into endogamous marriages, marrying members of the families of Bîtu and Ion, others made exogamous marriages to '*rudari bulgarii*', which already in the 1920s (years of the marriage of the first sister Vana), seem 'stationary' in the Silistra area.

Did the sisters of exogamous marriages meet their future husbands during a transition that saw them gradually leave an itinerancy linked to their profession to work permanently for the *boieri*? Or were the husbands' families of origin already 'stationary' and did only the men go into the *boieri* woodlands to fetch the wood and work it for the owners and not to make artefacts and sell them from *sat* to *sat*?

In any case, the meeting could have taken place in *baltă*, as it would in the future for Stan and Luminiţa. Aurel explains: 'the *rudari* when they went to *baltă* they met with the other *rudari*, with those other groups, you know? They knew each other; they came from other nearby villages; they talked to each other, they exchanged information';[8] they could, therefore, choose to move to one village rather than another; to one wood or another, depending on the opportunities they offered, also from what was reported by the *rudari* from other groups.

We now follow our *rudari* in the years of the Romanian Dobruja (1913–1940) and in the movements following the Treaty of Craiova.

From 1913 until the Treaty of Craiova, 7 September 1940

At the end of the First Balkan War, with the Peace Treaty signed on 10 August 1913, Southern Dobruja became Romanian. Map 2.3 shows the

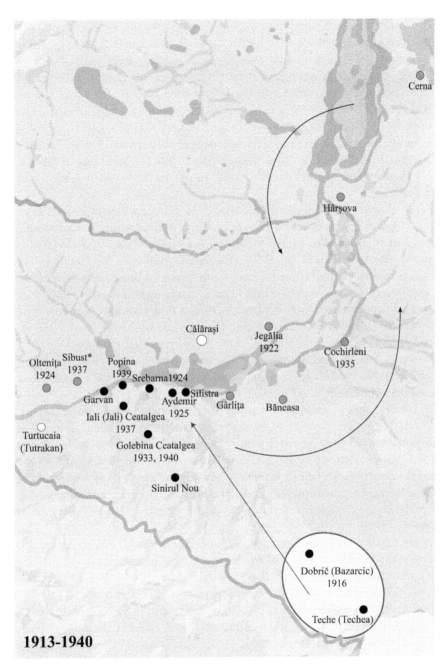

Map 2.3. Period of Romanian domination over the whole of Dobruja. © Sabrina Tosi Cambini.

areas where our *rudari* are in the period until the Treaty of Craiova. The places that appear on this map are those mentioned by my interlocutors in their accounts and those reported in the birth and marriage documents at my disposal, which helped me to note some reference dates.

One area, shown on map 2.3, is the southern districts of Silistra and Călăraşi, on this side and the other side of the Danube. The other follows the course of the river toward its mouth, from the west of Călăraşi to the province of Tulcea, reaching the area of Ostrov and Hârşova. I recorded above that Pena (the sixth of the nine sisters) was born in 1925 in Aydemir and married Ion B., born nine years earlier in the surroundings of Silistra, and then moved to the area of Ostrov, in particular between Gârliţa and Băneasa.

We also record the presence of families in Techea where Nacu was born in 1933, the future husband of one of Bîtu's granddaughters, Constanda, daughter of Bîtu's son, called Nicolae in the family (Nacu and Constanda would marry in Pelinu in 1957). Constanda was born in Cocherini in 1935, along the Danube not far from Cernavoda, while one of her brothers, Gheorghe, was born two years later in Sibust* (facing Popina, on the opposite bank of the Danube), and was later registered under another surname. The father of Constanda and Gheorghe, in fact, appears in the various documents with three different surnames and three different names.

Nacu's father's brother, Petre E., was also born in Techea, while his children – Nacu's cousins – were born in Popina (Tanasa and Joiţa), Golebina Ceatalgea (Gheorghe) and in Iali Ceatalgea (Stefania).

The branches of the *rudari* families preferred some territories over others, especially for the type of economic activity. Those who had the job of *lingurari* moved with the whole family along the Danube, from *baltă* to *baltă* and from *sat* to *sat*, although, at some times of the year, they worked with the *boieri* – proving a very flexible vision regarding the methods of acquisition of material resources (consumer goods) and economic resources (money). Map 2.3 shows the continuous movements in the territory with the two curved arrows.

Those who, on the other hand, worked mainly with landowners tended to remain in one village, and in this case, men procured wood from the woodlands for the *boieri*. Some even bought (before 1940) a plot of agricultural land with a building. This is the case for Petre E. and Mitea E. (born in 1905), who are owners of rural real estate, the first in the municipality of Iali Ceatalgea, and the second in the municipality of Golebina Ciatalgea (deeds issued by the Ministry of the Interior – Central National Historical Archive).

Explaining the relationships to me, Gogu di Vadrea* indicates under the name of his father '*bulgar*' [*rudar*] and under that of his mother '*rudar*' [*lingurar*]. And he does the same for other family branches in the genealogy.

From the Treaty of Craiova in 1940 to the End of the Second World War

The different relationship with the territorial space – one tending more toward mobility, the other toward stability – which reflects the economic strategies of the families in the network, is also found in the testimonies concerning the time of the establishment of the border in 1940, which convey a different experience.

> Gogu: I was in Alexandria between the two wars. It is clearly stated that on September 11, 1940, the forces of law and order [*jandarmi*] took us away. In 1939 [1940], when we were deported from Bulgaria to Romania and from Romania to Transnistria *la Bug*.[9] I have a list of those who were transported from Alexandria in *bug*. They made requests for Alexandru's parents to the Bulgarians, … [indicating] the place from which they left [*au plecat*]. …

Here on my list is the location and village where they were accommodated when they returned from Bulgaria. Mânăstirea in Romania. Daminovca [location of Bessarabia, shown to be incorrect, indicating, however, the deportation to Transnistria]. Then they settled in 1943, and were located in Romania, municipality of Albești. His [Alexandru's] adoptive father was Bulgarian, his [mother's] husband. (Vadrea*, August 2011).

> S.: Why did you come to Romania?
>
> Dumitru: When the border was created, so it remained, like when it was not yet there. Our old people used to go to relatives in Bulgaria. Our old people were born in Bulgaria.
>
> V.: They went with the goods to be sold in Romania but when the borders were closed, they remained there.

No one took them [forcibly] to Romania. Half remained in Romania, half in Bulgaria. In Bulgaria they stayed to work. They went there to sell spoons, spindles, all very well made of wood. That was before the borders were closed.

> D.: They remained [in Romania] because they had more freedom, while in Bulgaria they were forbidden to sell wood. They put them [*i-a bagat*] in school to study, while in Romania they still went to make spindles, spoons and so they stayed here.

…

> D.: The majority who came to Romania were from here, Dobruja [*Cadrilater*], Rudari and Macedonians. They also stayed with relatives but in the woods to raise many sheep. They left their land, their houses, everything. They lost the *bordei* [huts or underground houses]. I have received compensation from

Bulgaria. Only those who were born in the years 1944–1945, in the period of the border. Many old people receive pensions from Bulgaria.

Ghe: My mother had two sisters in Bulgaria, and she has another one who lives, and still has a house, in Silistra, near Ostrov. I think she has 20 grandchildren. They remained after the war … There were the Russians, when with the war they won they were both occupiers. Half the Danube was taken by the Romanians, half the Danube by the Bulgarians, even now it is so. There's a border on the Danube …

My mother was born here in Romania, but we have relatives there [in Bulgaria]. (Sibu Mare*, October 2010).

Map 2.4 shows the movements of the family network. There are two forms of directionality and two main forms of territoriality that I tell through some fragments of family stories.

Forced displacements for many families did not end with the transition from the Quadrilateral to Muntenia, but continued due to the Nazi policies begun in Romania by Antonescu for the 'purification' of the nation. It is for this reason that for many of our *rudari* the two events, population exchange and deportation, independent though contiguous in Romanian history, became a long and painful single event in their micro-history.

Together with Gogu, in Vadrea* in 2011, I went through the documents on the displacement of fifteen families (plus one which did not live in Vadrea*), for whose members Gogu used the term 'deportees', both because they were destined for forced labour in Transnistria, and for the transfers from Southern Dobruja and for those within Romania. Table 2.1 is the reworking, with additions and modifications, of a first table drawn up by Gogu at the end of the 1990s.

In the transcript of the events made by Stana, with Gogu's support, it seems that the exit from Bulgaria and the deportation to Transnistria coincide, presumably anticipating the latter by a year (that is in 1941).[10] Reconstructing, we can say that in Bulgaria (Popina-Garvan-Ceatalgea area), his family and others had been forced to climb onto their wagons and, then, on barges, to cross the Danube, transferring them across the border.[11]

Similarly, in the spring of 1942 (1941?) his family was taken together with others and transferred to Transnistria, always using their own means (animal-drawn wagons), to be placed first in the Trei Dube camps and then moved to another location – perhaps Dubnica Nad – where the family was employed in forced labour at the *kolkhoz*.

From what Gogu tells me, the Authorities recognised the violence that Stana and her family suffered, but there was no chance of finding the relevant documentation among her papers.

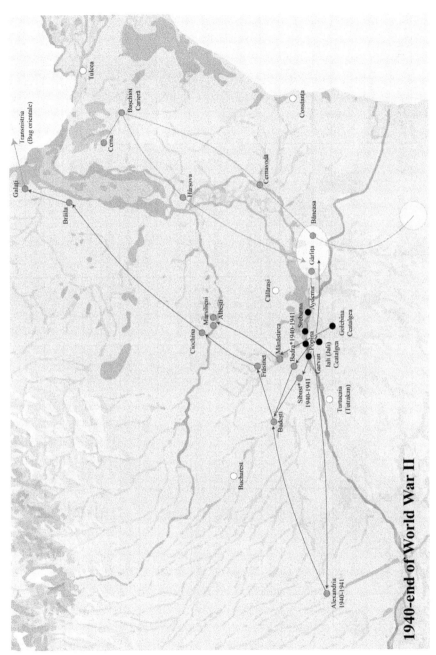

Map 2.4. From the Treaty of Craiova to the end of the Second World War. © Sabrina Tosi Cambini.

Table 2.1. Displacements of sixteen families. © Sabrina Tosi Cambini.

No.	Name	Month/Year of Departure	Place of Departure	Displaced in	Then housed in	Year	Any Later Forced Displacement	Year
1	Alexandru	1940; then 1942 Bug	Bulgaria	np	Marsilieni/Albești	1943		
2	Dimitra	September 1940	Garvan-Popina, Bulgaria	Mănăstirea	Marsilieni/Albești	1941		
3	Pena C.	1940; then 1942 Bug	Sibust*, Romania	Transnistria	Marsilieni/Albești	1943		
4	Stefana	September 1940	Iali Ceatalgea, Bulgaria	Mănăstirea	Marsilieni/Albești	1941		
5	Pena E.	1940; then 1942 Bug	[Bulgaria] Sibust*, Romania	Transnistria	Marsilieni/Albești	1944		
6	Radu	September 1940	Bulgaria	Mănăstirea	Marsilieni/Albești	1941		
7	Gheorghe E.	September 1940	Iali Ceatalgea, Bulgaria	Mănăstirea	Marsilieni/Albești	1941		
8	Costanda	1940; then 1942 Bug	Sibust*, Romania	Transnistria	Marsilieni/Albești	1943		
9	Nacu	September 1940	Techea, Bulgaria	Mănăstirea	Marsilieni/Albești	1941		
10	Stana	September 1940	[Bulgaria] Sibust*, Romania	Transnistria	Marsilieni/Albești	1943	Pelinu	1948–1949
11	Vasile	September 1940	[Bulgaria] Sibust*, Romania	Transnistria	Marsilieni/Albești	1943	Pelinu	1948–1949
12	Gheorghe I.	September 1941	[Bulgaria] Sibust*, Romania	Transnistria	Marsilieni/Albești	1943		
13	Juița	September 1942	Iali Ceatalgea, Bulgaria	Mănăstirea	Marsilieni/Albești	1941		
14	Tanasa	September 1943	Iali Ceatalgea, Bulgaria	Mănăstirea	Marsilieni/Albești	1941		
15	Constantin	September 1944	Romania	np	Sibust*	1940		
16	Maria	September 1945	Alexandria	Transnistria	Alexandria	1944	Bucharest	1960s

For five other cases, however, we have more complete documentation: two documents concern deportation to Transnistria and the others the forced movements to Romania. The first ones involve Constanda and Maria.

In 2004 – about three years after the first request was made – Constanda was awarded compensation for the forced labour to which she had been subjected (*compensatia pentru munca in regim de sclavie*) of €7669.38, paid by the International Organization for Migration (IOM) under the *German Forced Labour Compensation Programme*.[12]

Concerning Maria, following the request submitted by her son, we have the certificate issued in 2001 by the Romanian Ministry of the Interior, National Archive, which declares that Maria, together with her husband and four children, appears in the table drawn up in September 1942 by the Alexandria Police Station referring to the *gypsies* (*ţiganii trimişi*) sent to Transnistria.[13] Maria, with the other members of the family, then appears in the 1944 table of the Turn Măgurele Police archival fund, referring to the *gypsies* evacuated to Transnistria, returned to Romania with the withdrawal of the troops from Transnistria, and who came to Alexandria – registered by the local Police Commissariat – in June 1944.

The other cases are linked to the displacements from the villages in Romania and from the Quadrilateral and concern Gogu's father (Gheorghe, born, let us remember, in 1924 in Srebarna), Stefania's family (who was born in 1937 in Iala Ceatalgea) and that of Tanasa (born in the same area in 1933). By decisions, all three issued in 2003 by the Commission of the Province of Călăraşi, for the application of Law 189/2000, it is recognised that Gheorghe, Stefania and Tanasa were displaced [*strămutat*], in accordance with the provisions of art. 1 paragraph c) of the law, in detail: 'Art. 1. – Benefiting from the provisions of this ordinance is the person, a Romanian citizen, who during the regimes established from 6 September 1940 to 6 March 1945 suffered persecution on ethnic grounds, as follows: … c) was displaced to a location other than their domicile.'[14]

Stefania, Tanasa and Joiţa are sisters, and daughters of Petre, mentioned in the previous paragraph. The brother was awarded compensation for the loss of his rural property in Bulgaria in the municipality of Iala Ceatalgea (Durostor district).

The same applies to Elisaveta, whose father owned a house with a courtyard and one hectare of farmland in the municipality of Golebina Ceatalgea.

The fact that, at the time of the exchange in 1940, they were not recognised as holders of property rights can be explained, as well as any factors that we do not know, because of the location of the properties themselves in the *rudari* part of the villages. It is possible that, despite the declarations made in September 1940 and accompanied by the document of the Bulgarian municipality describing the property (*Declarația și Situația de averea imobilă rurală*) and its value, they were discriminated against because, despite being of Romanian mother tongue, they belonged to a minority considered *gypsy*.

The daughter of Pena C. in 2003 with Gogu reconstructed the stages of her forced displacements, until the deportation to Trei Dube in Transnistria: after being displaced to Sibust*, Pena C. with her husband and children were moved to Budești, then to Frăsinet, Ciochina, Brăila and Galați – localities, Gogu told me, which return in other family stories (see map 2.4). The family of Pena C. returned to Romania in 1944, and was placed in Marsilieni (now in the municipality of Albești). The families listed in table 2.1, except two, were transferred to Marsilieni, both before Mânăstirea and after their return, after the tragic experience of deportation.

The *rudari* who, as we have seen, during the period when all of Dobruja belonged to Romania, moved along the Danube to Tulcea, were forced to leave the Quadrilateral or not to return, if they were in the north of the region, but did not undergo subsequent forced displacements or deportations to Transnistria.

Tudorița, born in Bulgaria in 1939, says that her family had moved from Bulgaria to the area of Gârlița and Băneasa, and that at the beginning of the war she was in Bașchioi (near the quarry); while fratele Gheorghe, cousin of her cousin, son of one of the nine sisters, told me that he was born in Cerna. The two localities are very close and are situated in the district of Tulcea, in the landscape of forests and waters designed by the expansion of the Danube, a favourite environment of our *lingurari*. Valeriu, son of the son of one of the nine sisters, told me:

> the *rudari* moved around in Dobruja, in particular to Călărași and Tulcea, always near the Danube, with their wagon. They stopped in places depending on the duration of the contract for usufruct of the forest that the *padurar* gave them. They moved with their wagon and oxen.

He explains that during the Second World War the *rudari* went to the municipalities of Cernavoda and others nearby where there were waterways, especially along the Danube and its ramifications, and asked the *padurar* to be able to cut down the trees. They worked the wood, making spoons and other kitchen utensils, and then moved during the summer between the various countries to sell or trade them with other objects (mainly foods such as flour and cheese, which they then consumed during the winter). They also worked for the *boieri* (the owners of real estate and land) both at their houses and in the fields.[15]

Vasile, who comes from Badra*, relates:

> V.: The father [of my father-in-law] left in a boat to Romania, some were expelled ... My father's brother ... swam across the Danube to Romania; otherwise he stayed in Bulgaria. It has been difficult. Some of us had relatives in Bulgaria.
>
> S.: Where? Near Popina?
>
> V.: in Silistra
>
> M.: Yes, in the province of Silistra, municipality of Popina.
>
> V.: ... Her [his wife's] father was born in Bulgaria and had a house there, properties, the father of my father-in-law.
>
> S.: When your father left for Romania, he was making spoons, wasn't he?
>
> V.: Yes, yes, he was.
>
> S.: And when did he stop?
>
> V.: No, no, this is a craft, it doesn't end. I too make spoons ... From our ancestors, it's a custom, a habit.

Rudari Traces, Bulgarian Traces

For our families, what are, therefore, the significant traces of their past in Southern Dobruja, represented today by that attribute 'Bulgarians'? Bulgaria emerges as a significant element of identity for the outside world, that is, in relations with larger society, at two moments in their history: when they passed through Romania in 1940 (as we have seen) and, almost sixty years later, when, at the end of the 1990s, they began to collect documents for the formal recognition of this link, thanks to which they can receive compensation, according to the legislation gradually promulgated by the Romanian government.

> S.: Why is the documentation proving that you have been displaced important [*strămutat*]?
>
> G.: Yes, yes, it was important that they should recognise us as Bulgarian citizens. So we could benefit from the pension money [contribution].
>
> They [the Authorities] have granted us the right but not totally. Only part of it. Because we are *rudari*.

To ask ourselves, however, about a deeper meaning of 'Bulgarians', within the groups, we must take a step back.

With respect to the possible date of the arrival in Southern Dobruja of the group of *rudari* that we have called, on the basis of the emic definition, '*rudari bulgarii*' – and who in that territory would meet the families of the *lingurari* once the latter crossed the Danube – there is no historical memory among my interlocutors, even among the elderly. The authors usually believe that the *rudari* arrived in Bulgaria at the end of the nineteenth century (see Marushiakova and Popov 1997; 2013), following the end of slavery in Wallachia in 1856. Since in those years we still cannot talk about Bulgaria but about the Ottoman Empire, under which the whole of Dobruja was at the time, just as the Principalities themselves were, 'politically', we could think that some *rudari* living in border areas had already crossed in the 1960s. In the National Archive, Bucharest Regional Centre, there is a document dated 1862 that concerns the correspondence between the sub-prefectures based in Balta and Vădeni and the Prefecture of the Buzău district regarding the entry into the country of a group of ten *gypsies* from Turkey (Dobruja), where they could no longer earn a living by practising their trade as manufacturers of *copaie* [big tubs] and spoons.[16]

This document records the existence of a reverse displacement, in which the specific *rudari lingurari* to whom it refers moved between the borders of Dobruja and Romania as early as the early 1860s. It is therefore not entirely inappropriate to imagine that the '*rudari bulgarii*' who 'mixed' with the *rudari lingurari* arrived in Southern Dobruja at least starting from those years. Moreover, as stated in the previous chapter, the *rudari* during slavery, as well as being the property of the prince, could also be owned by monasteries and nobles, which usually implied a qualitative difference in the life they could lead.[17] This fact is interesting for us since some of our *rudari* interlocutors in Vadrea* and Burdu* know the expression *țigani de vatră* referring to their 'ancient' history. *Vatră* stands for hearth and *țigani de vatră* are usually considered in literature the 'settled' *gypsies*. Here too, the 'classification' principle leads us to think statically of events that may instead have had a possible fluctuation/mobility: diversification of the destinies of families in various territories and probably transition from certain professions to other more convenient ones at a given time. This could have happened precisely in the years when panning for gold in the rivers was no longer profitable work. The authors usually converge on a sort of linearity of the transition from the profession of gold prospectors (hence the denomination of *aurari*) to that of woodworkers. However, at the moment there are few studies that have directly investigated what actually happened and, if generally agreed and linear, this passage risks homologating the destinies of thousands of people, who may have found themselves in different work niches.[18]

Precisely because they enjoyed a certain organisational freedom and bargaining power that the other *robi* (slaves) did not have,[19] it is possible that groups of families, in some periods, had worked under a boyard, with a gender division of work duties – men as lumberjacks and woodworkers, women as domestic servants. This was in the same way as they did later, at other times in their history (e.g. between the two world wars), when woodworking did not allow them to obtain sufficient goods to live on. This does not mean assimilating the *rudari* to the *vătrasi*. The confusion generated between the overlap – sometimes a forced synonymy – of the 'categories of craft' during slavery that we find in the Archives, the 'ethnic connotation' of the *gypsies* starting from an external classification and the lack of a fluid vision of the groups, at least with regard to our reference groups (the *rudari*), seems to have generated cages for which the groups or families cannot be thought of in the context of changes that led them to move between different occupational possibilities at different times in their lives.

The group of families today in Sibu Mare* – as mentioned – had practised, both between 1913 and 1940 and between the two wars, a mobility linked to the craft of *lingurari*; while among the families who crossed the Danube (freely or forcibly) in 1940, of the group that belongs to the Silistra area there are more *'rudari bulgarii'* relatives. Now, among my interlocutors who are familiar with the phrase *țigani de vatră*, it emerges that among their ascendants there are many more *'rudari bulgarii'* than *'rudari lingurari'*. Taking into account the data reported so far and the fact that the *rudari*, as we said, are not to be considered a monolithic block, but groups of families, with their own vicissitudes, trades and reference territories, we can assume that the *'rudari bulgarii'* had moved with greater compactness than the families of *lingurari*, and after arriving in Bulgaria they had negotiated – through the *vătaf* – the terms of their work with the landowners, according to the internal organisational methods developed during slavery, and therefore deciding to 'stop', and settle in the villages.

What, then, does the 'mixing' entail? Surely some of the members of the *lingurari* families began, also like the 'Bulgarians', to settle in the villages, changing their profession: into the woods went only the men on behalf of the master, while women and men reduced themselves to carrying out woodworking only for their own domestic needs or for those of the *boieri*.

The *settling*, as would happen later in time, led families to dedicate themselves to agricultural work and, as we have seen, in some cases, also to buy rural real estate: small plots of land and houses.

It has been noted that this 'mixing' brought with it a different sense for our interlocutors: a sense of loss for some, that of change for others. These are two different perceptions that we also find in the statements reported by Chelcea (1943). Some perceived the risk of losing their trade (in this case linked to the gradual disappearance of the woods – ibid.: 91) or they felt dispersed in a majority, that of the Romanian peasants, and in living conditions worse than they had before (ibid.: 98); or, again, they felt the risk of losing themselves: 'there is nothing left for us but to die'(ibid.: 91), 'all that remains for us is to let ourselves perish' (ibid.: 98). On the other hand, the few who built houses and were, therefore, 'stable', interpreted this change as an advance: positively coming closer to the life led by Romanian peasants.

I will return to this point later in the text, when some of our *rudari* speak of the changes in the way they lead their lives as the result of 'modernisation'.

Chelcea carried out research in 1959 – so in a very different period from those of the best-known, published in the early 1940s – on behalf of the Village Museum (*Muzeu Satului*) of Bucharest, on the *rudari* of the Danube Valley, between the lower course of the Olt River and that of the River Mostiştea. In this portion of land, there are also villages that we know have been inhabited also by our *rudari*: Alexandria, Chirnogi, Budesti, Mânăstirea. The author divides the *rudari* of this territory into 'vlahuti' and 'turcani'. The latter represented by those who

> have left the Quadrilateral more recently, for example, or even from within Bulgaria, further away from Turkey – or to remember their long experience under the Turks – they will be called 'Turks', as for example, we find in the village of Mânăstirea (few huts, *bordeie*). These rudari claimed to speak Turkish and Bulgarian, which surprised local relatives and also the other inhabitants. (1969: 11)

Under the name of 'turcani', Chelcea may have inserted *rudari* from different families, who, for example, could have intermarried in Romania. Our *rudari* families, in those years, were no longer in Mânăstirea, but we know that there were some in Alexandria and, although they left the Quadrilateral 'more recently' (to use the words of Chelcea) and despite speaking Bulgarian, they certainly cannot be assimilated to the others who speak Turkish or even defined as 'turcani'.

In the available literature, the most evident Bulgarian trace in *rudari* groups was usually found in the presence of the ritual of *gurban*, ever since the study of Nicolăescu-Plopşor in 1922.[20] Calotă speaks of it as 'the ethnographic element through which the Rudari Albieri and the Rudari Rotari differ, both from the other categories of gypsies – including the other category of Rudari, the Corfari – and especially from the Romanians' (1996: 49), even if only brief descriptive hints are given.

Our *rudari* from Vadrea*, among whose descendants there are more 'rudari bulgarii', told me that they heard this term from the Turks; but a more intriguing reading, and that leaves us with open questions, comes from the conversation with a member of a younger generation of Vadrea*. When I explained what I meant by *gurban* or *gurbane*, I received the answer: '*Praznic*!? But so do the Romanians. In Romania everyone buys a lamb for Easter'. The point is that Mihai had immediately connected the meanings that *gurban* brings with it (not the actual practices of the ritual) to what he identified with *praznic*[21] and when it is held (Easter).

Since he and his wife were guests at my house, I had the opportunity to immediately submit to Mihai what Calotă wrote, in the part of his volume dedicated to the glossary, to define the term *gurban/gurbane*, which we read together:

Praznic that the rudari albieri made on the day of St. George or of the Ascension (in the ancient ways, *pe stil vechi*), which consisted in sacrificing a white lamb and reciting a prayer to the saints (*Sfinte*),[22] to heal a sick person, usually paralysed, or as a sign of thanksgiving to heal a disease. (1996: 218)

As we read, he nodded and said, pointing his finger at the text: 'see: în ziua Înălţării (on Ascension Day)!', and continued: 'yes, we too, it was done for the sick, children who have diseases, to help them heal'.

The line is thin. Surely what Mihai told me has very little to do with the complex ritual that Neagota and Benga (2016) or Nicolăescu-Plopşor (1922) described; perhaps it has something in common with those de-ritualised versions of which Sorescu-Marinković (2007) writes, but we are not able to say more. We should take into account, in any case, two moments of passage in the history of our *rudari* that led to the partial disappearance of their 'magical world'[23] and that may have strongly influenced the transformation or abandonment of this rite, provided that it was actually present. The first, which concerns everyone, is the long period under communism, particularly that of the Ceauşescu dictatorship. The second, still in progress and involving many of the families, is the conversion to the Pentecostal movement. In any case, today we do not find any 'identity' feature in the uncertain past existence of *praznic-gurban*.

In conclusion, we can argue that the term 'Bulgarians' is a trace of the 'mixing', between '*rudari lingurari*' and' *rudari bulgarii*', and of the simultaneous establishment of a network of families whose current members place the 'nine sisters' as the beginning of the formation of this network, the boundaries of which, to date, are maintained by the practice of endogamy.

In relation to larger society, a transferred meaning through a 'public' use in its own favour, 'Bulgarians' has a very specific strategic importance in the relationship with the institutions, for the possibility – as we have seen – to see the compensation recognised.

From the End of the 1940s to 1970

In this period[24] we witness the movements that gradually led to the configuration of the presence of our *rudari* in the areas of the current locations (see map 2.5).

From Mânăstirea to Marsilieni/Albeşti there was a forced movement; the same thing, from there to Pelinu or Pelicanu; while if from Marsilieni/Albeşti, the families went directly to Vadrea* it was by strategic choice (we shall see this further on). From Pelinu and Pelicanu, the families also moved to Vadrea*, to be reunited with the others.

From the area of Garliţa and Băneasa, families moved to the area of Tulcea; some then returned to Garliţa, and then moved to Pelicanu (it was a mobility linked to trade and marriages). From Pelicanu to Vadrea* they always moved due to internal dynamics, while from Pelicanu to Burdu* (in 1970) by the will of the Authorities, that year they dismantled the locality of Pelicanu.

The other families stayed longer in the areas of *baltă* and among the villages of the district of Tulcea; then from the area of Brăila they went down toward Pelicanu (where they stopped, and then they were transferred to Burdu*); or they went to Sibu Mare*, where they were joined by relatives who lived in Pelicanu.

S.: You were brought from Albeşti. Did you then come here [to Vadrea*]?

G.: … I was in Albeşti where they gave us a place/land to build the house [*locuri de casa*], in the year 1950.[25] Then we moved here [Vadrea*] and we have stayed here until now.

S.: Why did you move here?

G.: They gave us land in Albeşti. Then the *boieri* who were from Albeşti owned land also here in Vadrea*. There was no transport there, we moved here because there were means of transport, that is, the train, thanks to which we could travel and work.

Thanks to the Agrarian Reform of 1945, the then municipality of Marsilieni (then annexed to the municipality of Albeşti), recognised for some dozens of *rudari* families (41 heads of families) the right to be assigned a plot of land, from 2 to 5 hectares, of which, therefore, they became owners.

Stahl also notes in his survey that some families had land (1991: 56–57), which was then quickly taken away for collectivisation, as had happened for the peasants: 'It would have been interesting to know', writes the author, 'how the life of these domestic groups that became owners developed later' (ibid.), concluding that: 'it can still be said that the Rudari who went to

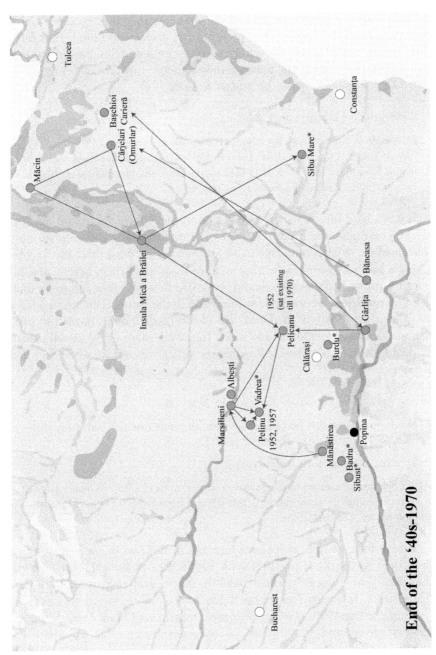

Map 2.5. Main movements between the late 1940s and 1970s. © Sabrina Tosi Cambini.

live in the Romanian villages have become agricultural workers after the collectivisation of the lands, while those who remained in their settlements have continued … their ancient profession of craftsmen' (ibid.). Basically, this process took place for the *rudari* who later settled in Sibu Mare* (taking into account, of course, the pressure of the communist government), but it also emerged previously for the '*rudari bulgarii*'.

S.: When did your parents settle in Sibu Mare*?

D.: In 1965. Our parents have been all over the country. And I was born in Cerna, Tulcea. I was born there. I was in Călăraşi, village Pelicanu, and then I was in Sibu Mare*. In 1965, after Gheorghiu-Dej,[26] the Head of State, died, I came to Sibu Mare* at the time of Ceauşescu.

It was a hard life. We always went around the villages: we stayed outside to sleep at night; the mosquitoes bit us. Life was really difficult, no one welcomed us. We slept in wagons, slaves [*robi*], poor, what can I say. In the spring a boss came and took many men to work, paid them before, and in the autumn we had debts again and so we had to work again and so we had debts all our lives. We worked for them and in the spring there was a party, it's called the Sabbath of the Dead. The *rudari* made spoons, bowls and sold them in exchange for clothes and food. They went twice a year [to sell], then worked for the *boieri*. The CAP came, the collective, and we worked in the CAP. That was 1956.

S.: Were you forced to stop doing *linguri* (spoons)?

D.: Authorisation was necessary, but when they saw that you had many children, they left you alone, they were good

S.: You did not have the authorisation?

D.: No, it was black work. There was no school to [learn] how to make spoons in order to get an authorisation. You learned from father to son. (Dumitru, Sibu Mare*, October 2010)

Valeriu told me that his parents had met in Băneasa in the early 1960s, then they had moved, together with his father's parents, to the area of the district of Tulcea, to the village of Macin and to that of Omurlar (Carjelari).[27] Then they headed for Brăila.

Since the late 1950s – with progressive measures of State control, forced sedentarisation and the process of collectivisation – his grandfather's brother, together with other men from the extended family, began to work at the Agricultural Cooperative of Sibu Mare*, where they also stayed to sleep. They were paid from Monday to Friday, while – Valeriu reported – Saturday and Sunday work was paid with flour and other food products.

When Valeriu's grandfather's brother called Luminiţa (Valeriu's mother) to Sibu Mare*, she was pregnant with him (it was 1966): 'They were in Brăila [to be precise, in Insula Mică in Brăilei] and therefore they had to cross the river with the wagon on the boat and Luminiţa was afraid of falling into the water and losing her child, that is me'. Ion, Valeriu's grandfather, obtained 2,000 square metres of land and they settled permanently in Sibu Mare*.[28]

Tudoriţa, while we were in her home in Burdu*, built with remittances from her children and grandchildren's migrations to Spain, explained to me that at the age of sixteen, that is in 1955, she married in Gârliţa (after having been in the district of Tulcea). Tudoriţa is a cousin of Valeriu's father, who in turn is a cousin of the Gheorghe brothers, their mothers being sisters (two of the 'nine sisters'): 'From Gârliţa we came to Pelicanu; there we rebuilt a house, they demolished it and we came here [Budru*], and in 1976 I built the house.'

> S.: Did you make *linguri* (spoons), spindles …?
>
> Ghe: Yes, I made *linguri*, I am *lingurar*. I made spoons out of wood from the woodlands; they were made everywhere, in the woods, at home, in the fields … Pieces of wood, roughed down and roughed down again, worked with the *teslă* [a sort of billhook] and taken with a knife [that is, hollowed with a typical knife of the *lingurari*], scraped with a file … [he mimes with his hands and shakes his head, sighing] … We went to many villages, and sold them. We had the wagon with oxen.
>
> S.: How long did you stay in one place?
>
> Ghe: We would stay two days or more. Until we sold the merchandise, based on how much people bought. If we sold, we stayed even a week.
>
> S.: How did you get the wood? Did you have to pay?
>
> Ghe: We had to pay or we worked to get the wood. We did what was needed and instead of money we took the wood.
>
> S.: So the forester paid you directly with wood. During communism, did you have any problems selling the merchandise, for example with the police?
>
> Ghe: in some places [the police] did not let us sell, they asked us for authorisation to pay a tax to the State, an authorisation for wood processing. We worked without authorisation. Just like now with a store.[29] …

The police asked us where we got the wood. You had to get a 'voucher' from the forester to take with you to prove that you hadn't stolen …When communism began, the craft of *lingurari* began to be lost because we had to work at the CAP ... With the police we had problems, we ran away because they asked us for our documents, where we worked ... they stole the merchandise from us.

From 1970 to 1989

Luminița: During the time of Ceaușescu, we no longer did anything; there was no wood, we did not have the materials; in Sibu Mare*, the acacia forest had a guard who shot you if you took the wood; it was forbidden; he hit you, he hunted you; they [the *rudari*] could no longer make spoons, spindles, vats, they no longer could. Only at the lake in Brăila, Fetești etc. ... [my husband] went to the horses, he worked with the horses; he carried the beets, the corn from the field, there were no cars, there were the wagons; there were seven rudari, Simion, my man, Bairam ...; the rudari where we were carried the beet, the maize with the wagons; at the collective there were three tractors and a trailer and a tractor driver, that's all. I loaded the apples for the people of the collective ... I collected the fish in crates ... What you did [worked], gave corn, sugar, peppers, cabbage, beans, wine, everything came from the CAP. ... potatoes for the winter.

Nicolae: Didn't they give you money?

L.: We took the money every three months; 17 lei; it was money! As 100 million would be now, seventeen thousand;[30] 17 lei were every three months; but you built two houses; with 1 leu, like 100 thousand are now; you did the shopping and you also came away with change; if you took 2 lei you could clothe the children; a belt, a shirt, a costume, they did not wear *fesuri* (a type of hat); they had astrakhan hats of a good make; you gave the children hats, belts, boots,... everything, everything ... you clothed the children ..., and you came away with the change.

N.: and did you work every day?

L.: at the CAP you worked; if you did fewer days, the percentage, if you did not have 17 percent you did 80 days; ... if you did not have 50%, points, you did not get the wheat, the maize; it did not give you food in the autumn. You went to the collective, with the horse belonging to the collective and you loaded and you brought the maize home; you took a cart of wheat 500 kilos or 1,000 kilos, you had nowhere to put them. You brought the wheat home; you made bread, you didn't buy it; you built the ovens; we had the oven outside, there. You used to make bread, crackers for the children, cakes, not like now: now it's not good. Today's bread is not good, it has no taste, but if you make it in the oven outside ... but the oven must be good; it smells good; but like this it doesn't smell good.

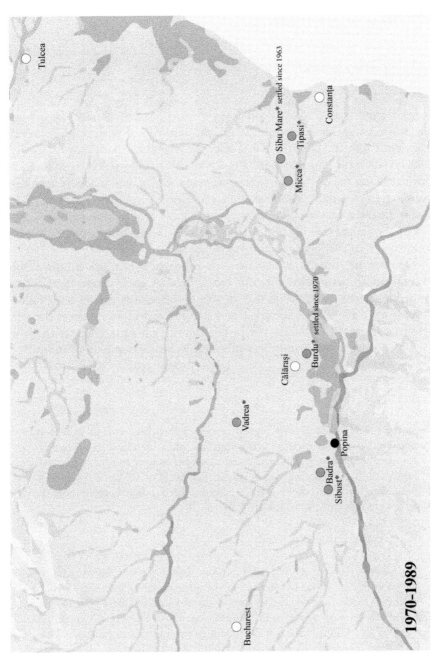

Map 2.6. During communism. © Sabrina Tosi Cambini.

N.: and who found you a job, the first time when you came?

L.: The collective, the brigade.

N.: Were you obliged to work? … if you did not have a job …

L.: You always had a CAP; if you stayed at home they would fine …

[my husband] was employed milking the cows …; he was with the calves, the cows; I went at three o'clock at night and milked with him; I carried a little milk to the children, I hid it in the manger, I put the milk in the bucket; when the cow had a calf I took the colostrum [which is produced a few days after the birth], the dense one, you boiled it, you made fresh colostrum, you made half a cauldron, you made a cake, *cocoline*, it was good; it was to be eaten by the children; we made cheese, we put it in jars, earthenware pots we had that big pot, we put two kilos, three and we made yogurt. You could cut it with a spoon, it was thick.

Despite the difficulties experienced, the period of work in the CAP is remembered as a 'safe' time, in the sense that some elements of social protection were guaranteed, that in the post-Socialist period have failed completely.[31] However, the vision is not uniform and also reflects the territorial contexts. In Vadrea* the perception of that time is better than in Badra*, a town in a territory less affected by the development of industries and production.

Vasile told me:

In the time of communism there was money but there was no light, food, bread, oil, sugar, salami, rice, everything was sold with a card. You had a card for each person and it gave half a litre of oil per month and half a loaf a day and if you had children it was much more difficult. It was good if you found work, you had money but you didn't have anything to buy. Because the wealth of our country was taken abroad (Florence, 2015).

And, again, Vasile explained:

If they saw you working, you were free, but if they saw you not working, you were not free … It was not like today, the boys with long hair, there were the civil police and they controlled you, it was forbidden to have long hair or a beard. They'd send you straight to the barber to get a haircut. 'Do you have money?' 'No I don't'. 'The first time I will give you the money and then I want to see you trimmed'. That was the discipline. You had to work. They captured you once, they forgave you, the second time the same, but then they put you in jail for a few months, it means you don't want to work and they would find you work …

This is how we were treated and this racial hatred has remained until today. I don't know until when … what can we do with this racism and wars always start with racism (Florence, 2015).

Notes

1. It was 8 August 2012, the evening before my departure by bus for Romania with Dana, Ionica's daughter. 'It's not written anywhere' refers to the fact that in Romania the *Rudari* are not recognised as a separate minority and therefore the term does not appear on the census sheet as a possible choice. Given that they are considered as *ţigani* (gypsies) by the Romanian majority, they would be assimilated to the Roma minority, to which they do not attribute themselves. The word *rudari* emerges in my reply to the question from Rodica's husband who asked me, 'What are you going to do in Romania?', so Ionica explained to him about my research. During dinner, curious about the connection between me and Ionica, Rodica's husband had asked me, 'How can you be Ionica's friend if you are not a believer?' In fact, he was unable to understand this relationship, since I was neither Romanian (*rudăreasă*) nor Pentecostal.
2. See, for example, Calotă's doctoral thesis (1974) which saw the published version over twenty years later in 1995.
3. And it was Ion Chelcea, one of the main references among scholars, 'who would become the "Gypsyology" expert of Gusti's school. Influenced by the Nazi ideology of Traian Herseni (incidentally one of Gusti's favourite students), Chelcea (1944a: 100– 101) also supported the sorting principle, as well as that of sterilising and deporting Gypsies to Transnistria' (Asséo et al. 2017: 37).
4. To be precise: '*Suntem* [we are] *rudari lingurari bulgarii*', '*suntem rudari bulgarii lingurari*' or '*suntem rudari lingurari*'.
5. See Mladenov (2007); Dorondel (2007).
6. Zaharia Stancu cited in Magris (2011: 426).
7. Some of the younger sisters' children: Angelina from Popina, *fratele* Gheorghe from Sibu Mare* and Petre from Badra*.
8. Conversation held in Florence, March 2014.
9. *Bug* is used to indicate deportation. In fact, the *gypsies* were interned in camps at the border or within villages located on the shore of the eastern Bug.
10. The same interpretation is assumed by the International Organization for Migration (IOM) in the reconstruction of Claimant's story. Claimant, in fact, also says that he was taken to Transnistria with his parents on the wagon in 1941, first to Trei Dube and then to Varvaloca. As regards the year, the IOM writes, 'Although Claimant states 1941 in his personal statement, IOM believes that, consistent with the deportation of other Roma from this area and the historical record, either Claimant was probably deported in 1942 and, with the passage of time, has become confused about the current year of deportation or because the official persecution of Romania began in 1941 after Antonescu's speech on 8 July 1941 about the elimination of national minorities, Claimant due to his young age and the passage of time has not distinguished the two events.' Holocaust Victim Assets Programme (Swiss Banks), Group XII

Submission, Slave Labour Class I, Representative Case Summaries, Representative Case Summaries For Romanian Romanies Who Were Deported To Transnistria, document available online: http://swissbankclaims.com/Documents/2017/IOM%20 SL%20I%20Case%20Summaries.pdf.

11. 'Both the Bulgarian and Romanian states, to organise transfers, divided the populations concerned into three categories in consideration of their place of residence. Those belonging to the first were moved by means of sea voyages using mainly the ports of Constanţa in Romania and Varna in Bulgaria; for those included in the second category, rail transport was used; finally, for the populations included in the third category, simple land transport (with wagons and more rarely trucks) and, of course, barges for crossing the Danube were used' (Basciani 2009: 169).

12. 'The German Parliament passed the German Foundation Act establishing the German Foundation "Remembrance, Responsibility and Future", whose main purpose was to establish a compensation programme for slave and forced labourers of the National Socialist regime. The Foundation was capitalized by the Federal Republic of Germany and by German companies with DM 10 billion (€5.1 billion). In July 2000, IOM was designated by the Government of Germany as one of seven partner organisations of the Foundation "Remembrance, Responsibility and Future"; rendering IOM the first permanent international organisation directly engaged in the implementation of a large scale reparations programme. As a partner organization, IOM was responsible for all non-Jewish victims of slave labour, forced labour and personal injury belonging to the so-called rest-of-the-world' (IOM: 2007).

13. The family had been deported to Balta.

14. The other paragraphs state: a) they were deported to ghettos and concentration camps abroad, b) they were deprived of their liberty in places of detention or concentration camps, d) they were part of forced labour detachments and e) they survived the Death Train.

15. Valeriu, Sibu Mare*, Romania, October 2010.

16. Judeţului Brăila Prefecture BR-F-00027-1-1862-183. The specification '(Dobruja)' is contained in the text.

17. On the other hand, we also know that during slavery, groups of *robi* (slaves) sometimes fled beyond the borders of the Principality towards the Ottoman Empire, which was less iron-fisted towards the *gypsies*.

18. The research conducted by Julieta Rotaru, Södertörn University in Stockholm, reveals new historical evidence in this regard. Rotaru, since 2018, was part of the larger project 'Mapping the Roma communities in 19th century Romania', https://ostersjostiftelsen. se/project/mapping-the-romacommunities-in-19th-century-romania/; MapRom www.maprom.se; Rotaru (2018). The seminar held in spring 2021, entitled *Unlocking the Golden Past of the Rudari Woodworkers in Romania (Methodological Remarks)*, aimed to advance a paradigm for the reconstruction of the history of the *Rudari* in the manner of the *histoire à la rebours* by Marc Bloch, taking as a sure moment of their past the professional reconversion recorded in the demographic sources of the early nineteenth century. See Rotaru and Gaunt (2023).

19. This was linked to a flexible/mobile social organisation that comprised an organisation between families with a *vătaf* – responsible for the agreements – but also the possibility, as we have seen, that a family took other paths considering them more convenient (a strategy that they have kept alive for a long time, as our interlocutors tell us).

20. Nicolăescu-Plopşor first indicates the *Gurban* as a ritual present among people known as *rudari* – which he names with the term *caravlahi* (as did Filipescu (1906) – and not among all Romanians, which occurs on St. George's Day or Ascension

Day. 'The Gurban is a magical-religious ceremonial complex found with the south-Carpathian Rudar communities (Mehedinţi, Dolj, Olt, Teleorman, Giurgiu, Gorj, Vâlcea and Argeş) and the south-Danube ones (the Bulgarian and Serbian Timok and the Morava Valley), where woodworking is the traditional handicraft: Albieri/Rotari (wheelwrights) and, sometimes, Corfari (basket-weavers). Within the crossing-border communities of Băieşi (miners) from Transylvania and with the Lingurari (spoon-makers) from Moldova/Bukovina who did not participate in the Balkan migration that brought them into contact with Muslims, this ritual does not exist [*Gurban*, in fact, derives from *Kurban*, an Islamic sheep sacrifice]. Therefore, the Băieşi from Croatia and Hungary, of Transylvanian descent, do not know the Gurban. In Serbia, north of the Danube, the ritual is scarcely attested: in Grebenac, Vojvodina, it is celebrated during a certain feast (Ascension, Whitsun or St. Peter's), for the recovery of sick children. South of the Danube, the ritual is attested more often, during the Old St. George (celebrated on 6 May), but with de-ritualized local versions – praznik, gurban, gropan' (Neagota and Benga 2016).

21. The *praznic*, Stahl explains (1986, 1992), is an annual family rite that coincides with the feast of a saint recognised by the Orthodox Church, patron of a region or of the local church. The family is here understood by Stahl in the sense of *household*, the smallest social unit, which the author connotes with the ancient French term *maisnie*.
22. Creatures present in both Romanian and *rudari* folklore.
23. What remains, above all, is the importance given to the dream and its interpretation.
24. 1970 was chosen instead of 1965 (the year in which Ceauşescu became secretary of the Communist Party) because they settled in Burdu* that year, completing the spatial configuration that we find today.
25. The year 1950 is when their land was probably expropriated as a result of Law 83/1949. On collectivisation in Romania, see Iordachi and Dobrincu (2009); Kligman and Verdery (2011).
26. Gheorghe Gheorghiu-Dej, General Secretary of the Romanian Communist Party, was President of the Council of Ministers and later President of the Council of State from 1961 to 1965, the year of his death. He was succeeded two years later by Ceauşescu, who in 1965 had become Secretary General of the Communist Party.
27. Toponym that no longer exists: the town has been incorporated into the municipality of Carjelari (Citzer 2012: 157 et seq.).
28. The story is taken up later in the second part of the text. Valeriu uses the verb buy ('buy the land'); Ionica, his sister, on another occasion told me that the land had been bought by another *rudar*, when they came to Sibu Mare*.
29. See also later in Part II, chapter 12.
30. The elderly *rudari* often refer to the old leu (Rol) in use until June 2005. A new leu (Ron) corresponds to 10,000 old lei.
31. Teodorescu also reports: 'the Rudari of Valea lui Stan, who in the state-socialist era was active on the collective farms … This lifestyle was remembered by some older Rudari interviewees as prosperous and secure. Not secure from farm relocations, but secure in that everyone was forced into employment and therefore not "dying of hunger like nowadays in democracy"' (2020: 103).

Chapter 3

ETHNOGRAPHIC *MORCEAU*

Memoriale

Since the policy of ethnic recognition in the Balkans has been overvalued and considered a fundamental instrument of redemption, there has been an alliance of the *rudari* with the Roma, who unite in the same political parties or jointly present their claims (Șerban 2007; Alexa-Morcov 2013).

> Gogu: I was president of the Roma … So I did some research and wrote the request. I wrote down [the names of] all the families who had settled here brought from Bulgaria. Please issue the birth certificate to obtain the compensation money.
>
> In Bulgaria, persons who were deported [displaced] to Romania had to prove with a birth certificate that they were born [came from] Romania.

Today (2 February 2015) Mihai's parents were going to Timișoara to get documents for the compensation, about which Mihai first tells me: 'they [the *rudari*] took slaves', then he adds: 'they took their land and their house in Bulgaria'. 'And where do they take the documents?' I ask. 'They go to Sibiu, to Cioba', he explains, 'the king of the gypsies, who managed to get Germany to give the compensation money. He's very powerful'.

Gogu had been a local councillor for the 'pro-Europe' Roma Party for about a decade, until 2004. Only names of *rudari*, 245 in all, appear on the list of the 'founders' of this local Party cell. The main reasons for joining this association, essentially through Gogu, were linked to the possibility of access to resources allocated little by little for 'the inclusion of the Roma', from economic subsidies to land in the municipalities, and to the obtaining of compensation related to the events we have seen previously, granted by the laws that have followed and been amended over the years.

As for the actions of Gogu, many *rudari* have been critical, especially as regards the reconstruction of the right of ownership of the agricultural land that with the collectivisation of Romania had been taken from the families, thanks to the possibilities arising from law no. 169/1997, subsequently amended by law no. 1/2000.[1] On the issue of land, further possibilities for accessing new land were granted in 2003, linked to the Romanian government's strategy for improving the social and economic situation of the Roma. But even on this matter, many families felt that not enough had been done.

Here is an ethnographic document written in 1998 by Gogu to present the cause of the *rudari*.

Memoriale

For the love of the Romani Rudari Nation which was deported during the period of the Second World War and for which certain relief [compensation] measures were not taken by the Romanian Authorities

From the content of this memorial it is clear [it is assumed] that the Roma Rudari, as well as the other categories of Roma (*Ursari*, Argentari, Calderari – bear trainers, silversmiths, boiler makers, etc.), found that the Romanian Authorities had no interest in taking action or highlighting the social problems that all the Romanians in the country experienced during the period of the Second World War. I care about this problem because ever since I have known myself [I can remember], the social situation in this country has always been put at the bottom of the agenda or has even been forgotten.

Gentlemen, who feel you are dealing with these problems, and it is in your power, resolve this cause because you are undermining the laws and the Constitution of the country that binds itself equally with the rights of every man on earth, in a justly democratic state.

I write these words to remind you to give the justice that the minorities of this country (Macedonians, Jews, Germans, etc.) deserve. More related to the problem of the Roma Rudari in my area of the municipality [omissis] in the province of Călărași, because, although there are many deportees in this area, they have not benefited at all. Their situation is very critical, like the Roma *Ursari*, we are nobody's, there have already been depositions and meetings on this issue, but no action has been taken, why?

Gentlemen, I have reached the conclusion that this country is dominated by that form of shame with which the Roma have been, are and continue to be seen, and why? Perhaps when they made the army, when everyone took part in the defence of the country's homeland, they were good craftsmen (goldsmiths, silversmiths, spoon carvers, etc.), musicians, and above all the best in the world, to whom did they belong, Gentlemen? For whom is it that we have tried to behave in a certain human and respectful way toward the nation, the laws, but I have the impression that some figures in Authority at the head of the Country infringe the good conduct of the democracy of the nation, why? To keep us Roma on the sidelines and to get money from us [literally: on our backs].

Why, Gentlemen, won't you help us? Think that for us too there are so many talents who want to help the country to get out of this discomfort, and we suffer, certainly especially we Roma, who do not feel the support of this municipality [omissis] nor I believe, of the whole nation.

Our teachings are also yours, Gentlemen, you give us permission to apply them, because we have come uselessly to be insulted, if you refer to the colour of our skin my principles/teachings fail [lose their meaning], but the progress of the Romanian nation also fails.

So, in other words, Gentlemen who are at the helm of the State, I ask nothing more, in the name of all Roma of all categories, than to stop creating differences among the Romanian population, because it is also our mother's, ...when there has been misfortune in this country our ancestors, our parents have fought, and we will fight too. Here I am addressing the coordinators of the entire Roma nation throughout Romania and the whole world because at the moment when a nation needs a people to fight against another people it mobilises everything that means Romanian, in our case 23 million [people] have been asked, including us Roma, but they have always done this, since I began studying the history of Romania.

In the time of Alexandru Macedon, when we are supposed to have come here to Romania, in our day, who shaped iron, who worked wood, gold, silver and our music in particular: who sang and supported the Romanian Games? What minority comes and takes from us [deprives us of] this right, who takes from us this right that we have in our blood and we have supported this country in all the rights [from all points of view] especially in the regime of sad remembrance. Like them, this regime has hidden a large part of our rights from us and has humiliated us very much, and now in democracy we would like you to grant us, as well as all other minorities, the rights we deserve. Because most of the deportees are Roma if you think about it, along with them the Jews were taken and sent all over the place and they killed them, and derided them all over the world.

How is it possible that in one country ... not recognising the right to compensation for everything that [a person] has left behind from a life in another country, and is transferred to another country, to make another future then in other words to rejuvenate his life and to start over again from when he was aged 18–19.

I will continuously document with exact data what happened to these Rudari men and I believe there are also many *Ursari* or other categories of Roma, throughout their lives and especially when they were not allowed to carry on their meagre life where they were born, where they built their nest and obtained a social position for a fairly quiet life without prejudice from anyone, but this is how it had to be, especially for us Roma, when we had the same fate as the Jews.

In 1939–1940, my grandfather together with his children and other relatives … lived in the Bulgarian Republic, born and raised with a stable domicile, where the Romanian language was active … who formed a municipality and all lived together and formed a province or a village etc. But it did not happen because in this period came a mobilisation, a force, which either willingly or against their will, they embarked them on their own wagons and with something to eat they were exported by the Bulgarian troops or better expressed by the Bulgarian Authorities, they embarked them … and sent them to Romania.

Gentlemen, if my ancestors lived on the opposite bank of the Danube and have the Romanian language just like all the Romanians why not compensate us too. Based in the provinces of Durostor (Călăraşi, Silistra etc.) there existed a whole series of species of Romanians mixed with a whole series of nationalities that when they crossed from the Romanian side they benefited from all the rights. Well, Gentlemen, let us assume that it was Romanian territory, and that the country was in a situation like the current one, but because the others received and the Gypsies did not or because the Romanian Authorities simply lied when they took some of the Rudari, Argintari, etc., we who obviously did not have a place to escape to, they made them get on their wagons and embarking them again they took them to the Bug in Transnistria, because they would be given back their houses and plots of land in Bulgaria.

Because Gentlemen, whose fault is it, ours because we wanted to live as God made heaven and earth and left a place on earth for every life, but words to a man?

From the stories of all the Roma who have been heard, it emerges that they were angry with them, with their lives and with their habits/customs. The Roma in general have a simple life without involving themselves in the life of others, a life without too many complications, because [a Roma] sees that because of these he must withdraw or because of the complicated problems he has with his family, this is his life, so he had to get on wagons and be transported, like cattle, or on ships or cardboard boats, or beaten up without mercy. A whole series of makeshift boats were used for crossing the Danube, they lost human lives, some responded, some kept to the obvious, some assured them of towing more or less when they arrived in Romania or there in Transnistria.

Gentlemen, from the reports and discussions held about them, only bitter problems have come to pass, deaths from hunger and epidemics, from tuberculosis, and so many dead, shot and buried in the fireplace or left on the spot under the open sky in the hands of God. Gentlemen, you have thought why there are so many tuberculosis patients among the Roma, psychological illnesses, and other diseases harmful to the nervous system, … they come to despair, and to crime and are in prisons! They, Gentlemen, because of the problems that still exist, have seen terrible torments, they have seen and experienced on their own skin, sufferings, problems and misfortunes. They have seen how they mocked their own children, soldiers torn to pieces, left in the open air without food and water, until they ate animal droppings. Why, Gentlemen! At school when we studied, we were teased, some teacher out of God's pity or out of love for culture said that we are intelligent people, and maybe that's why they kept us in the shadows.

Gentlemen, therefore, the departure from Bulgaria to Romania, and from Romania to Transnistria was not made at the behest of the Roma, to leave their homes, land, agricultural equipment, etc. and to be humiliated in front of the soldiers to be fed with faeces, to leave brothers, sisters, children, parents, relatives who died on the way, or were shot.

In other words, you must find ways to help these people who feel they belong to no one but God and must be respected as any democratic state would.

Details of their suffering are found in their demands and statements, but this is nothing if you come and discuss with them to hear their problems and all the tribulations that have happened.

These tragedies of the Gypsy memorial could mean the definitive end of the problems of national insult, and that there shall no longer be discrimination against us in Romania, if the entire population recognises our human rights, and gives us all their support, without differentiation of nationality, in all domains of activity of this nation that is the only mother for all the 23 million people who form the Romanian Unity …

Today 16.09.1998

Note

1. On land reforms, see Cartwright (2001); Fay and James (2008); Dorondel (2016).

Chapter 4

MARRIAGE RITES AND PRACTICES

A joyful life for me is when you have a wife with children
or else who do you work for? What else do you do: work
and eat and spend your life like this?
—Marian, one evening in Medgidia, August 2011

In this chapter we see the practices related to marriage, that is, 'how' one
marries and what rituals take place. Within our family network, the union
between a man and a woman coincides with their first sexual relationship.
In this context, the virginity of the young woman represented, up to the
members of the fourth generation, an essential value, at least from an ideal
point of view. In fact, it would be the very loss of a woman's virginity that
unites the two in the husband-wife relationship.

Șerban commented: 'Until our generation [the third] it was very
important; now young people behave differently. Now the Internet eats the
brain.' His mother-in-law added: 'I was a virgin until Vasile, my body knew
only him for 32 years [her husband has been dead for some years]. Then
after 35 years I saw another man' [the last statement is made with irony and
everyone present laughed].

In the third generation, the vast majority of the marriages we know
occurred by eloping. In the fourth there are some changes, which I will
deal with shortly, although this practice still prevails. In the stories about
elopement, almost always someone has advised the girl or boy about a
young man/woman to marry.

During dinner at the home of Ionut and Mariana, in Florence, Ionut
narrated how things went when he got engaged to his future wife:

I met my wife when I was 18 … Someone introduced me to her because she was a beautiful girl, and told me that it would be good if I met her and married her. I went to Sibu Mare [Ionut is from Vadrea], I saw two girls, they were beautiful, and I said to them 'who shall I choose between you two?' [Mariana had gone to the disco with her sister for the first time], because they had long hair down to their shoulders: 'who shall I choose?' First I managed to talk to Monica about Marius, two, three words [to know something more about Mariana].

The first evening I kissed her.[1] The second evening, I told her that I loved her and that I liked her and that I wanted to get married and that I wanted her to come with me. Without my going to ask her parents for her with my mum and dad. We just ran away. That's how it was.

The second night, I had friends with horses and a wagon and they took us to Madgidia station. We spent thirty minutes waiting for the train and left for Vadrea. We arrived home. My parents were very happy and so were all our relatives and neighbours. I said "ve got[2] a beautiful girl, everybody liked her. She was a virgin. After a while we had our first baby.

I asked Ionut if, after taking her to Vadrea, his parents had spoken to Mariana's parents.

'Yes', he replied and continued: 'His parents talked to her parents about having a party: *logodeala*.[3] It means that we all come together to have the engagement party. Because that's what you do when the girl's a virgin. You have a big party only if she's a virgin. If she's not a virgin, there's no party. She was 16.

I asked him, 'Did your parents give Mariana gifts?' Ionut replied, 'Yes, they gave her two pillows, two sheets, a quilt, money, both from [my] parents and from Mariana's… My parents didn't know anything [at first]. Only my mum knew because my mum had laid eyes on her before I met her and said 'I've seen a beautiful, hardworking girl' … She fell in love with me at first sight and the second evening we eloped [*am placat*] [everyone laughed].

Even in the second generation, we know that elopement was practised. 'When I met Vasile' – Mariana's mother-in-law recalled – 'he told me that he would be with me for 3–4 days, and I replied that it was fine because it was enough to be able to say that we were engaged. Then we were together 32 years.'

Looking back through the generations, from the fourth (at least for the older children) to the second, we find that from the enormous prevalence of elopement, in the second generation this practice coexists with an equal number of previous 'agreements' between the families of the two young people – agreements that took place in a very simple way, as reported by both Stahl (1991) and Chelcea (1943).

Dumitra: At first I liked him and I did not like him [Stelu, who then became her husband] …I was 18 years old when I arrived in this municipality [Badra] … He was much older than me. I hadn't had a relationship with him until I got to his [parents'] house. My cousin was married to his sister, and he knew the family situation of my [future] husband. My cousin spoke of me to his parents; I did not know that my cousin intervened by talking to his mother, to his parents, and that they had spoken of me to him. [My cousin] convinced me that he was a good boy and from a good family. He fooled me.

… this man of mine, I was 16 years old, he stayed three days with me, I did not want him; and my father and mother said: 'take this boy, we know his parents from Bulgaria' … I did not want him. My parents and his parents knew each other from Bulgaria. And they [the parents] say, 'Take this boy.' My uncles came, my father's brothers. My father had seven brothers. They lived in Bulgaria. There were seven brothers, and they got together, took a bucket of wine and drank. At home, in Băneasa there is good wine … There are many vineyards here. And the collective and the people from the village. My father had a lot of vineyards … Yes. That's what people had at the time. It wasn't called *tuica* but *rachiu* [a distillate]. That's what they said, at that time they said *rachiu* (Luminiţa, Sibu Mare, March 2015).[4]

Luminiţa's story allows us to glimpse two scenes: one relating to 'convincing' the young *rudăreasă*, after her parents and those of the young *rudar* had talked together, to make them marry; the other, that of the celebration of the marriage itself, with the arrival of relatives, wine and *rachiu* to celebrate.

For the first generation, from the folds of two testimonies emerges *en passant* that there was also the practice of *bridewealth/bride-price*, for which the verb 'buy' is used by my interlocutors. Though both women who talk about it place it in the sphere of a remote past, in a conversation the fleeting reference to this practice is immediately dropped.

Sabrina: At the engagement, did his parents give some money for her?

Mariana: No, no, Sabrina, he didn't buy me like it was a hundred years ago. Without money.

Elena [the mother-in-law]: That's what the gypsies do.

Ionut: With us, you don't buy, you don't use.

Mariana: Only the gypsies do these things. With them, girls are bought. (Florence, 2015)

The next day I went back to Mariana's and in the absence of her mother-in-law and her husband, I returned to the subject of marriage and asked her, very delicately, for some clarification about the previous conversation. Mariana explained to me:

Sabrina, we are Romanians, but, you know, in Romania they call us gypsies, but we [are] not. We've had a lot of trouble because of this, you've been with us, so you know. We have nothing in common with them. We've always worked, we are honest. Our old people came from Bulgaria, maybe it was different in Bulgaria. I don't know. In the time of our grandparents, with us too, girls were bought, not always, it could be done or not. Then it wasn't done anymore. (Florence, 2015)

Ionica narrated:

There were traditions when my grandmother got married – I have to figure out the years; I don't know when, I think 70–80 years ago. She was from a family of nine sisters;[5] with them, when they got married, the boy's family had to buy the girl from her parents. They were 13, 14, 15 years old. At that time it was very important for the woman to be tall, robust, because the *rudari* thought [of the need] to be able to carry a large sack on their shoulders, without letting it touch the ground. My mother also told me that her father-in-law, when my father married her, said: 'Ah, leave it, Stan, look at that beautiful girl!' My mother had long hair because with the *rudari*, a serious woman does not cut her hair, only whores cut their hair. Or so it was thought. 'Stan, the girl is beautiful', said [the father-in-law] 'and good, because she is tall, solid and can lift a sack onto her shoulders: Dogs do not eat them from the sack' [a *rudari* saying]. Had she been small, the sack would have fallen off her shoulders onto the ground. They made cloth bags, with long straps, to be able to put them on their shoulders – it is called 'traistă făcută de rudari' [bag made by the *rudari*]. When they went into the country with spindles and spoons, they put them in their bags and also put in their bags what they carried for food, since the wagon did not go from one door to another, they left it on a street and continued [on foot] through the streets, at the doors, and shouted: 'Spoons! Spindles!', and what people gave them, they put in the bag. And my mother's father-in-law said: 'it is good because dogs do not eat it from the bag'. Grandma was tall, beautiful and sturdy. Grandpa married her. She was praised for her beauty and skill. Then, it was important for a girl to be a virgin. If she hadn't been, he would have sent her back to her father's house and all the *rudari* would have made fun of her. It was a big disgrace. (Florence, 2015).[6]

The genealogical level of the 'nine sisters', therefore of exogamous marriages, also seems to have seen the presence of a nuptial practice that subsequently disappeared, that of *bridewealth*.

Let us now look at the fourth generation, which has an adult group, a group that is still very young, not yet of marriage age, and one that could be. Among the couples who got married, and who in turn already have children, some sanctioned their union by eloping. Others, on the other hand, spoke to their respective parents about their wishes, and the boy's family invited the girl's parents to agree on what to do. In the latter case they are children of Pentecostal families. Being part of the Pentecostal movement, in fact, has not so far affected either the endogamous tendency (with whom you marry) or the virilocality. But we can see that it is beginning to change the ways in which people get married and also the ritual.

At the moment of their return, the elopement involves, now as in the past, going together to the home of the parents of each of the two young people, asking for forgiveness and acceptance of the union. The latter, usually, is not hindered, but there is not necessarily a great feast. This has also depended a lot on the situation of poverty in which the *rudari* have lived for a very long time. Valeriu (October 2010) explained to me that they have the *masă*, that is a dinner, usually held at the house of the girl's parents, in which the respective households take part.

The couple will be able to go to the town hall to 'regularise' their union and then contract civil marriage even after several years, often when the children start attending school. This formal passage is not called marriage, but defined through the phrase 'making documents'. From that moment, the woman changes her surname to that of her husband. Also in this case the *masa*, with the *grătar* (the barbecue) is held, attended by the closest relatives.

Among the Pentecostals, on the other hand, the engagement is followed after a few months by a religious wedding ceremony, which is held during the day at the church with collective prayers and songs; while in the evening, the families go to the restaurant, without accompanying the dinner with music by *lautari* and dances, but only with 'inspired' songs, that is, always connected to religion. At the microphone, people take turns to dedicate thoughts and wishes to the young couple. The bride, however, and also the groom and the guests, can devote themselves to the choice of clothes, lavish like other parties, to the embellishment of the places of the reception, as well as to engaging professional photographers for the images and the video.

Thanks to the earnings of the migrations, couples who have been married for a long time and who have already built their new house, decide to give the great wedding feast and, therefore, to celebrate the wedding (*la nuntă*), in the village in Romania during the month of August, when almost all the emigrant families return.

'There are two witnesses, the husband and wife, *nasu* and *nasă*. If the bride is a virgin, *mere* and *mereasă* each sleep at their parents' house; if it is not so then they sleep together in [their own] house'.[7] In the case that Valeriu narrates, the witnesses were he and his wife, while the couple who were to get married have been living in Spain for a long time, they have a teenage daughter and other children, and therefore, in the evening they slept together and in the morning 'she helped him to get dressed, then she stayed at home to prepare herself, helped by the women'. The relatives invited by the groom go to the house of the witnesses: 'we toast, drink, eat some sweets, the groom gets shaved and we dance the *hora* [the collective dance in a circle]'. Then they all go to pick up the bride, forming a procession in the street accompanied by the 'musicians' (*lautari*); often the favourite instrument is the accordion, 'because everyone must see and know that they are getting married'. Arriving at the bride's house, every person who enters is offered a drink and a cake, and the women dance in a circle (the *hora*) while the bride prepares herself. The women, during the dressing, gather around the bride, while the witness (*nasă*) makes her up, combs her hair and, finally, puts a tiara on her head. Subsequently, the groom must lift up the bride also lifting the chair where she is seated, as a sign of good luck. Then they reach the church, where the marriage is celebrated with an Orthodox rite and then all go to the *Camin Cultural*, where all the marriages, baptisms and festivals of the village are celebrated. Between the church and the *Camin*, the women stop to change their clothes, in particular the *nasă*, for which the expected garments are three. The groom and bride stop at the entrance, waiting for the guests and greeting them one by one – 'all, until the last guest arrives', which includes a greater number than those of the morning and afternoon.

Valeriu explained all this to me as we began to watch, together with one of his daughters and Dana, the video of the wedding with his wife Anabela, who occasionally looked from the next room to add some comments about the guests, the clothes, the musicians.

The tables are arranged in a horseshoe shape, so that the room can be left free for dancing. The spouses sit together with the witnesses at a table exclusively dedicated to them, in front of all the others. The party, which lasts until the next morning, is a succession of dinner and dances, alternating dances in pairs, collective dancing and the *hora*.

Then there are two special moments. The first is represented by the public proclamation of the gifts received: the singer gradually says the name of each invited family (name of the husband, wife and their surname) and the gift they have given to the spouses, followed by applause and exclamations: a fragment of joy and exaltation for each guest.

The second moment represents the staging of the bride's abduction. The sign of the disappearance is represented by one of the shoes – which in the speed of the abduction would have slipped from the foot of the young woman on the threshold of the place of the party. It is the witness who 'kidnaps' the bride.

The groom must then look for her in the streets, in the shops still open (which in summer close very late), staging anger, asking around, left and right, who has stolen her. Meanwhile, the witness takes her somewhere else, even to a nightclub (the wedding is always held on a Saturday).[8] When the groom returns empty-handed to the *Camin*, and the witness is also back, the two stop in front of each other, to the excitement of everyone. The groom then asks the witness: 'Did you steal her from me?', and he replies: 'Yes. If you give me the money, I'll give her back'. The young man must, therefore, give a certain sum to the witness to get his young woman back. That money, then, by internal circulation, will go to the bride.

The bride, in the morning, at the end of the celebrations, sits down. A new scene begins: the witness tries to put a handkerchief on her head, as a sign that from that moment she is no longer a free girl. For three consecutive times, as soon as they put the veil on her, she must remove it, with a jerky gesture, to represent the fact that she wants to remain free. Finally, it is put on and tied behind the back of her neck (in everyday life it is only worn by elderly women).

At this point only the women dance in a circle: *hora miresei* (the *hora* of the bride).[9] The *nuntă* has ended.

Notes

1. The children, who were listening, laughed; Dana opened her eyes wide and said to Ionut: 'Look, you didn't have to tell the whole truth!'
2. Ionut used the verb '*a luat*', which the *rudari* often use and which has a strong sense (it is used daily with objects) of emphasising that he didn't ask anyone for her, he took her. The verb, in the various stories, is also used in the plural, emphasising both the action and the will of both, man and woman, to take each other.
3. The Romanian word for engagement is *logodnă*.
4. Interview conducted during the *MigRom* project.
5. She is talking about the 'nine sisters': Ionica's father was the son of one of them.
6. Interview conducted during the *MigRom* project.
7. Sibu Mare*, October 2010.
8. At the wedding I attended as a guest in August 2011, the bride was taken to a party at a club in the nearby town (about 5 kilometres from the ceremony venue).
9. The 'bride's ball' also often ends the Romanian marriages that are not of *rudari*, with a different execution and the participation of the closest relatives. In this regard, it should be noted that the *rudari* have their own *hora*, an element also noted by Stahl (1991). Similarly, the *hora* of the women is found during the dressing of the bride even in traditional Romanian marriages (this time in the feminine in both contexts).

Chapter 5

ETHNOGRAPHIC *MORCEAU*

Ionica's Conversion

Since the late 1990s, the Pentecostal movement gradually began to enter the lives of some of our *rudari*.[1] Initially in a marginal way, then through various members of a family and subsequently involving entire domestic groups. Among the people, even in the same nucleus, there are several variations and shifts in the attitudes toward the belief itself, the commitment toward its precepts, and the impetus with which people take part in the religious meetings. The spirituality that is conveyed in our context, referring to Spittler (1988), is based on the high value given to the religious experience, the spontaneity in the collective service or during private prayers, on oral communication from the pastors and on the authority of the Bible.

What is remarkable about the power of this form of ritual revitalisation is that although it is rather simple, promising a reversal of social positions, it is nonetheless exceedingly efficient in deeply penetrating social structures without relying on additional resources or preconditions (e.g. hierarchical social structure, common cultural features). The cultural requirements for this form of ritual revitalisation are basic: ideas of an open human heart and the Spirit that can fill this heart (Fosztó and Kiss 2012: 62).

What we could call the 'low-threshold' access to Pentacostalism seems to suggest to people that they should make an interior change, which would enable them to 're-signify' the uncertainty of their lives. In the village assemblies (*adunări*) which I have attended, special importance was given, above all, to two moments/spheres: participation as an emotional, transported experience, through singing; and the words of the pastor, who through the Bible seems to provide a model for a 'good life'.

These two aspects are the centre of the following ethnographic account from Ionica, collected in an interview in Florence in 2015.[2]

Sabrina: Ionica, tell me about your conversion.

Ionica: Converted means attracted, changing from one religion to another. After I married, after twelve years, because I got on very well with my husband. He worked at the tractor cooperative 'Agricola Castelu'. He had a job. We got married 1985. I was 17 years old and he was 17, he was born on 1 November 1967 and I was born on 17 November 1967. A difference therefore of 16 days: we were both children.

He was respectful, he wasn't a drunkard, he drank very rarely, once or twice a month, when he received his wages, because he was with the guys who did the transfers and together with two of my brothers and a cousin of mine, who worked at the Port of Constanţa. In 1999. He smoked, but little, he never created a scandal, except that he liked women. He was calm, a model husband ... He didn't offend me, he never swore at me, he didn't hit me, we got on very well.

An example: when he got his wages, he shopped at the market, also for the children, chocolates in particular, and for me a bigger one [chocolate]. Also new kinds, of different brands. He was careful about everything he did. When there was something, we did it together, we arranged it ... let's do this, we'll buy that ... he would buy food that the children liked. Sweets.

Before I converted to this religion, being, *pocăiţă* [Pentecostal], I had only four children ... After 12 years of marriage ... I became ill with hepatic, splenic echinococcus and cholecystitis. A disease without a cure. But I wasn't afraid that I would die. I was like this for many years, about five years.

With me at Sibu Mare, there was a large group of Pentecostal Christians, I had known them since I was 14 years old. I was together with the girls in my street because their parents were Christian. At the meetings where they gathered, they sang beautifully and they prayed. This attracted me. The girls with whom I went to the canal, to the woods, always, ... with whom I went on the streets, we knew each other very well. And I went with them to someone's house, they sang, they didn't do bad things, I liked it.

I was 29 years old when I had a dream, I dreamt about a pit, in fact. I went to a *pocăiţă* friend's. Petra was her name; she was five years older than me, a serious woman. Different from other *rudari*. She was very well off, she had a beautiful house, they were organised and were doing well. I became her friend in the field, when we were hoeing. When my children were older and stayed on their own, I sometimes went to the field and was paid for the day's work. Virgil was at work and we went there to get out of the house. I hoed. That's how I got to know her, taking the row of maize next to her. She invited me several times to go for a coffee; I went to hoe only then, for a few days. A year had passed from when I had met her and she heard about my serious illness. I dreamed and I told her my dream. I forgot to tell you: I liked her, for seven years I went to my mother's, I would go down that road where the *pocăiții* gathered, they sang with their windows open in summer. As I went to my mother's, I stopped to listen to their songs. There were some Romanians who gathered, *pocăiții* and *rudari*, and they sang. My heart would fill with joy and this calmed the anguish/stress of my thoughts and my mind became calm, when I was angry that is, it gave me peace of mind; I was like a new person, who didn't know good and evil. A newborn without worries. Ah, how well I felt! Total relaxation; I was in a new world when I listened to their songs; I paid attention, I understood them, my soul recognised them and it was a soul fully at peace.

Without my entering the meeting, even though I had known them since I was 14, I went with the girls, but I didn't decide to repent [convert]. Every Sunday I went down that street, to my mother's, and I listened to the songs, they attracted me.

I had the dream and told it to this girl. She was a Christian, she had four children too. She told me that dreaming means life and death: 'The pit you dreamed of is yours! You will be in it if you do not return to God! He will save you, because you have a difficult disease.' This girl did not know what illness I had, I had not told her anything, I only told her about the dream.

This dream troubled me for a year and I believed, I felt that I would die. I went to her house; I sang with her, with her daughters, aged 13–14; these girls are in Italy [now].

I always went to her, because I had no one better than her. Because they were all gossiping … Virgil was at work, the children were small, I was on the edge of the village, with the older neighbours. I had no friendship with them, … I did not leave home, but since I met Petra, she was serious, I went to her house, she called me to her, I went to the religious *adunare* [gathering], but when I entered, the believers were praying, I stood with my eyes open and laughed at them. *Adunare* means a special home for those who pray, sing, no one lives there. It is a holy place. They gathered on Thursdays, Tuesdays and Sundays. There, in the hall, was a priest who knew the word well. He sang very beautifully, well, his family was in order, that is, as it was written in the Bible. To be a priest you must have good qualities: these people had them.

But, at first, I went with her because I was ashamed to refuse. It was funny and I laughed: 'Come on, come with me?'; 'Alas, I can't, Virgil is coming home from work, I'm going home.' Once, twice, how many times could I refuse? I was ashamed.

So, until 1997, July 5, when I underwent surgery for echinococcosis, a liver cyst and cholecystitis (gallbladder). I was very ill, that disease was without a cure. Female cancer. It had spread to the spleen, gallbladder and to the liver. Both lobes. Very tough. But since I believed and believe so much in God – since I was little, I told you [in a previous conversation], I caught the children to beat them, and I couldn't [beat them], I had pity, an unknown gift guided me. I felt sorry for the poor, who were suffering, and did not have what they needed.

I went to Constanţa, to the district, to have the operation; the doctors told me: 'Good, do a ten-day treatment, we will operate on you!' For those ten days, I got to know better, although I knew it by sight, a *pocăiţ*. And I talked to him, because he was from my country. He spoke to me about God; I learned from him three songs that I wrote down, and I sang along with the other patients. Many were seriously ill with cancer. And I thought it would be good to tell them about God too, to know and not die without God (because man in difficulty, in despair, seeks God). It was very, very tough.

S.: For how long were you in the hospital?

I.: I was there for 40 days, 14 of which were in intensive care, where you are monitored 24 hours a day. I had three drains (tubes): one from the liver, one from the gallbladder, one from the spleen …

Before I had surgery, when I entered, I entered without fear, with trust in God. I said, 'If I'm for Hell, God let me die now! If my name is written in the Book of Life and I am for Heaven, let me live!' I was on the operating table for four and a half hours …

This time of 40 days after surgery, they removed me from the room with a blood perfusion, a treatment perfusion, a thread on my mouth and three drains. Imagine, full of threads. I was ill. After two weeks, they got me out of bed, stood me up, made me walk; they helped me. Being drugged with sedatives, I did not feel pain, but I heard myself moaning in my sleep. And I couldn't wake up. They moved me to another ward after the intensive care.

Before the operation, I had a dream. About the pit. Two weeks after the operation, I dreamed of three particularly bright rays, like the sun [fire], of a particular light, like those of the lighthouse of the big port. A soft warmth, that calmed me, relaxed me from the pain. It went straight into my liver. From then [1997] until today [2015], I have nothing anymore. God healed me. I didn't understand the dream. But, thinking about it, I realised from where and what: it is because I believed so firmly in God and I still believe today. And I felt well. I have been cured. Everyone was amazed! The doctor said: 'You were going to die, you wouldn't wake up after the operating table, but God made you get up, because I never operated on what you had. When I was a student, I witnessed these cases. But 1 in 1,000 succeeds. But you: God has raised you from the sleep of death! What more do you want to believe?' I received healing and the doctor said so. What do you think I did in the hospital? I went together with that *pocăiţ* because he stayed for a long time in the hospital, because he was operated on. I reported the dream … 'Look what I dreamed …' 'God has healed you.' I know. Because I felt it, no one told me, but I know it's healing. And it turned out that I haven't fallen ill anymore. But, I say, why has God healed me? That I might repent [convert].

When I got home, I forgot, and for three, four months, those who saw me said I was going to die. Because they saw me and knew what I had had (they didn't know I had received healing, because I didn't tell them). No. I was yellow, like wax, and very thin. However, I was like a person after an illness. It's been four, five months and I met on the street that *pocăiṭ* man from the hospital. He was with his wife and pointed his index finger at me, amazed, and asked: 'Did you keep your word?' He said that to me while walking and didn't say anything else. And he left. We knew each other. We didn't speak to each other. I said that I did. But I hadn't kept my word, I had forgotten about it. And then another person came to me, in my thought, and reproached me. She was right. A promise made, I must keep it. And I decided to go to the *adunare*.

Moreover, after having surgery on July 5, I left the hospital in September, and went directly to another hospital, in Mangalia, Eforie, since Virgil had fallen from a height of 4 m, while at work, because he worked at the Port, in Constanṭa … Falling, he cracked the heels of both his feet. God protected him, because if he had fallen differently, he would have broken his bones … He was released from the hospital, but not cured. He was told not to use his legs for three months; it was difficult. He obtained medical leave: September, October, November, December. Being winter, he stayed only in the house. I have recovered.

He alone, without a team, without the away guys and without drink, he was not a drunkard, but on Sundays, after work, he drank with the guys who had the same job, 'stevedore' … Friends no longer looked for him, because he had no more money. He no longer met with them. He was bored, he was alone in the house …

One day, a friend, the one I told you about, Petra, … sent one of her girl-friends to call on me: 'Come to us, because a *pocăiṭ* brother, pastor of Negru Vodă, has come. He is called Mirică'…

Then Virgil also offered to come. That pastor asked him some real-life questions. 'How old are you?' He was 29 at the time, and so was I, but he hadn't asked me. 'What have you done in these years, what have you achieved'? It was true: we had done nothing. Just four children and a little house. Do you know this, Sabrina? Everything is an escape following the wind: can you catch the wind? To catch it, you run in vain.

We worked, we ate, we didn't have a nice, good house, we weren't even in line with the world. Because so many young people of our age had fun, were fashionably dressed, went dancing, to weddings. We with the children, poor, only to survive, not lacking our daily bread, we went too, when we had no children, at the beginning; after having three, four children, who went dancing? We couldn't do it anymore. When I had a child, my mother or mother-in-law was there. But then, who left? We rarely went to weddings, only to a close friend, or a relative.

Being bored, he [Viorel] has come too. Those questions were like an awakening, from a dream to reality, so it was. All a race behind the wind. Let us think of eternal life, of the soul. So Virgil went to a wake night. The evening of the vigil there is a meeting, a gathering of several Christians, from all over the nation … in a village, in a large hall, from afternoon until morning. All night long, singing and praying, for the sick and those who believe in it are healed. Prayers for what you need in everyday life.

After that evening, since Virgil was invited by that *pocăiț* to his village, to that party, he returned determined to make the bond with God, to repent: 'I've decided to repent.' To tell the truth, I loved God, but I wasn't going to repent so young, at 29, because I was afraid I would have to have so many children. But when God came to my heart, I no longer thought of these earthly things. When I realised that there is eternal life after death, I decided. That human life is like a vapour that is dispelled. And after burial, man passes on to another life. I believed and believe even now, I decided with him to make the bond with God. In March, 17 March 1997, we made the bond, the oath, a baptism in the water, dressed in white, we entered the river. And he [the pastor] asked us, 'Have you decided to follow God forced by others or out of love for Him? How long do you want to follow Him? Until March or until death?' We replied: 'until death'. And I want to keep my word.

We immersed ourselves into the water. It means: immerse an old person, full of sins, and come out of the water a new person, full of love for God. And we really changed into new people, with new lives, being in the world with small worries, problems; we were with a heavy soul and it weighed like a sack on our shoulders. But knowing and having a bond with a Father in heaven, all that is necessary I ask Him and He resolves it for me. I am with a quiet soul and full of peace, even if I am in difficulty and my soul is sad, oppressed by the things of life. We prayed, sang, and felt our souls freed from a weight that was like a heavy sack carried on our shoulders. Now I no longer have that oppression because I give it to Him, and He, God, carries it in my place. An example: it happened sometimes, very rarely, when Virgil was about to get some money, that he no longer had enough to make the children's dinner or lunch. One day, I prayed to God and told him. There are times when I don't have anything at all. I was expecting Virgil from work that pay day. Your mum lived far away, who went to see her? I never went to my neighbours, not even to my brothers … I had nothing. I woke up in the morning, I cleaned up. I had four children … Faith is great and I knelt on my knees and prayed: 'God, I have no food today, but You know it and I ask You the favour of taking care of it.' I had even forgotten that I had no food. It was 11:30. And I went to see a sister [Pentecostal friend], this girl, Petra. Without asking her anything, without telling her anything. She was washing, I remember, and it's been years since then. 'How are you, Ionica?' And I said: 'Fine'. Talking to her, she said, 'Here, I have some cabbage that I'm not using, and I want to give it to you, because I want to wash the barrel and clean the warehouse. You take this cabbage and, here, my husband bought me some pork. One piece is enough for me. You take a piece too, to make it with the cabbage. And I took them, I had kept silent, and I said, 'God, thank You! Thank you, thank you' ... God has worked so much in my house. My son was ill. We have witnesses, Dana and Raluca, the girls were big and they know it. Ioan was very ill. I was with him at night holding him in my arms, to silence him; they were also there when I prepared meals. Virgil was at work. He cried out that he was ill; he had a fever, even during the day, even at night. I didn't know what to do for him. He was one week at home and two in the hospital. So I went behind – we had two rooms, a corridor and a summer kitchen behind – to prepare food. I cried and prayed, being in the kitchen, I said in my prayer to God: 'God, You touch this child! I've had enough of myself; he's always ill. You take him with you, you make him healthy, you let him live.' Right after the prayer was over; Dana came with him in her arms, since she cared about him. She said to me, 'Mum, Ioan is asking for food. He is not ill any more, Ioan.' He had been ill for three days, had a fever and was not eating. The sign that God heard was that he asked for food. This is what happened. God heard me.

Twenty years ago, Romania wasn't like it is now with telephones. There was a woman who had a telephone in her house, she was rich, she didn't have anyone, and there was a factory with its headquarters on the edge of the village, about three km away. He usually fell ill on Friday, Saturday, when there was no one at the dispensary, and in town it was the same. Just the doctor on call. And my hope was in God, I prayed. When he asked for food, I thanked God for touching him. So, I believe in God. Because I personally went through Him. So it was my return to God. I became ill and He healed me. I have been through so many things in my life, and with troubles, and joys and sorrows, but God is with me and I thank Him that we are healthy and on the right track. And I'm waiting for a new life.

S.: I'd like to know, why do you think your mum believed in myths and you didn't? What changes have been made from your mother's generation to yours?

I.: Yes, my mother believed them when she was a child, being in the Orthodox religion. She didn't practise it, but she was Orthodox. Since in Romania, during communism, you had to have only one religion. Not a God. The people had to believe that the president of the country is their father and their God. You went to jail if word got out that you were a Christian. So many things have happened.

S.: I didn't mean religion. I was talking about the traditions, *rudari* customs. Why don't you have them at your mum's?

I.: Mum lived in a generation that was isolated from other more educated people ... Since they did not read the Bible, which was not to be found anyway. Read, believe, know the truth. The Bible is the book that points to the truth, they learned from their elders, from one generation to another. From dreams, from their mental inventions ... They had no school, they were illiterate. They lived like this, from their ancestors, with these rituals of enchantment, the evil eye ... Mum believed so much in the customs of the *rudari* ... She heard from her parents, but for the evil eye, disenchantment, she left when she thought it was necessary, with the children, when we were little (me and my brothers) ... The Romanians also believe in these things. We, when we were kids, mum was very strict. Children must be children. Parents respected as parents. Mum respected old people and was serious like them. Her mother and father-in-law, her brother and sister-in-law, her parents should not see her in a nightgown or barefoot or when she was breastfeeding her baby. So, a huge respect for the elderly. Now, everything is normal. They have kept [these habits] in my family's generation, for them, to us they have not passed them on; they went out in the morning, they came back in the evening from the field. They didn't ask you what you did or what you want. She came, she made food, and she took care of her children, her husband, the house and everything ...

So, in my generation, 35–40 years ago, habits were no longer as they were 70–80 years ago. But, in some families, they are also maintained in the same way now. I went to school and those of my generation were sent [to school] every day. We didn't have many different clothes, like today, just a few changes, for school. But Mum washed them, took care of them, because she is a clean, very tidy woman. She took care of us, the cleaning, especially when it was a holiday. I remember when it was Easter, the mother painted the walls outside with lime, with a brush in her hand she made a *brâu*, a thick line at a distance of 30 cm, which was invented by the old *rudari*. Instead of colour, she put the ash in the lime, and the lime turned grey, a grey colour. Then, she would put some kind of wallpaper (roll) on the walls, very nice. A house with walls full of flowers. So, I learned from her to make bread, to paint, to put the roll on the walls ... When I went to the shops to buy sweets – you would find the things you needed. Children were obliged to go to school, otherwise there would be fines. There was religion, since God existed. This was under communism, in the year 1990. Ah, no – I didn't believe in customs, myths, rituals, nor do I not believe. That is the difference. Mother, when she was little, was not in a family, a meeting of Christians. She bent down and prayed to an icon (a drawn picture), to a wooden cross. Nor did anyone know about the Bible, really. But I, being a ten, twelve-year-old girl, I heard about God really, together with the girls on my street. But I believed in it. And when I was a child, for example, when I cried so much, and I probably had the flu, I was ill, she didn't go to the doctor. And she [my mum] would say, 'Alas, let's go to Sister Tudora', an old *rudăreasă* from the village, 'we will do something for her, we will free her [*o-descântăm*], we make the crying pass'...

The old *rudăreasă* pulls the baby, gives him a massage and then with a razor blade scratches him, and the baby recovers, he no longer cries. But the child being massaged for 30–40 minutes, it is normal that he is tired, and after he is massaged, he falls asleep. They interpret differently. What do you reckon? This is the truth! The children being chubby, crying is normal. My mother, when I cried, took me to that old woman, pulled me, made me a 'disenchantment', cut me, fatigued me, and then, children sleep, being tired. Ah, you're ... I have been cut with a razor on my shoulders and chest. See, that is a custom: '*leac băbesc*' [old wives' cure]. I, on the other hand, know the word of the Bible, what is written: it is not okay, it is a sin to shed blood and I have not used even a 'disenchantment', because this is magic, from other gods. Mother lived among other customs, habits, religions, we are of another generation, more emancipated, ordered, with our body and mind going to schools, towns, countries, we have seen the world, and we have learned too.

Notes

1. Here only some elements from the ethnographic field are reported, without looking at the scope of these religious movements for which there is an abundant literature, which focuses on the spread on a world scale of Pentacostalism, with its multiple facets and political implications. Besides the classical Robbins (2004), Marshall (2009) and the volume edited by Coleman and Hackett (2015), please refer to Schirripa (2012) and for Romania to Rubiolo (2016), above all for the implications in contexts of migration with a focus on women, as well as to Fosztó (2009), to Fosztó and Kiss (2012). See also Slavkova 2021.
2. During the research in the *MigRom* project.

PART II

The Time of Migrations

Home, Mobility and Transnationalism

Prologue

Mihai comes from a small village in the south of Romania, located along the railway line that connects the capital Bucharest with the city of Constanța. He has been in Italy since he was 18 years old; he worked as a labourer, then mainly as a bricklayer and, finally, as a courier. At the beginning, more than 15 years ago – paraphrasing his words – he was having a good time: he was in Montecatini (province of Pistoia) and per month he managed to earn a salary ten times higher than an average of his context of origin. He sent a little money home and he spent a lot: on clothes, clubs, discos … '*Eram prost*', 'I was stupid', he comments.

Now, he has been married for several years and since 2015 also 'with documents',[1] he has three children – a boy and two girls – the last born in February 2020. In Florence, he lived mainly in occupied buildings, the last of which was cleared following a fire in 2018. It was a former hotel, closed and abandoned, which shortly before the evacuation housed over a hundred people, most of them families from Morocco and Romania.

And who is Mihai's wife? A strong young woman, Dana: after so many years that we have known each other, we are now good friends. She is about ten years younger than me, but I – in her and her family's opinion – seem younger and so at their home in Romania we may both look thirty. This was an idea of his grandmother's in Sibu Mare, *mamaia* Elena, who repeated it with great conviction, especially in the period when I was *singure*, that is, unmarried, perhaps to find me a husband … so I joked and commented that it would take me only two hours by plane to recover so many years! And it all ended in collective laughter.

People laugh here. They smile. People make fun of each other. There is no lack of irony when they are sitting together outside, in front of the door or in the *gradina* (garden/vegetable garden), under a tree, a willow tree as when they went into the woods, my *rudari*. Perhaps it must be 'my' for an anthropologist after many years of knowledge and research, passing through and being with them in the most diverse environments of their lives. On the other hand, when I talk about it, I use the phrase 'my Romanian family' and if I had to do my genealogy, I would probably include relatives of 'choice', people who have built a relationship with me thanks to my fieldwork. And they too, reciprocally, are witnesses of my biographical vicissitudes, the last represented by my marriage, in which Mihai and Dana were also present, while I had previously gone to the municipality at Vadrea and to their *gratar* (barbecue) that they had organised for the event that, from an external perspective, is called civil marriage.

Marian, on the other hand, Dana's brother, married in 2015, not in Romania, but in a village in the province of Florence. A marriage, to tell the truth, *sui generis* for this family network because his wife is 'Romanian-Romanian' (as the *rudari* say of the Romanians who do not belong to any minority), and this division was evident, also reflected in space: the area of the tables where they were sitting, the one and the other clearly separated; the noticeably unrelaxed atmosphere and the different *obiceiuri* (customs, habits). I had gone there alone, without anyone accompanying me; even this is strange for a woman who is no longer young: I was part of the family!

Many things have changed over the years, they are part of my life and I am part of theirs. This testimony, in my case, is also transformed into a disciplinary work that, on their part, is immediately depicted in the writing of a book: 'So, have you written *cartele*?' And they did not fail to mock me because, until now, I had not completed it: it was from the year following our meeting, in fact, that they told me to write this book *despre* (on) *rudari*.

The marriage in 2013 of Raluca, Dana's sister, and second in age of the daughters, was quite different: it was, in fact, the first marriage celebrated in Florence and was Pentecostal. In the restaurant in Piazza della Libertà, rented for the occasion, everyone came, the entire network of relatives who are in Florence, emigrated from the four Romanian places of reference in my research: Sibu Mare, Badra, Vadrea and Burdu. It's June: a wedding dress bought in Bucharest, photos in front of Florence Cathedral and on Piazzale Michelangelo. A few months earlier, in March, however, she and her husband had also 'got their documents' in Badra, and had – on that occasion – laid the *masă*, the table, that is, they had celebrated at the house of her in-laws, with her parents and closest relatives, in addition to friends and the closest brothers and sisters of the church, making a *gratar*. And it was no longer, since then, Raluca di Sibu Mare, but Raluca di Badra.

And, again, two years earlier (in 2011) I had been to a big wedding in Romania, in Sibu Mare: that had definitely been the most engaging wedding. It was held at the *Camin cultural*, building of the municipality built with European funds, which is made available to the public for festivities. And where people remain – after a day of celebrations spent elsewhere – from the evening to the next morning, having dinner and dancing in continuation.

On that occasion, I had been accompanied by Dana's first cousin, Nicolae, not without first asking permission from her grandmother and other family members ... Yes, because if I was considered almost like a daughter, a cousin, a granddaughter, it is also true that in reality I wasn't ... Therefore I had to be careful not to create embarrassing or 'shameful' situations for myself, that is, not appropriate for a single woman and of which, therefore, I could be 'ashamed' and make people 'ashamed' of me. I therefore went as a 'cousin' accompanied by a first cousin, also alone, *singure*, having separated from his wife. And having been appreciated for how I danced, especially in the *hora*, I made my family look good. Among other things, the witnesses of the spouses were the family's neighbours in Romania, Ştefan and Ana, in turn the godfather and godmother of Nico's brother. In 2019, on the occasion of Nicolae's coming with his new wife, we had met for dinner at their home in Florence and the photos of the wedding eight years earlier, which they had been able to find, had again been an opportunity to make fun of each other (including me).

Continuing on from the previous one, I started this part on the migrations with what is most important for our *rudari*: with their children and with marriages. And to complete the picture, I should mention the home, in Romania, where the formation of one's own family finds visible, material consecration: everything else comes afterwards and depends on it, including the decision to migrate. At least for now.

Note

1. We have seen that this expression is used to indicate that the marriage is formally registered, but it is not the equivalent of *nuntă*, that is, the wedding feast.

Chapter 6

LEAVING

What have we gained from the revolution? Nothing. We couldn't take care of ourselves, we had no work, no money, nothing. Our children, we didn't know how to dress them, feed them. We had become poor, poor.
—Ionut, Vadrea, August 2014

They closed everything, everything. There was nothing left. There was only work left in the fields, casual labour. You were just earning money so as not to die of hunger, but just not to die of hunger, I swear.
—Mălina, Sibu Mare, August 2014

The end of the era of the socialist regime, as in other contexts in Eastern Europe and the former USSR, and also for a very high number of Romanians living especially in rural areas,[1] marked a socio-economic collapse in the lives of our families.

Sabrina: What was it like for you after the revolution?

Florentin: Very difficult, I had no job, so many poor, unemployed. Romania was rich, many worked in agriculture, there were factories, but after the revolution they sold everything: the factories, agricultural land, agricultural machinery, everything was ruined! Having no work, I went to work days in the bosses' fields, I did not know how to make spoons, the tradition was lost, [I went to work in the fields] because in Ceaușescu's time if you did not have a job you went to prison! When I was 14, I went to school and worked as well, I gave the money to my mother, but when I had my family, I didn't have a job, I left for Turkey, Serbia and worked there. (Florentin, Florence, January 2015).[2]

Several times the testimonies show the reference to the trade of *lingurar* as a heritage lost in the generational transition during the dictatorship of Ceaușescu, in Vadrea and Sibu Mare, less in Badrea and Sibust, as we have seen. The perspective is not nostalgic but very practical: knowing how to do this craft as a resource to be recovered in case of need. Not that Florentin thinks – like the others – that this trade would have allowed him to live well and not have to leave, but it is the comparison between the work in the fields (done by the day, with no contract or protection, with a spade and without any machinery) and that of *lingurari* (as the unique bearers of a know-how, wood craftsmen) that emerges from Florentin's point of view. The perception of having had to suffer, men and women, a situation of labour exploitation, without respect for the person, instead of a decent job, that they felt 'their own', carried out by their fathers and fathers' fathers.

In fact, in Badrea and Sibust, where families had not stopped transmitting their knowledge related to woodworking, some *rudari*, with the end of the regime, had resumed the craft, with the making and itinerant sale of the goods:

Vasile: It is a tradition for us, a trade, if I am without work tomorrow, I can buy wood, because I know it and I can work to enhance it. I'm a licensed craftsman. In Romania I was out of work and I had to learn the craft from my father, from my grandfather, from these two generations … There is a festivity in April … people buy dishes, pots, put spoons in the pots and we sell them. Those who had money [gave] it to us, and those who [did not] gave us goods … This [was done] even after the revolution. It has remained like a never-ending bank fund, so this craft has continued. Now I don't know [for] the fourth generation.[3] I carried on [doing it], my grandfather, my father and I don't know if the children …

Ionica: What did you have to do [in Romania] to get a licence [licensed craftsman]?

Vasile: I had to document myself so as not to say that I am …[rudar] I declared myself a craftsman because I know how to make spoons … I had to bring proof. There was only one type of rudari cooperative [in the] district [Călărași] and they came to our municipality [Sibust] and we showed them our work. Because we went from village to village, I had to show it because if they found me without a licence they confiscated the goods. Because when I left with the merchandise, spoons, spindles, stools, I left for even a month, [I even] went to another district … We went with the horses and the wagon and if the police stopped me they asked me to present the documents to show that I was licensed and that I had the right to sell, I presented them with the authorisation; I went to the municipality and paid a tax that showed that I am from there, from that area and they knew about me, otherwise I could not sell without a licence … [It was] after the revolution, after 1990 that they began to ask for the licence.

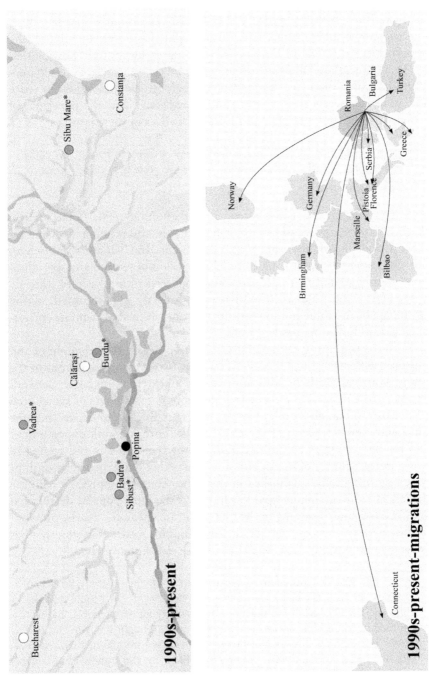

Map 6.1. Romanian villages and migrations. © Sabrina Tosi Cambini.

As resources dried up in their own life context, our families got back on the road. Their mobility territory is expanding enormously, first by taking into account neighbouring countries and tight timescales, then by seizing opportunities throughout Europe and opening up longer term possibilities.

We will therefore follow the times, ways and thoughts related to different migrations over the years, trying to keep together the dimensions of space and time, connecting the transnational perspective and the paradigm of mobility to the past, present and future of the lives of these families.

> Since the revolution we have spread, we have arrived here in Italy ... We came here for three months [2001] and 14 years have gone by. (Vasile, Florence, 2015)

A few years after the revolution, around the mid-1990s, some men in the families began occasional cross-border migration, going to work for short periods in neighbouring countries – Serbia and Turkey in particular, but also going to Greece. These are jobs that do not require any specialisation, mainly related to the construction and agricultural sectors. Already at the end of the 1990s the first departures to Italy were recorded, taking advantage of the three-month permits for tourism, with a temporal investment always linked to seasonal work.

With the beginning of the 2000s, migration began to be thought of and practised differently: longer periods, but also better living conditions in the places of arrival. Both an both internal and an external migration network began to function: on the one hand, neighbours or brothers of the church (Pentecostals) but, above all, relatives, who were the first to depart, became links with new territories of Western Europe, both for work opportunities and for the necessary accommodation (however precarious and related to work) in the country of immigration. On the other hand, new relationships were beginning to be established in the arrival contexts, especially with the owners of construction companies. Italy was the most popular destination and, in particular, Tuscany, in the Florentine area or in the nearby province of Pistoia, in this second case for employment on construction sites that has attracted many young men, one after the other, from our network.

> Ionut: Life was like this, after we got married, I left for the army for a year [military service]. We had a son. She stayed home with [my] mum and the children. Then I came out of the army [finished my military service], and was baptised by Christians, not as before.[4] Afterwards I bought a wagon and two horses and we went to get wood from the forests and we sold it. I remember Mariana being pregnant with our second child. She also came with a belly and helped me because we could not do otherwise. We worked and ate with everyone. Then after Miriana was born we stayed 12 years at [my] parents'

house. Afterwards, since I said it was time to leave for a foreign land, I spoke to someone who told me that it would cost me $200 to come to Italy. I paid $200 and I came to Italy. I met an elderly Italian and worked two weeks in Florence. It is now 'only' 14 years that I am in Florence ... A church brother told me to come. He was in Florence and he told me to remain in Florence, and he found me and helped me get a residence permit. After this, I went to Montecatini Terme where I worked for a year. (Ionut, Florence, 2015).

Florentin: ... in 2002 I arrived in Italy.

Sabrina: Who recommended Italy to you? Did you have someone who called you to Florence?

F.: Yes, some friends told me that in Italy you could find a well-paid job and I decided to come here too.

S.: Who were your friends and how did you get to Florence?

F.: My friends were *rudari*, my relatives! I came in a car with six guys, there were six paid seats and one free, and I went for free, I was the seventh! I was lucky!

S.: Where did you live?

F.: In Scandicci, under a bridge near Torregalli [the hospital]. If the police found you, they'd send you home with an expulsion order. I stayed only for three days, the days I worked, then I finished the job, and I went back to Romania. I returned to Italy in 2004, after about ten days I found a job for three and a half years with a good Italian, he was like a brother!

S.: What kind of work?

F.: On construction sites ... (January 2015).[5]

Even in these years, as in the first, migration involves only men: it is a spatial shift of an activity that, following the 'classic' division of roles, concerns the man: if there is no possibility of working in your country, you look elsewhere. The woman remains at home with the children and relatives, in the dual condition of taking care of the other family members (of the nucleus or extended family) and being protected by them. Moreover, the context of arrival – in these early periods – is too uncertain, it is a sort of advance discovery, it is inconceivable to leave the woman alone (and that the woman herself can think something like that) for a new context, far away, foreign, without a secure base of support and in a situation of promiscuity (such as shacks or shared rooms in apartments).

Sabrina: Stelu, when did you come to Italy? Where did you live? Together with whom?

Stelu: I came to Italy in 2003, on August 4. I arrived on a Friday evening, at my brother-in-law's; at the street – I know it very well – Francesco Redi. In those days, when I came to Italy, it was dangerous: we had to have a residence permit as a tourist. They wouldn't let us through customs. We weren't EU members. We had to pay a fee, give it to the driver. At the customs, a ticket was about 350 euros. I borrowed the money, [to be returned] with interest and came to look at Italy.

S.: Who brought you to Via F. Redi?

Stelu: My brother-in-law, Marian, brought me to Via F. Redi. Who is now on a trip, far away, at Gorgona, on Gorgona Island [Petre jokes: on the island of Gorgona there is a penal colony, where his brother-in-law was sent].

S.: Ah, Cornelia's husband. I understand.

Stelu: I came because he lied to me. Yes, I'm telling the truth. He lied to me. When I was in Romania he phoned me, from Italy to Romania. He called me and told me he would give me a job when I came. I quit my job [in Romania], I borrowed some money, and I got on the bus, in two to three days I left. Already on the bus, when I arrived in Austria, he said to me: 'Brother-in-law, if you don't have a tie here, they don't accept you at work. Put on your tie!'

S.: What job?

Stelu: Bricklayer. He was making teasing me [laughs]. Yes, to wear my tie. So, when I came here … I said, I came on a Friday, in August 2003, I arrived late at night, late; we slept together with 20 other people. It was a three-room apartment.

S.: Where?

Stelu: The one in Via Francesco Redi.

S.: Ah, yes, yes, Francesco Redi. The same street. Francesco Redi.

Stelu: The next day I went around the city, I knew the city as a tourist. Then [my brother-in-law] took me to eat at the Caritas. When I entered there, he showed me [the photo of the] Pope, as he was there, receiving us with both hands. I was afraid to eat, because I was holy at that time [joking, they laugh]. [The phone rings, Petre converses with a policeman, nicknamed Gumă.]

Where were we? At the Caritas. Ah, yes. Afterwards, we ate; I saw some *rudari*, they had changed a lot. They were better dressed here. After a day, two, three, I settled here in Italy. I went to the religious meeting [*adunare*]. Then from Monday I had to start again, because everyone went to work. Because all the Romanians who came to Italy in 2003 had jobs. And I, along with some other people, just arrived in Italy; we had to go looking for work. We had many promises, you called [and they tell you]: 'So, come tomorrow, come the day after tomorrow.' Then, they said: 'the jobs are taken'. They were telling us lies. [Some told us] that we didn't know Italian, others to wait longer. And what happened was that I too got a job. In Barberino [Val d'Elsa], near Tavarnelle [between the province of Florence and Siena]. I got a job there, worked for a while until December.

…

Stelu: Then, to come to Italy, I borrowed money from people and came on January 25–26, 2006.

S.: By yourself?

Stelu: Alone, because my wife, she was afraid to come. She wasn't used to it. She stayed at home with the children. I came; I looked for a job for a while.

S.: Where did you come to work? Where did you sleep?

Stelu: Always for the same boss. And I slept at the boss's.

…

Stelu: When I came, I slept at the house of a woman from Peru. I didn't live in an occupation. Now I do.

S.: Weren't you under the bridge [ponte dell'Indiano, with other *rudari*]?

Stelu: No, I was not under the bridge, I had money, and I paid the rent [for the room]. In 2004, in August, I stayed for a week. And I went to work. I called the boss and he took me to a Sicilian, Pippo, for work. In Campi Bizenzio [municipality near Florence].

S.: How did you meet him?

Stelu: How did I meet him? He's a friend of my brother-in-law, Vasile, the one with the lean belly [jokes].

…

S.: Ah, yes, Raluca's father-in-law.

Stelu: How do you say 'cuscru' in Italian?

S.: We say 'consuocero' [co-father-in-law]. That is, *cu s (o) cru* … [joking, between Romanian and Italian, about kinship, everyone laughs, Petre teases his wife, a little sarcastically].

Stelu: Then I started working with Pippo, and then I left this Pippo. And I went back to Mario B., to my friend and his father, Donato. I also worked in the countryside, in the city too: I would put in windows; I'd give a coat of white paint. I did everything. Meanwhile, when I was working, we were not in Europe in 2004. And the carabinieri, if they caught us on the street and we didn't have a residence permit, they sent us home.

S.: Could you explain? Were you controlled? [laughter]

Stelu: [starts talking very low, always joking]

S.: You have to tell me! [laughter continues]

…

Stelu: In 2005 I started working, and in Italy I worked well. I made good money. My boss thought to send me home every three months [to keep within the time for the visa]. He got me a tourist permit. With this permission, I had nothing to do with the carabinieri, with anyone. Three months, tourist permit, for when I went home to my children. He paid one trip for me, I paid for one. And when I came home, my wife would say to me, 'Are you coming home with such little money? You always come! Others have even stayed for more than a year …'

S.: At home, always in Spanțov?

Stelu: Yes, always, in Spanțov, yes. In Sibust, I used to go there all the time. In 2006–2007 it changed [the situation]; I got angry with the boss and told him so. In December, when the boss sent me home, I said: 'I don't go home anymore; here are my documents – my name and surname, the city, the house number. You go to my wife's house. I have 6 children and I can't go there anymore with such little money.' Then he got upset and gave me another 500 euros. And I went home with 1,200 euros, I stayed for the festivities, I came back in 2007. After that, a lot has changed. Problems. I have no longer paid the rent … (Stelu, Florence January 2015)[6]

Although, therefore, the Romanian *rudari* are part of the same migratory flows as the Romanians, as Slavkova notes for the Bulgarian *rudari* in Spain and Greece (2017), unlike the Romanians, the situation recorded by copious literature on the subject[7] does not occur, except in very few cases, of transnational families where the woman is the only one to leave, for a long time, maintaining – with her work of caring for the elderly in foreign homes – the entire nucleus and often the newly formed families.

The work of *rudari* women[8] takes over later, due to two interrelated factors, linked to the prolongation of migrations over time and changes with respect to the accommodation in the arrival contexts. Since the local context does not produce changes in terms of possible economic resources, but at the same time it is observed that emigrations, although they require sacrifice, can give the hoped-for good results to achieve what they want for their family, the migrations in the history of these families are prolonged and expand, making them progressively become a 'structural' aspect of their lives. From a spatial point of view, it is the housing solutions in the host country that change, in the event that a condition occurs in the new context that can accommodate the wives (and then perhaps, in the future, it depends on how the situations evolve, the children). But the change of accommodation, from a material point of view, is directly linked to their reasons for departing. Therefore, the maintenance of the place where people live must not, first of all, employ huge monetary resources, that is, the improved housing condition must have low costs, or even zero, if possible, since the earnings are for home, for Romania: people do not leave because they do not want to stay in their country anymore, people do not leave because they want to go and live in Italy or Spain. They are not interested in Italy or Spain as such, they are just places where they can find those economic opportunities that they are looking for to fulfil their needs and life aspirations. They really would rather not leave. They do this because where they live it is not possible to access a labour market that allows them to eat properly, take care of themselves, make themselves a home, fulfil their wishes as husband and father, wife and mother. The arrival of the woman who, in fact, usually needs a more dignified housing context (therefore, not a shack under a bridge), but above all not promiscuous (housing with strangers and men), is linked to the increase in her chances of earning: the woman, too, comes to work. This aspect should certainly not be seen as a subversion of the rules: if, in fact, in the ideal division of roles, it is the man who works (i.e. it is the man who is responsible for the material maintenance of the family) and the woman is the one who takes care of the house, the husband and the children – in practice, *rudari* women have always contributed to production: in the traditional profession as *rudari lingurari* (spindles were made by them, for example) or in the work at the houses of the *boieri* or in the fields both before and during communism.

In mid-2006, for this vast *rudari* network there was an opportunity for a major change in connection with the occupation of a large building, the result of an expansion of external contacts and in which, and here lies its peculiarity, the internal migration network is solidified also spatially.

> F.: In the same year [2004] I also called Sandra [my wife] and after two months came Simona, our daughter! In 2006 we brought the whole family; we lived in the Luzzi, at Pratolino.
>
> S.: Who told you about the Luzzi's occupation?
>
> F.: When I was still renting with Sandra, we heard from friends about the Luzzi, and we too occupied a room from day one, and then I went to pick up the children [from Romania]. (Florentin, Florence, January 2015).[9]

But before we start discussing the experience of this occupation, it is appropriate to broaden our view of other migratory possibilities.

Notes

1. The so-called 'transition' from the communist economic system to the capitalist one turned out to be a polymorphous period, overflowing with contradictions, in which corruption made its way to all central and local institutional levels – from government politicians to village health service doctors. The de-industrialisation of entire areas of the country and the destructuring of every form of protection has deeply affected people's lives, consigning them to a situation of poverty, and in our case to a high vulnerability emphasised by the discriminatory component against the *rudari* because they are considered *gypsies*. See Gunder (1991), Țichindeleanu (2010), for a critical reading of the concept of post-communist 'transition'; Burawoy and Verdery (1999), Buchowski (2001), Kürti and Skalník (2009), West and Raman (2009), for a broader overview of post-socialist transformations, also in a comparative key.
2. Interview collected with Mara Stînga during the *MigRom* project.
3. Vasile is the husband of one of the daughters of the youngest of the 'nine sisters' (see chapter 1). The generational levels to which he refers exactly match those of the reconstructed genealogy, so they are his children, who now all live in Italy, in a municipality close to Florence, with him and his wife or independently if already married.
4. Pentecostal baptism (he had already been baptised with an Orthodox rite).
5. Interview collected with Mara Stînga during the *MigRom* project.
6. Interview collected with Mara Stînga during the *MigRom* project.
7. See Cvajner (2018), Vietti (2019), Anghel (2013).
8. I will resume that later, see chapter 11.
9. Interview collected with Mara Stînga during the *MigRom* project.

Chapter 7

MIGRATORY *DÉCALAGES*

The migratory 'passages' and the various situational 'configurations' of which I have spoken above, should not be seen either as linear or as homogeneous: they are, in fact, traces that can tend toward a generalisation only if considered as one of the possibilities through which migratory processes are realised. That is, they can take place in the way described so far – and we have seen this for a wide network of people – but also through other paths, which denote internal phase shifts, lines that draw multiple directions and possibilities.

The knowledge of the migratory and mobility experiences learned among the members of the families I met in Romania has given me the opportunity to avoid the danger of making inferences from one context to another, that is, from the migratory 'trend' found in the history of the families who emigrated to Florence to that of their relatives.

The family members of one of the brothers of Ionica (Dana's mother, and at whose house I was predominantly a guest during the research periods), Valeriu, composed of two spouses and four children, have emigrated for several years for limited periods. This is linked not so much to the question of the possibilities offered by the context of emigration, but to their wish not to leave their own *sat* for very long periods, not to find themselves 'displaced'. These intermittent emigrations are linked to the possibility of earnings that are reinvested almost immediately: something sent to relatives to stock up or pay for utilities – if the period of their stay abroad is a little longer – but more frequently the use of money on their return to buy appliances, add a room to the house, build the bathroom … And also put something away to get through the winter.

The migration in this case is 'contained', in the form of a 'migratory opportunity': as if they did not want to expose themselves to the danger of being eaten by migration, taken, stolen; as if they felt the danger of the 'loss' that a longer-term migration can bring with it. A feeling that seems to be condensed in the words of Sandu (brother of Mihai's mother): 'We are fine there [England], but happiness is here in Vadrea, where all my relatives and friends are.' He told me this on a July evening, as we sit with many others in his sister's backyard, and I asked him how he is getting on in Birmingham.

'I'll make some money and then I'll go home.' This statement, however, is from Valeriu's second son, when he informed me that he had just returned from Germany where he was with his wife for a month and a half, both employed in picking strawberries (in the greenhouses).

'Where in Germany?' had been my question: he answered me in the north; she, on another occasion, told me that she does not remember the name of the place. So, always in a vague way, she told me about Spain: there she is a little more aware of the territorial location of the company because she has been to Spain several times, but the point is that the place, understood as a city, where you will go to work is not important: if it is beautiful, ugly, north, south ... Without a doubt it is a pleasant discovery to be able to go out and about in one of the few free moments, but they are not there to visit: they are there to work.

What does become important, however, is the place as a work context: what accommodation is provided by the farm, where you can cook, where you can wash your clothes, with how many people you have to share a room ... but you get to know this in detail only once you arrive at your destination.

The first of the family nucleus to have an experience of working abroad was Valeriu's eldest son, Nicolae, who, shortly after he had married and had a son, left for Spain for a longer period of time than those he would face later, hosted by his uncle. Since that time, he departs occasionally for various countries, using not only the possibilities offered by the family network (also in Italy), but the opportunities that come from the *ţigani pletoşi* who live in Sibu Mare in their own neighbourhood, adjacent to that of the *rudari*. Nicolae, on behalf of the *ţigani pletoşi*, has been a driver for over ten years: the *ţigani* often have means of transport, but cannot drive them to go do their business in Bucharest or other parts of the country or abroad because they do not have a licence, and therefore need reliable people who they pay for this service. With them he has been both to Germany and Britain, encountering a series of difficulties and adventures.

Nicolae: November, December [2014]. Two months [in Germany] ...

I went as a driver, always for the iron.

Sabrina: With the gypsies?

N.: Gypsies from Cuza-Vodă.

S.: What do the gypsies do there?

N.: They collect iron. Old iron.

...

S.: In Dortmund city? Or nearby?

N.: No, we were in ... a village ...

S.: And where did you live?

N.: I used to live like everyone else there, renting, at 400 euros a month. I was there for two months.

S.: Then, did the police come?

N.: Later, the work didn't go well, the police found us, they said it's forbidden, and that we don't have the documents to collect the iron. And they fined us, 1,000 euros. If we didn't pay the money, we'd go to jail. And we stayed in the police station until we paid.

S.: For checks, for ...

N.: What checks ... in prison!

N.: We were outside, in the [police] car: 'If you don't bring the money, go to jail'. We paid bail, 1,000 euros. And then, what could we do? If they did not give you permission [for the iron], you could not do anything, it was a foreign country. I came back home. (Nicolae, Sibu Mare, March 2015).[1]

The experience is very different, of course, if you stay with a relative or not, and in what housing situation. In the first case, and in particular if you have the possibility of staying in a real house, and not living precariously (such as occupations of buildings), the location takes on a more important value; the city does not remain so anonymous, you have the possibility of being in a protected context. Nicolae, for example, having lived on his first migration with his maternal uncle's family, in an apartment for rent in the city, remembers the locality, enveloping it in a unique beauty:

N.: At the age of 18 I left for Spain.

S.: In Spain, where?

N.: At Logrogno [Logroño].

S.: Logrogno [Logroño], where is it? North, south, centre?

N.: I don't know which area. But the area was good, where there was a vineyard. The best wine: Rioja ... At Rioja. Zaragoza, Logrogno [Logroño], Bilbao, nearby.

S.: Was it nice?

N.: Yes, I liked it. The most beautiful city in all of Europe. I liked it a lot. The most beautiful country. (Nicolae, Sibu Mare, March 2015).

Those who emigrate in the same way as Nicolae, used to alternate periods of precarious work in Romania with others of employment abroad.

Since the beginning of 2010, some *rudari* have opened a new channel of emigration, already consolidated some years ago in Romania. There are private agencies that connect foreign companies – which require unskilled labour for strenuous tasks and which cannot be found in the surrounding basin – with potential Romanian workers who, on the other hand, do not have access in their own country to a labour market that can guarantee them a continuous wage commensurate with the cost of living. Sometimes, drivers are also sought for the transport of foreign workers to foreign work-places. These agencies conduct interviews to select staff, who will then be sent to the companies. Through a *rudar* friend who he has known since childhood, Nico became aware of this opportunity, especially for England; they looked together online and they each sent their CV. Among those who sent them, he was the only one called because he possessed several driving licences. Subsequently, and from here on I was able to follow the story directly, they contacted him by phone, but the outcome of the call was not positive: he does not know English and – in all probability – they heard the *rudar* accent of his Romanian.

After a week, however, they contacted him again for an interview, this time presumably as a labourer, at least this is what Nico thinks (even if he always hopes as a driver) since nothing is mentioned about the possible job: neither where, nor the pay, nor the conditions. But all this, after all, was secondary for the moment and, at that point, in view of the interview, he had to solve the problem of how to find the money to leave. To go to England, through these formal channels, the costs were high: the commission for the agency, insurance and plane ticket. Plus a few pence for when he arrived waiting for his first week's pay. Until the day before, we did not know if Nico would be able to go to the interview or not: there was little time and we needed to find about 500 euros. To resolve the matter, his mother talked to her sister who, in turn, talked to her husband, who was in Norway where he had a well-paid job. The transfer of the necessary money arrived via *money-gram* the afternoon before the morning of the interview: we could go!

We went by car to Bucharest with our friend, who should have remembered where the agency's headquarters were ... we drove around in a suburb of the capital for a while, and finally – between questions to passers-by and reminiscences – we found it. We entered, without our friend, and waited a quarter of an hour, then an official ushered us into a room and gave Nico a questionnaire to fill out – which he did with some difficulty – in which some personal and health-related information was requested. After a further, slightly longer wait, we went up to the first floor where a secretary received us.

The contract related to employment on a farm at Stratford-upon-Avon, and was summarised in a few details: the work would begin on 27 May and end on 30 September, unless the company proposed a further period to the worker, and the hourly wage was as expected, the basic £6.31. Nico read, here and there, the hygiene and health rules to be kept, some information on insurance coverage, while I translated for him the parts in English on the contractual conditions and accommodation on the farm. Actually, all of this took about ten minutes. Then we moved on, to book the plane ticket: Nico would leave with four other young Romanians from Bucharest on 23 May, and for the first few days, until the 27th, he would be informed on the spot about the specific methods for carrying out the work.

In the farm data sheet, the following indication was given about the wage: 'Basic rates of Pay – National Minimum Wage – Pounds 6.31 per hour'. In addition to the information, always in English and which was not translated by the agency employee (but which I explained to Nico), there was no guarantee of a minimum number of working hours per day, as there could be considerable variations from one period to another.

In the section 'Terms and Conditions' of the 'Work Placement Application' under the item 'Payment', we read further, but contradictory, information: 'Most work is paid on piecework basis. Piecework rates will, at minimum, equate to the minimum wage (£6.50 per hour)', followed by point 1.4, in which it was specified that 'Actual piecework rates will fluctuate according to the crop, its condition and the season'. The evident difficulty of making the payment for the amount harvested equivalent to the minimum hourly wage was also noted in the following point of the document.

The expense incurred by Nico to obtain this job and to depart was exactly: 689.85 Ron (£115.32) for the agency service for the programme called 'Concordia 2015'; 239.11 Ron (£49) for Concordia *membership*, which included insurance, up to one year, for travel and employment in England, a travel package with a British SIM card and additional, theoretically optional insurance, but which was instead presented as mandatory; and finally 489.49 Ron (£110) for the airline ticket.

Figure 7.1. First page of Nico's notebook: daily notes concerning income (how much collected and the amount earned) and expenses (cigars and food). © Sabrina Tosi Cambini.

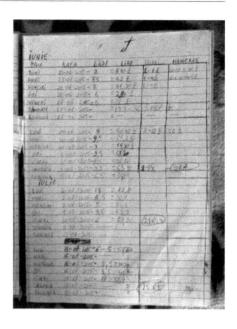

Figure 7.2. Containers where workers are housed and view of the field. © Sabrina Tosi Cambini.

After leaving, Nico wrote to me every now and then about the hard work and how fast he had to go. On one occasion he also told me that he would stay longer, until mid-October or perhaps longer.

When I visited him at the end of September 2015, in the Stratford-upon-Avon countryside, he explained to me that the remuneration was only based on the quantity of onions harvested, and that therefore the speed with which the work was done was fundamental to earn as much as possible: he was bent over, on his knees all day, with his hands in the ground. But he didn't work regularly. Nico recorded his income (paid weekly) and his expenses every day (see figure 7.1).

The accommodation did not correspond to the description on the agency sheets: it was not a hostel, but a field with containers (see figure 7.2), with bathrooms outside and a large kitchen in the main building. Inside, the containers had the minimum essentials: a bed and a locker each, a small fridge, a hotplate to warm something up and make coffee.

Note

1. Interview conducted during the *MigRom* project.

Chapter 8

The Interweaving of Migration and Fights for the Right to Housing and to the City

The Occupation of the Former Luzzi:
A *Sat Rudar* on the Outskirts of Florence

May 2006 marked a very precise point in the matter of the networks of *rudari* families in their migration to Tuscany, and coincided with the beginning of the occupation of a large public building, immersed in historic woods on the outskirts of Florence. Some of the men from our families who occupied in 2006 came from an unauthorised settlement composed of parts of abandoned buildings and barracks, located in a part of the 'Osmannoro' industrial area called 'Osmatex', between the municipalities of Florence and Sesto Fiorentino.[1]

This period of the occupation and the years that followed, of living in what had been a sanatorium, represented a great change in their lives – as well as for the ethnographer who met them during that occupation, a year and a half later.

In the history of our network of families, this occupation represented an opportunity for life that intersected with the history of other immigrant groups, but above all, from that moment, it linked them to a citizen movement of protest and a fight for the right to housing. This immediately shows how their housing situation was configured within a local housing framework where housing was a problem for several 'types' of population groups, united by the impossibility of accessing the real estate rental market and the absence of serious policies in this regard.

On 14 May 2006, hundreds of people of 11 different nationalities – significantly including the Romanian nationality of our *rudari* – occupied the main buildings of the former Luzzi hospital, which had been abandoned just under eight years previously. Organising and supporting the action was the Movimento di Lotta per la Casa (Movement for the Fight for Housing), which sought through this operation to provide a solution for hundreds of people who until then had lived, in most cases, in self-constructed artefacts in the industrial area of Osmannoro or in makeshift shelters on the street and in various interstices of the city: 'stories of people, affections and hopes that intersect with places abandoned to neglect and degradation, which come back to life with the work and hopes of the new residents'.[2] The families transformed these abandoned spaces into places for their day-to-day life, into their home: *Casa Luzzi*, to be precise. Problems related to the plumbing were solved and some renovations were made. Many men worked in the construction sector and were therefore able to make significant improvements to the buildings and to 'model' some rooms according to the needs of families or individuals.

The institutions' and the citizens' reactions to the occupation were, from the outset, reluctance to grant these people the possibility – in the absence of alternatives – of creating a place to live, of carving out a space within the city that was not urban waste, but a dignified place to be made habitable again. In the newspapers, in public statements, the occupiers were portrayed as unwanted and undesirable, with links to criminality, in a status of illegality, distant in their language and way of life.

As Foucault teaches us, space is fundamental in every exercise of power, and power techniques are at work in architecture.[3] The people who live in *bidonvilles*, in the *slums*, on the streets, in the occupied former factories and so on, are agglomerated in a sort of unit from an external perspective, and called marginal, non-persons, asocial:

> These expressions do not describe a way of life. They suggest a notion of danger, of infirmity, of abnormality ... Even those who incriminate capital or urbanisation, even those who accuse society of deliberately fabricating its marginalised people, even political militants, trade unionists, or the clergy, who deplore injustice, do not express any doubt regarding the existence of a phenomenon of which, in so doing, they provide proof. (Pétonnet 2002: 20)

Reading the various appeals of the 'Luzzi Interethnic Community' (the name that the inhabitants had given themselves a few months into the occupation) – aimed at involving citizens in an open management of the former hospital, for aid related to aspects of health and schooling – and comparing them with some political communiqués or some associations on the occupying families and the speeches of the citizens reported by the newspapers, I think by analogy of what Colette Pétonnet wrote in the 1970s on the Parisian *bidonvilles*:

If we just do not let ourselves be stopped by the external aspect and penetrate the streets or the courtyard of a bidonville, we immediately perceive the signs of organised human activity: smoke coming out of the chimneys, laundry on the washing line, piles of wood, vegetable plots planted with cabbages, but no trace of rubbish. A group of men declaiming, women who come back from fetching water, wash their clothes together, knit on the doorsteps, announce a social life. Contrary to the opinion that is as false as it is widespread, the bidonville is not a mass of shapeless shacks that are unworthy of man. Even an imperfect observation like mine (interrupted as it was by the systematic destruction that has raged in recent years) immediately leads me to think that the bidonville is comparable to an old neighbourhood, which meets the same criteria regarding its organisation, its role, and its precise functions. The bidonville is a suburban neighbourhood that still corresponds to a rural way of life. (Pétonnet 2002: 61)

In the fog of information spread by the mass media in the months that followed, there is also a constructive redundant message which is both an appeal and a desire of the occupiers: 'It is important that people get to know us and realise that we are good people.'[4]

The intertwining of speculative interests on property, national and local security policies, the construction of a racist narrative on the situation – that of immigrants – outlined as dangerous and a source of social problems and economic waste, the ever greater difficulties to which families (Italian and foreign) had to respond, created a tense atmosphere: even the ARCI[5] circles in the area wrote against the occupation, and there was little response from the local population to the occupiers' appeal; in fact for a long time no association entered the Luzzi, no volunteers. The municipality of Sesto, on which the property lay (and still does) administratively, adopted a stance of strong opposition and – in addition to not granting residence to the inhabitants – refused to make a school bus available for the children.

Families tried to 'belong to the territory', to establish a bond with the inhabitants of the area and with the school and health services. With the former, in particular, they wanted to build a relationship, an active exchange, placing themselves within a *common history*:

When we arrived we were only 'homeless' of different origins, today we are a multi-ethnic community that has found a place from which to start afresh, tangible prospects starting from 'philosophy of the essential, recycle and reuse'. The problem is that our primary needs clashed with economic interests, the entire Luzzi was auctioned for 17,000,000.00, there were still no buyers and there were no bidders at the last auction.

There was a fear of building speculation, in which the historical-cultural interest, the environmental importance, the constraint of transfer of the property, would be left in the background.

Parallel projects for common needs within the neighbourhood, the fight against speculation, questioning the use of the Luzzi, which solved a real housing problem, where a self-managed community tried to find its own dimension while respecting the environment.

An open invitation to the neighbourhood: come and meet us and find out about our peaceful and spontaneous reality, let us join in common battles; we share for example the problem of distant schools, buses that skip their rounds, etc., and we support the refurbishment of the Banti as a public, multifunctional building.

… We are raising common problems involving a large number of poor families.

You cannot ignore our voice, you cannot extinguish our hope of finding support to defend this house that we are struggling to improve with the few means we have. Today we are no longer homeless, we are inhabitants of the Luzzi and this first form of identification allows us to recover a kind of dignity that is denied us daily, being poor and often marginalised by a system ready to exploit us as a workforce but without guarantees. (from the Luzzi's manifesto)

The public gaze – political and public opinion – placed on the Luzzi's people restricts them to an impersonal marginality often accompanied by a discriminatory approach. When defined as 'marginal', they are considered to be in need of rehabilitation and of being assimilated; when the attribute of 'dangerous' is also added, there are requests for them to be sent away from the buildings, without any alternative housing; some may possibly remain in the territory, but incessantly demonstrating their 'good conduct'. The residents of the former hospital, on the one hand, are strongly stigmatised and on the other hand are considered as shameful evidence of poverty.

But the Luzzi, in the discourse of our *rudari* is *la* [feminine article in Italian] Luzzi, because in Romanian the names of the localities are feminine. This means two things simultaneously: the re-building and the identification of the large complex as a village, a *sat*, and the development of a feeling of territorial belonging.

When I first went in 2008, from my very first steps, the Luzzi appeared to me as an almost fulfilled possibility of the subtraction of space, in which there are 'productions of subjectivity escaping the powers and knowledge of one dispositive to reinvest themselves in another through other forms to be created' (Deleuze 1989: 20).

As Deleuze pointed out in his last public intervention, among the dimensions of a dispositive, that of subjectivation has given rise to more misunderstandings, but at the same time perhaps the study of its variations is also 'one of the fundamental tasks that Foucault left those who came after him' (ibid.: 29). The other dimensions of a dispositive are the curves of visibility, the curves of utterance and the lines of force; the latter are 'the "dimension of power" and power is the third dimension of space, internal to the dispositive and variable with the dispositives' (ibid.: 15).

Space for Foucault is:

> the pivot of the physicality of control aimed at capturing under itself the triple relational game of knowledge, power and the capacities of the self ... What is at stake is to ensnare the threefold relation of Knowledge/Power/ Subjectivity in a space delimited by state-like concatenations, that is authoritarian, normative, and heteronymous, with which every possibility of organising life is articulated by channelling it according to a verticalisation of the meaning produced [biopolitics] ... It is necessary to move from here in order to subtract space from the capture of the state-form so as to escape the paralysing dichotomy of utopia and heterotopia. (Vaccaro 2002: 14–15)

The lines of subjectivity, in our case, indicate to us the cracks and fractures, and at the same time, the processes of identification that manage to escape, for a given period, the power relationships in a specific field-context.

The occupation of the former Luzzi had, in itself, some elements that made it a very special and extremely interesting experience. The property, immersed in a park on the outskirts of the city, on a hillside, included several buildings, in a generally good condition because they had been unused for a few years, with a well-functioning electrical system and a slightly poorer water system that suffered in the summer season.

But the most important peculiarity of the occupation was the creative organisation and methods of management of the spaces and of the communal living that the occupiers had given themselves; in March 2007 they exceeded 350 people (of whom about 80 were children), with a total of 71 families. Of these, most came from Romania, but there were also about thirty people who were Eritreans and Ethiopians (who slept here in the same building, door to door), a dozen Italians, a dozen Somalis, a Tunisian family and so on. One day a week the assembly was convened, with a high turnout: it discussed the Luzzi's life, relations with the institutions, and developments in the situation with respect to a possible eviction, the likelihood of which was becoming increasingly imminent.

During the winter of 2006/2007 there was a playroom for children and on Wednesdays and Sundays there was a cineforum: everything was self-organised. The role of mediation with the local authorities was mainly played by Italians, including Camilla, who had been a point of reference for families both for the schooling of children and in relations with the health services.

It is the creativity within families that has made the former hospital a village: creativity understood as 'know-how', which has materially changed the place; and a creativity that we could define as 'know-how' supported by relational resources: the recreation of a real *sat*.

Mariana would say a few years later:

At the Luzzi I had a good time, well ... Sabrina, you know, we were all together, like at home [in Romania].

... It was nice [the occupation]. I had a good time like at home [in Romania]. It was a good life at the Luzzi because I gave birth to three children there: Ana, Daniel and Andrea. At the Luzzi it was a very nice life, the children were free like at home. (January 2015).[6]

And Ionica told me:

In March [2006], I found the [church] brother Constantin, with a group of *pocăiți*, and he had in his hand a notebook with a list of people for an occupation [of a building: the former Luzzi sanatorium]. He said to me, 'Won't you join too? Give me photocopies of the passports'. I gave them to him and I signed up. Whoever wanted to, could stay in occupation, go to the demonstrations [of the Movimento di Lotta per la Casa]. When I signed up, it was just me with Șerban [her son]. Virgil [her husband] was [at that time] in Romania. After three months, on May 20, 2006, the occupation of the Luzzi took place. I was [there] for 8 months, in September I went home, because the children started school. Virgil and Șerban remained in a large room, without water. We lived on the first floor, with shared bathrooms, no showers, but habitable. Virgil had no job for as long as he was there and in 2008 a Moldovan found work for Șerban, as a courier for Posta Italiana S.D.A. [the express courier S.D.A. also carries out the service for the Post Office]. While Șerban found [a job], I was at home [in Romania], with the children, and in May 2008, Virgil also joined the same company, at work, with Șerban. After a few months, I came too with the children. On September 6, 2008, I enrolled the children in school. Virgil was already working. Șerban was working. We made a few euros, Șerban got a car. I also brought [to the occupation] the oldest boy, he got married and lived separately with his wife. He worked for a Romanian on a construction site. I was sending money home to Mum, to pay for the electricity. She was home alone. (Ionica, Florence, February 2015)[7]

The buildings began to look more and more like condominiums, with a good flexibility of transformation of the internal space according to the families' needs: in each of the buildings accommodation almost like apartments had been prepared (in some of them, sometimes, there could also be a bathroom) and minor renovation or maintenance work had been done;

the surnames were indicated on the doors and next to them a number like a sort of street number, useful to the organisation linked to the Movement; there were planned shifts for cleaning the communal 'condominium' spaces, while Saturday was the day dedicated to the cleaning by everyone of the streets and the surrounding green areas. Along the road that goes through the former hospital, some hand-written signs (in Romanian or Italian or mixed) urged people to be careful, owing to the presence of children (i.e. 'atentione bambini'). While just before entering, in plaster on the asphalt, there was the exhortation '*pastrați curațenia*' (keep clean), which invited everyone to take care of the place. And it was clean for a long time, until the external pressure began to prevail (Pétonnet comes back to mind).

In the evening, in the summer, amidst the smoke of the outdoor barbecues, we walked among the fathers and mothers with their children playing around; and the girls who came out of the door laughing and joking. The music rose slightly to accompany the evening return of many workers (who arrived after 21.30 by bus from Florence). At the beginning of July 2007, some *rudari* had set up an outdoor bar: a gazebo with a fridge, stereo system, light. And intra-group relations of a different nature were established: a Tunisian lady made bread and sold it to the other inhabitants. Camilla tried to promote the Luzzi externally by also organising parties, markets and self-financing initiatives, such as the recycling of clothes 'made in Luzzi', open to all citizens And then there was the church – locked to stop the children from going inside. In the space of about a year and a half there were very few moments of tension among the residents.

In a theoretical-practical vision of the city, this experience has represented the testimony that it is possible to build a city capable of changing, of leaving spaces for negotiation and experimentation of forms of 'spontaneity', in which the lines of subjectivation can escape – even if not definitively – the dimensions of power and knowledge, tracing original paths of creation: the Luzzi, therefore not only as a former sanatorium, but as a portion of the city self-organised by its residents, according to their needs. Later we will see how this reading was the basis for an attempt – lasting a few years and following a very difficult process – to transform a space left in decay into a place for the whole city: a social and environmental reuse capable of giving some answers to the multiple needs of many different residents.

For the *rudari*, organised in family networks, it was a little village a few kilometres away from the city, like those from which they came in Romania (near Călăraşi or Medgidia or Piteşi), able to fulfil the needs of human settlement. This statement recalls what Colette Pétonnet wrote after the comparison of the *bidonville* with the district of the Porte d'Aix in Marseille, through which the profound meaning of that settlement appeared. The careful observation of what is in the streets, in fact, revealed a rhythmic distribution, 'the old neighbourhood responded in the same way as the slum to the needs of human settlement' (Pétonnet 2002)[8].

Pétonnet, through an ethnographic approach, had managed to go beyond what was already a given, beyond the ordinary meaning of public opinion, beyond some approaches of the social sciences. Entering into the intimate and hidden tenor of those realities, she had demonstrated the regulatory role of the spontaneous habitat and at the same time its ability to accompany the arrival and the complex passage from one part of the world (that of departure) to another (that of immigration).[9] The Luzzi has also had for its residents this function of protection and support in facing new social and cultural contexts, partly similar and partly very different from those of their origin. The bond of solidarity within families and the flexibility of the reception of the place has given many families the opportunity to try different strategies of mobility between Romania and Italy, to gradually face the new realities of the country of immigration, to try more opportunities of life between the two countries, to try a path of life *here* without jeopardising the fulfilment of their dreams *there*. Self-management has made it possible to maintain that right to action, already largely limited by the imposition from the outside of identity characteristics that did not belong to the occupiers.

In the spring of 2009, 334 people lived at the Luzzi, 239 of whom were of Romanian nationality,[10] mostly represented by *rudari* (178 people, 46 families formed only by members of the nucleus – spouses and children – or even members of the extended family – grandparents, cousins, children and grandchildren), in addition to some Roma *lautari* and *ursari*.

Tables 8.1, 8.2 and 8.3[11] show the number of members of the *rudari* families divided into adults and minors, coming from Sibu Mare (including some also from Micea, a nearby town, but under another municipality), from Burdu, and from Călărași (Badra and Vadrea). Given that floor plans of the occupied buildings had been made, the presence of the families had also been marked with the relative location, accommodation by accommodation (i.e. room per room), therefore the identification (ID) indicates both the family and the accommodation; the total of this column indicates the total number of families. The item 'displacement 2009', concerns the involvement of the family in the first 'agreed' displacement (according to an agreement between the institutions and the occupiers), which took place between August and October 2009.

Let us now look at the first year of arrival in Italy of individuals and families, indicating the year they went to live at the Luzzi occupation.

The quantitative data in the table and graph fully confirm what was detected in the field research. The numbers increase until 2003 and 2004, the year of major arrival, before falling in 2005 and resuming in 2006, the year of the Luzzi occupation, and then gradually falling again. Since the data are on families and not on individual members, between 2003/2004 and 2006 there would be an even smaller quantitative difference since, as mentioned, many people (especially minors) arrived thanks to the housing opportunity provided by the Luzzi.

Table 8.1. Families from Sibu Mare. © Sabrina Tosi Cambini.

Family/Housing ID	No. Members	No. Adults	No. Minors	Displacement 2009
3	2	2	0	
4	4	2	2	Yes
6	13	6	7	
8	1	1	0	
9	3	2	1	
15	4	2	2	
23	2	2	0	
26	5	2	3	
29	2	2	0	
30	3	2	1	
32	5	2	3	
36	3	2	1	Yes
37	3	3	0	
38	4	3	1	Yes
39	3	2	1	
41	3	3	0	
50	2	2	0	
72	3	2	1	
73	4	2	2	Yes
74	2	2	0	
75	3	3	0	
Total 21	**74**	**49**	**25**	

Table 8.2. Families from Burdu. © Sabrina Tosi Cambini.

Family/Housing ID	No. Members	No. Adults	No. Minors	Displacement 2009
9	3	2	1	
14	5	4	1	
20	3	3	0	
21	6	2	4	Yes
23	2	2	0	
26	5	2	3	
28	8	2	6	
29	2	2	0	
34	1	1	0	
40	5	1	4	
48	6	2	0	
51	7	4	3	Yes
55	8	4	4	Yes
59	5	2	3	
67	3	3	0	
Total 15	69	36	29	

Table 8.3. Families from the Călăraşi district. © Sabrina Tosi Cambini.

Family/Housing ID	No. Members	No. Adults	No. Minors	Displacement 2009
7	5	2	3	
16	6	4	2	
44	2	2	0	
57	2	2	0	
58	3	2	1	
60	3	3	0	
61	4	2	2	
64	3	2	1	
65	2	2	1	Yes
100	5	2	3	Yes
Total 10	35	23	13	

Table 8.4. Year of arrival in Italy and at the former Luzzi. © Sabrina Tosi Cambini.

In Italy since	No. Families	No. People	At Luzzi since
2000	3	12	2006
2001	1	3	2006
2002	3	18	2006 (2 fam.) and 2007 (1 fam.)
2003	10	43	2006 (9 fam.) and 2009 (1 fam.)
2004	10	44	2006
2005	7	31	2006 (5 fam.) and 2007 (2 fam.)
2006	10	34	2006 (7 fam.) and 2007 (3 fam.)
2007	7	22	2007 (1 fam.), 2008 (5 fam.) and 2009 (1 fam.)
2008	2	6	2008 (1 fam.) and 2009 (1 fam.)

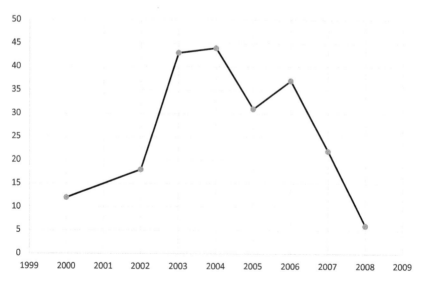

Graph 8.1. Year of arrival in Italy. N.B. The calculation of people per year is per household, but in reality some members may have arrived later. © Sabrina Tosi Cambini.

The Former Luzzi and the Institutional Treatment of Precarious Housing

Precarious housing, with its unsafe shelters in the urban interstices, represents the concretisation – (in)visible and uncomfortable – of the exclusion from housing. It concerns social groups who are not allowed, very often not even formally, a real status as citizens. It is a *history of suffering*, traced in that emerging tension between people's searches for a desired life and a territory that remains alien, unwelcoming, racist.

The area of this exclusion is highly differentiated, as are the factors that can contribute to it: relative economic poverty; forms of discrimination; situations of more or less temporary precariousness that concern work, the family situation, the network of relationships; being or not being a registered resident; and, for immigrants, the legal status of residence. The phenomenon, which in Europe has been believed to belong to the past, of the emergence of precarious or informal housing – slums, occupations of buildings of variable dimensions, portions of cities emerging in places of urban transformation and redefinition of real estate values – marks a critical threshold and a spread to such an extent as to question in depth the criteria, priorities and hierarchies that govern the choices of urban planning and building development, as well as the very foundations of civil coexistence, undermined by growing inequalities.[12]

Faced with this framework, in the field of social and housing policies, politicians at national and local level have opted for two types of response: on the one hand, an increase in laws and regulations that, without any transformative force, focus on very limited measures that are not even an attempt to find solutions. At the same time, these measures push toward a process of normalisation: the reference citizen is, in fact, the one who meets certain parameters, which alone can meet the criteria for the provision of *benefits*.[13]

The other type of intervention is in the area of control and repression, which through space as a form of power, finds its strongest application in a joint process of racialisation of bodies and racialisation of urban space. In this sense, we must read the displacement of the bodies of those who are considered marginal, unwanted and useless, through actions of various kinds ranging from violent evictions to census operations, from the Mayor's *ad hoc* ordinances to the folds of the legislation.[14] The latter, precisely because of the lack of visibility, seem less incisive, while they have great power over the lives of the people we are talking about. A clear example is article 5 of the Housing Plan, launched by the Italian government at the end of March 2014 (Legislative Decree 47/2014), with the declarative title 'Fight against the illegal occupation of properties' with retroactive effect.[15]

With this regulation, people occupying a property 'without title' are forbidden to request residence and connection to public services, requiring the cancellation of the acts already issued. The article, in addition to the obvious effect of making any solutions negotiated between occupiers and institutions more difficult and pushing the precarious housing settlements toward a condition of illegality, contrasts with the rules and the numerous judgements of the Court of Cassation that guarantee the objective and subjective right to residence. In addition, given the frequent and substantial presence of children in situations of occupation and illegal habitation, prohibiting them from accessing basic services such as water or heating is contrary to international standards and conventions on the protection of children.

The story of our *rudari* is embedded in this scenario, since, as we know, they occupied the large building in the Florentine metropolitan area in the spring of 2006.

The description that follows, sometimes almost in the form of a chronicle, of the process that led to ending the occupation in 2012, shows the institutional failure to put in place a good and competent local policy of city government. In this sense, the occupation of the Luzzi had raised a central question: the governance of housing needs policies, investments, innovative projects, political courage, technical intelligence and administrative skill.[16] The myopic and relentless alienation of wealth and urban resources for budgetary needs by public administrations is, in fact, causing incalculable damage to the ability to respond to the growing challenges of the city and its plural and complex identities.

From the Institutional Impasse to the First Agreed Displacement (2006–2009)

After the occupation, neither the healthcare authority, to which the former sanatorium belongs, nor the municipality in which it is located, Sesto Fiorentino, nor that of the metropolitan capital, Florence, took action for the families; everything was delegated to a body in charge of order and public safety, the Prefecture. An element that allows us to understand how, from the outset, this situation had not really been perceived by the institutions as a *social question* (housing, cultural, etc.), but, first and foremost, as a *problem of public order*. The subject/object itself disappeared: the tangible reality of people, with their needs for subsistence, with which to build a political response, was made inconsistent and transferred onto the plane of territorial control.

Faced with a game of ping pong for the responsibilities and initiatives under the responsibility of the owners of the property and the municipality, the Prefecture invited the latter, through its function of supervision over the Administrative Authorities, 'to adopt ... the appropriate initiatives ... in order to remove the causes of danger to the hygiene and safety of the people occupying the building' (note of 05.06.2006). The Municipal Administration, in turn, responded with the order of 21.07.2006, through which it instructed the ASL 10 'to adopt ... all the necessary and indispensable initiatives to remove the cause of danger to the hygiene and safety of the people who occupy, even illegally, the property owned by the same ASL' (local healthcare authority). The latter made an extraordinary appeal to the President of the Republic requesting the annulment of this order.

Meanwhile, the Tuscany Region convened two meetings to form – as per the minutes of the meeting of 7 September 2006 of the Committee for Order and Public Security – a 'metropolitan discussion table ... to address the issues related to immigration and integration, also in relation to current situations in the Florentine area'. The work continued with suspensions and was resumed: the meeting was reconvened only on 2 July 2007, followed by several meetings until mid-October 2007.

Unlike other initiatives promoted by the Movement, in the case of the Luzzi, the occupiers themselves were immediately, together with the Movement itself, seeking a dialogue with local authorities, associations, university. The request that came from the occupation is not only, like in other cases, the possibility of conducting an experience of self-recovery – which was very complex given the conditions and characteristics of the property – but also that of giving the occupiers the possibility of gaining access to a decent home, not necessarily in those same buildings. In addition, the proposal was also, at a broader level, to avoid privatisation of the former sanitarium (buildings and park) and its becoming a hotel or private accommodation destination, instead developing the potential for social use of the edifices and the surrounding areas. This attitude opened up an unprecedented opportunity for a participatory plan for the Luzzi area and buildings as a destination for social purposes. The meetings between July and October 2007 of the institutional round table were aimed at finding solutions that would avoid a forceful intervention, which would put hundreds of people in a serious situation and leave their condition of severe housing discomfort unresolved.

The chosen path established that the Movimento di Lotta per la Casa should be engaged in a gradual reduction of the number of people present in the occupation, that the Department for the Social Policies of the Region should set up an action of housing accompaniment for approximately 70 people, while the Tuscany Region's Housing Department should promote an inter-institutional discussion, with the presence of the associations, for the identification of a possible 'public and social' use of the Luzzi.

But until 2009, only the Movement played its part; *par contre*, the Prevention Department of the local healthcare authority on 2 October 2007 carried out an inspection and sent a report to the local Authorities, stating that the number of occupiers had increased and exceeded 300 people and that a situation of 'significant hygiene and health risk' as well as 'serious danger to public safety and security' remained.

In the first months of 2008, the number of occupiers decreased significantly following the occupation of the former Donati barracks in Sesto Fiorentino, in which between 150 and 200 people from the Luzzi participated, but due to the evacuation of the former barracks (and the subsequent evacuation of the former S. Antonino hospital in Fiesole, where many of the occupiers of the Donati had found shelter) some of the families who were left homeless returned to the Luzzi, whose population was increasing again.[17]

Following the acceptance of the appeal of the ASL, by presidential decree of 16.4.2008, on the basis of the considerations expressed in the opinion of the First Section of the Council of State No. 2878/07 of 23.1.2008, the Luzzi *affaire* returned to the hands of the Municipal Administration of Sesto Fiorentino. The latter quickly reiterated a securitarian attitude, entrusting the matter to its Municipal Police Command, whose agents carried out inspections of the facility at the beginning and middle of September. The relative service note (ref. 752R/200) states that 'nothing seems to have changed …' in relation to the state of the premises described in the communication of the ASL attached to the note of the Prefect of Florence of 29/6/2006, in particular with regard to the 'buildings' seriously uninhabitable state and dangerousness', with the consequent 'high degree of risk that this situation entails for the occupiers'. Also in the same note, reference is made of the danger to public safety of those who live near the occupation, as: 'inside these [accommodations] in addition to essential furnishings for staying overnight there are also stoves powered by LPG cylinders and cooking equipment. There are also various appliances, from televisions and PCs to stoves, all connected to the electricity grid with flying cables and in unsafe conditions'. To which is added the note from the ASL, regarding a possible health and hygiene risk also for public health, as according to the institution, where necessary, 'a hypothesis of intervention would be very problematic, linked to the monitoring of cases of contagious infectious disease (e.g. TB, meningitis etc.) in those conditions and in that community estimated to number over 300 people'.

In addition to the well-known issue of hygiene and the sanitation process as a body control strategy, the above also seems to me to represent a clear example of the modus operandi of what Appadurai has called the 'ethics of probability': those ways of thinking, feeling and acting that flow out to what Ian Hacking called the 'avalanche of numbers' (2013: 257), which 'takes risk to spaces of emergency and suffering' (ibid.: 260). A hegemonic moral and cultural approach to be replaced – suggests the anthropologist – with the 'ethics of possibility', which 'can offer a more inclusive platform for improving the planetary quality of life and can accommodate a plurality of visions of the good life' (ibid.: 261). *La* Luzzi, also in this sense, represented an unprecedented local experience.

On the basis of the service reports and the current regulations,[18] the situation of prolonged and serious institutional impasse was resolved only in a repressive way with the Mayor's order no. 611 of 23 September 2008: 'Eviction order and measures for the security of the area known as the former Luzzi Hospital'. The occupiers were therefore ordered to leave the property and were warned that 'in the event of ascertained non-compliance with the respective orders given, notice will be sent to the Prefect of Florence for the forced execution of the same and notice will be given to the competent Authority in order to apply the sanctions set out in art. 650 of the Criminal Code.'

No alternative housing and no social intervention were proposed in the Mayor's order, not even in a 'reductionist' key, such as the provision of shelters for the minors and their mothers.

The Prefecture, however, did not carry out any forceful action. Paradoxically, the body responsible for territorial control did not carry out the eviction, ordered by an institution that, on the other hand, has, among its functions, that of providing proximity, welfare and educational services starting from the most fragile population and in particular from children, whose protection is required regardless of any social situation. At the beginning of 2009, therefore, starting from the position taken by the Prefecture, the Tuscany Region began to give a substantive form to the 2007 initiative. The Department of Urban Planning and Regional Planning of the University of Florence and the Michelucci Foundation were asked to include in the research, then underway, self-construction and self-recovery, as approaches and means for housing inclusion, precisely the case of the Luzzi.

Therefore the aim of the research was to build a first framework of knowledge about the former sanatorium and its occupants, which constituted the prerequisite for the elaboration of innovative proposals involving concrete actions. In the background, as outlined earlier, the possibility of building with all the actors involved – from the occupiers to the institutions, from the 'old' residents of the area to the associations – a common path to transform a space abandoned by the institutions into a place for the whole city. A growth over time, a discovery of people and a rediscovery of places.

Unfortunately, the pressure for a forced eviction of the property increcased again. To avoid a violent solution, the Tuscany Region relaunched the discussions with those involved in the matter: the Department of Social Policies promoted and funded a programme for accommodating some families in housing managed by associations in various places in the region,[19] and at the same time the Movimento di Lotta per la Casa was committed to finding alternative accommodation for a more or less equivalent number of people. In two different phases, between August and October 2009, the agreed displacements led to the closure of two of the four former hospital buildings.

Particularly interesting, constituting the only action in real contrast with the institutional logic, were the methods through which it was possible to identify families destined to be transferred: at the negotiating table, thanks to social mediation carried out at several levels by the Michelucci Foundation, there were both the Tuscany Region and the ASL and the Movimento di Lotta per la Casa and numerous representatives of the families, in addition to the Foundation itself. Every proposal was reported and discussed day by day with all the occupiers at the Luzzi and in the weekly assembly: the involvement of families in the decision as to who among them would go away, and where, unfolded into a dialogical relationship, in which the institutional demands often put serious pressure on the occupiers. The decisions, in fact, were far from easy: some proposed accommodations were far away from Florence, and the prospects for so-called social and work integration appeared uncertain. One of the demands that emerged at the Luzzi, perhaps the most important, was to be able to keep family nuclei belonging to the same extended family close and, as far as possible, in the same territory. In fact, the protective network that denoted the Luzzi managed to keep alive some of the fundamental characteristics of a family of this type: economic unity, co-habitation and solidarity. Unfortunately, this request by the families, supported by the Movimento di Lotta per la Casa and the Michelucci Foundation, found little satisfaction, due only in part to the objectively limited offer of the apartments and, predominantly, to the inflexibility of the municipalities of Florence and Sesto Fiorentino, supported by the idea of 'redistributing' in other territories the 'burden' of the immigrant presence.[20]

Table 8.5 gives the quantitative picture of the two phases of the transfer of the *rudari* families, which took place on 7 and 17 August, 5 and 15 October 2009.[21]

As the table shows, only one family (ID 55/1) had the opportunity to move to the city of Florence, thanks to the repeatedly remarked insistence on the workplace of the head of the family. The two family nuclei of his children (ID 55/2), in their turn, were taken to a village about an hour and a quarter by car (their own car) by their parents, but in two adjoining apartments.

The ID 60 extended family was also divided into family nuclei in two lodgings in the same province, but about 50 km away from each other.

The strategy of the so-called 'territorial redistribution',[22] repeatedly implemented, continues to be pursued, although it has been critical in most cases, especially for the situation of isolation and loneliness in which families find themselves, which creates a condition of deep suffering, in particular for the women. This became more evident in very small and poorly connected contexts – such as the town of Bibbiena in the Casentino, and Massa Marittima in the mountain hinterland of Grosseto, Castelnuovo in Lucca – which do not even offer people the opportunity of what sociology defines as a 'city effect'. These paths, influenced immediately and densely by these factors, in almost all – some already in the short term, some in the span of two years – have resulted in unsatisfactory outcomes both for the families and for the territory.

The ID 38 family, transferred to the city of Livorno, despite the various difficulties, has managed to trace a migratory path that has led it to achieve its objectives of improving its economic living conditions: the head of the family works as a driver between Italy and Romania, his wife as an assistant beautician, both hired with a regular contract; even their daughter – after starting high school, but then dropping out – has found a part-time job.

Table. 8.5. Displacement 2009. © *Sabrina* Tosi Cambini.

Family ID	No. Members	No. Adults	No Minors	Place
100	5	2	3	Lido di Camiore (Livorno)
38	4	3	1	Livorno
56	4	2	2	Livorno
63	6	2	4	Empoli
37	4	4	0	Massa Marittima
55/1	5	3	2	Firenze
55/2	5	3	2	Seravecchia (Lucca)
60/1	6	2	4	Capannori (Lucca)
60/2	5	4	1	Castelnuovo di Garfagnana (Lucca)
86	8	2	6	Bibbiena (Arezzo)
72	4	3	1	Santa Croce sull'Arno (Pisa)
59	5	2	3	Montemurlo (Prato)
Total 12	61	32	29	

The Closure of the Luzzi: Defeats and Advantages (2010–2012)

This process was approached by the occupying families in a very active and courageous way: on the horizon there was still the possibility of negotiating the 'destiny' of the Luzzi – the project for the social and housing reuse of the facility. The families' readiness to move internally, from one building to another, necessary in order to close half of them, and the self-control in keeping two empty, were remarkable.

But despite the daily commitment of the individuals and groups involved, the participatory design process for the reuse of the Luzzi did not have adequate support, and ended up being openly opposed: in February 2010 the hypothetical eviction again loomed large, owing to a new order of the Mayor of Sesto Fiorentino, which also involved the Ministry of the Interior, at the time led by Roberto Maroni of the Northern League Party.

The atmosphere inside the occupied buildings became oppressive, strained by all these events. The care of the outside and collective spaces was gradually abandoned: the external tension began to cause internal disturbances, heightened worries and feelings of insecurity on the part of the families, whose fear of having to leave the facility suddenly and violently, due to a forced eviction, increased day by day.

The only possibility that remained was to fight to avoid the most violent solution: at that moment we were facing defeat. Evening meetings at the Luzzi increased, as did the meetings at the Region's headquarters. In addition to those already at the discussions, other families came to the regional headquarters: they protested outside the offices and were brought in to discuss their future. But the release of the structure by the occupiers could not wait any longer: the timescale of a possible eviction was dramatically accelerated.

The necessary funds were found by the Region in a strategic way, taking advantage of the European assimilation of this minority to the Roma groups: the *rudari* at this juncture became, in the programme presented, *undoubtedly* Roma, thus opening up the possibility of obtaining from the European Community extraordinary funds specifically reserved for them. This was a fact that should not have leaked from the negotiating table: since the reaction of the territory to the occupation was to exclude and the response of the municipality of Sesto Fiorentino was based on repression, the news that they were Roma would certainly make it even more difficult to avoid eviction without any alternative, in addition to the uncontrollable political exploitation that would ensue.

For the families still present, therefore, the Tuscany Region initiated further processes: support for renting a house or, for those who took this opportunity as a chance to complete their projects, to return to Romania.

It was not the solution that the discussion table had hoped for (that is, a participatory process involving all the actors), but it served at least to avoid police intervention, which repeatedly seemed imminent, and to provide some resources for families to conceive the most suitable solution for themselves in those constrained conditions.

Initially, the institutions pressed for proposing a return to Romania for all. This hypothesis was immediately questioned thanks also to the data collected during the research, which showed how many families have close working ties with the territory, as well as the existence of about 40 minors enrolled in school. In the face of limited resources and necessary solutions to be quickly put in place, a path called 'start-up' was therefore envisaged: an economic contribution deemed necessary to facilitate housing opportunities through the market channel.[23]

The other path, of the return to Romania, included a contribution to each family calculated on the number of members (1,000 euros for each person) and divided into four instalments, three of which were paid to the family at their home in the country of origin.

For both possibilities, the institutions instructed the Caritas in Florence to manage, evaluate and grant contributions; at the beginning of March, this body opened a special office in its own headquarters in the central area of Santa Maria Novella.

The two possible solutions – 'start-up' and 'return' – were the subject of an intense discussion within the Luzzi. One of the basic problems was the list of registered occupiers, given to the Caritas by the Florence Police Headquarters ('Questura') and drawn up on the basis of two checks carried out by police officers on 30 November and 9 December 2009. The names present were compared with the list that the occupiers, together with the Movement and the Foundation, very quickly drew up in their turn: the objective was that no one should be excluded from the processes because their name did not appear on the police list. Some people thought they were not there, they misunderstood ... a lady was taken ill, believing she had been left out: the assemblies were full of fear and anger.

The evaluation was up to the families: take the opportunity to fix up their house in Romania or even start the construction of a new one?

On the other hand, those who had been in Florence for some time, and who had a job, did not want to put at risk the opportunities that they had built over the years and, therefore, preferred not to leave, and wondered how to find a house to rent.

For days and days, the families were taking these difficult decisions. Meanwhile, the environmental and housing situation of the Luzzi deteriorated sharply. In the gradual abandonment of the building and due to the lack of any other outlook, the self-control inside became almost non-existent. Any material of economic value (electrical wires, installations, sanitary ware, fixtures) was removed from the buildings. The spaces freed by the departures of the families were partially occupied by new, often unknown people. A highly critical situation was the result of the evacuation imposed by Authorities.

On 22 March, Gelu died, stricken by a heart attack in Romania. The next day, the Movement in the person of Lorenzo[24] – so many times named by our *rudari* in the discourse and interviews that took place – wrote a long letter to the institutions, journalists, activists, calling the Luzzi a 'migrant occupation':

> Weighing things up, the ability to resist was failing, and a quick evaluation of the power relationships forced us to accept the very miserable proposals ... When the time came to rally around, the Movement was left, as often happens, with only some commitment by members of the Michelucci Foundation, not much to show in front of the claims of the speculative big politics and the new philosophies on 'security'.

And after summing up the choices of the municipality of Sesto Fiorentino, outside the rule of law and of a repressive nature, the mobilisation and 'militancy' of which the occupiers had been capable – '*The people of la (!!!) Luzzi* were always present' – and their limits in the management of the facility, he ends:

> Humanly speaking, more could not have been done, we tried to build a common and shared experience, we succeeded only partially, but the important thing is that the history of this occupation, for those who have experienced the occupation daily, should remain 'a living memory' in the future as a further small stock of knowledge and experience.

In March 2010, 27 families had chosen to return to Romania, receiving the last instalment of the scheduled contribution in October 2010. The first families, numbering 12, with a total of 45 people, left on 25 March, together with Caritas operators who intended to 'monitor the real situation of families and their housing conditions' (Caritas operators' report of 20 July 2010).

In Romania, all the families have tried to use the money from the project in lasting investments: for the home, in most cases, as mentioned before, or in the activity of buying and selling fruit and vegetables and transporting them.

The path called 'start up' involved 26 families, a total of 105 people. Everyone has found a house for rent in the city of Florence or in the immediate vicinity, but the high prices on the open real estate market has denied almost everyone the possibility of staying there without incurring arrears and a subsequent eviction order. Where the number of minors was high, the evacuation was carried out at a later time. Only one very large family, whose apartment had proved particularly unhealthy due to a sewerage problem, was then able to get access to public housing.

The families in Romania, for their part, have gradually returned to Florence; however this was foreseen from the beginning.

Except for the few cases in which it was possible to keep the rented apartment, the choice of the return route proved to be the best: many families found themselves with a few thousand euros, with which they were able to partly fulfil their desires, the pursuit of which had been their motivation for departing.

Some extended families also managed to enjoy both possibilities: for example, if the parents had a more stable working situation in Florence, they brought back their son's young family.

In the subsequent development of migratory events, it is important to emphasise that both families who suffered eviction and those who would later return adopted settlement strategies that were careful not to be swallowed up by other projects or institutional initiatives. All, in fact, apart from the fact that they may have drawn real advantages from the evacuation of the Luzzi, lived for months in the fear of being awakened at dawn by the police and they suffered a state of passivity that allowed no alternative to the conditions imposed.

At the Luzzi, after returns and transfers, five *rudari*[25] families remained, just the most fragile – as they were made up of single women with children, or people, adults and minors, with serious health problems – who, on the contrary, should have been the first to be included in more careful planning. In fact, the institutions left them there for a long time, in a huge structure that had become dilapidated: three of them until 2011 and two until 2012.

As was foreseeable for a property of that size, in the absence of self-control inside and in a new total abandonment, the Luzzi was gradually repopulated, but with very different modalities and types of occupiers, which did not allow the establishment of a good coexistence. Despite the enormous differences with the past, the former sanatorium, as an urban void, nevertheless again represented a possibility to occupy, practised also by some *rudari* families: some who had experienced the 'start-up' paths, others who had returned from Romania, but for the most part these were new nuclei that had come to know about it thanks to the circulation of information in the family network.

In November 2011 there were already over a hundred people. Among the 20 *rudari* families, 8 were composed of previous occupants of the Luzzi (also with a different family composition) and all the rest came from the same places as the latter and had kinship or neighbourhood relations with them. Six of the 20 families, according to the municipality of Sesto Fiorentino, were entitled to a contribution linked to a final phase of evacuating the Luzzi. These families were summoned by the Caritas, always responsible for the project and the disbursement of resources, in February 2012 and then again at the beginning of April. But the families rejected the proposals: they did not want to leave the Luzzi and Florence if they were not offered a safe housing solution, at least in the medium term.

The police carried out a new census on 28 June, 2012, which showed the presence of 108 people, 91 of whom were Romanian nationals. These, beyond a couple of nuclei (only spouses) of *lautari* and some presences of *ursari*, all came from 'our' families.

The Prefect convened for 1 August 2012 a Discussion table to which he invited a series of institutions (the Province of Florence, ASL 10, the South-East and North-West Zone Healthcare Authorities, the municipality of Sesto Fiorentino, the UNCEM[26] Toscana Department of the Tuscany Region), as well as the Michelucci Foundation and the Caritas: all the actors who, in various ways, had been involved in the regional project, except the Movement, whose voice was reported, however, by the Foundation. Again the problem of the lists was emerging and the solution of territorial distribution was still being presented. On the part of the occupiers and those supporting them, the margin for negotiation was minimal; for the institutions, the game had to be ended as quickly as possible. Most families refused to move to municipalities far from Florence (only a few nuclei chose to), and obtained the condition that none should leave the facility without having alternative accommodation. On 13 December, the closing operations of the Luzzi began.

These were bitter days.

Notes

1. The Osmatex in mid-January 2010 was the scene of a dramatic eviction that would leave about 120 people on the street, in support of whom only some associations of the Florentine territory were activated at the time (including, in particular, the 'Doctors for Human Rights') and, above all, the Waldensian community that provided hospitality for several days to more than half of the people.
2. From the 'Political Manifesto' on Casa Luzzi of the Movimento di Lotta per la Casa, from http://www.inventati.org/casaluzzi/
3. See, in particular, the interview with P. Rabinow (Foucault 1982).
4. *La Nazione Firenze*, 22 August 2006.
5. Italian Recreational and Cultural Association: one of the largest associative networks in Italy, founded in the late 1950s.
6. Interview conducted during the *MigRom* project.

7. Interview conducted during the *MigRom* project.

8. Pétonnet carried out further comparative research on a housing complex that involved people who had not moved outside the borders of their country – a Moroccan *bidonville* in Rabat, where she stayed for three months.

9. Pétonnet again writes: 'A *priori*, according to the opinion more generally expressed and which betrays the desire [*vœu*] of assimilation, this neighbourhood will serve to maintain the residents in a rural and traditional way of life that will prevent them from entering French society. But it's not so at all. The bidonville, on the contrary, ensures the safety and adaptation of newcomers. Just as certain neighbourhoods have a specific function (trade, hospitality, entertainment, etc.), the bidonville has its own: a function of transitory passage between two worlds' (2002: 80).

10. The rest were divided as follows: 56 people from Morocco, of which 1 family and the rest young single adults; 1 family from Tunisia (4 people); 9 Italian people; 1 Roma family from Montenegro (26 people).

11. Elaborations on data collected in the spring of 2009 for the Michelucci Foundation during the *Housing frontline* project, and for the Osservatorio sull'Abitare precario (Observatory on precarious housing), of which I was researcher in charge under the supervision of N. Solimano.

12. The copious literature on housing exclusion indicates that difficulties have been emerging for some time in the functioning of the processes and policies against poverty and exclusion, determined both by the appearance of new and extensive areas of social vulnerability induced by the post-Fordist development model, and by the crisis of the welfare state that has, from different points of view (including housing), reduced the scope of social protection, and by the mix of these with global processes. For the local context of our reference, refer to the Fondazione Michelucci (2014).

13. At the local level, the Tuscan Regional Law of 2 August 2013, no. 45 'Financial support for families and workers in difficulty, for cohesion and to combat social hardship' is a clear example.

14. See Tosi Cambini (2015).

15. 'Art. 5. – 1. Anyone illegally occupying a property … cannot request residency registration or connection to public services in relation to the property itself and the deeds issued in violation of this prohibition are null and void for all legal purposes. From the date of entry into force of the law converting this decree, the acts referring to the connection of electricity, gas, water and landline telephone services, in the forms of stipulation, title change, renewal, are null and void, and therefore cannot be stipulated or otherwise adopted, if they do not show the identification data of the applicant and the document that certifies the ownership, regular possession or regular holding of the real estate unit for which the connection is requested … 1-bis. Persons who illegally occupy public residential housing may not participate in the procedures for the allocation of housing of the same nature for the five years following the date of ascertainment of the illegal occupation. 1-ter'

16. Already several texts by scholars involved in the applied research project *Housing Frontline* (already cited), have dealt with the occupation of the former Luzzi and institutional choices in this regard, in particular until the second agreed displacement in 2010, see Marcetti et al. (2011), Marcetti and Tosi Cambini (2013). Therefore, once the frame of reference has been drawn up, I will focus more on those aspects that are not dealt with except, sometimes, marginally, in the aforementioned texts.

17. About 60 of 'our' *rudari* had temporarily moved, first to the former Donati barracks in Sesto Fiorentino, then, following the evacuation of this, to the former hospital in

Fiesole; again evicted, they went to the former CNR building and then, finally, to the former Ottone Rosai school and back to the Luzzi again.

18. In particular, according to art. 54 of the T.U.E.L. 267/2000 (and subsequent amendments) which gives the Mayor, as a government official, the authority also to take contingent and urgent measures, in order to prevent and eliminate serious dangers that threaten public safety and urban security; in addition to the provisions of the decree of the Ministry of the Interior of 5.8.2008 (published in the Official Gazette of 9 August 2008 no. 186), issued pursuant to paragraph 4-bis of art. 54 of Legislative Decree 267/00, which in art. 2 clarifies that the actions of the Mayor pursuant to the aforementioned art. 54 com. 1–4 must be to prevent and also counteract 'negligence, degradation and illegal occupation of properties' which, according to this government legislation, may lead to a situation of degradation, facilitating the emergence of criminal phenomena and causing damage to the property, including private property, with the deterioration of the quality of urban life.

19. Resolution of the Regional Council no. 709 of 3 August 2009: outline of Protocol and Agreement between the Region of Tuscany and the municipality of Sesto Fiorentino; Resolution of the Municipal Council of Sesto Fiorentino no. 144 of 4 August 2009.

20. On the political idea of 'territorial redistribution of Roma families', at various levels and territorial variations (European, national and local), see Piasere, Solimano and Tosi Cambini (eds) (2014).

21. In August, as agreed, the Movement transferred other families or individuals from the Luzzi, placing them in existing occupations; in all they were an extended family of Montenegrin Roma, composed of 26 people, 10 young Moroccans and 2 Italians. Five young people from Morocco, on the other hand, found a housing solution independently.

22. Applied in the Tuscan context for refugees and Roma in the 'Roma Tuscany' project. See Fondazione Michelucci (2010, 2014).

23. This contribution included: the payment of the deposit requested by the tenant; support for rental expenses for a maximum of six months (half of the rent cost for the first three months, then halved for the second three months).

24. Lorenzo Bargellini – to whom this volume is dedicated, together with Gelu and Christian – a person of great humanity, who devoted his life to the fight for the right to housing and to the recognition and protection of the dignity of every person.

25. Together with about 20 young single people from Morocco.

26. Unione Nazionale Comuni Comunità Enti Montani (National Union of Municipalities of the Local Mountain Communities).

Chapter 9

ETHNOGRAPHIC *MORCEAU*

Displacements and Evictions

Ian and Alexandru, together with their son, accepted the proposal by two local institutions to move from the occupied house on the outskirts of Florence to the municipality of Massa Marittima, in the Grosseto hinterland. It was 18 August 2009. After a week Iana called me, telling me that the house was not in the village but in a hamlet, which had yet to be restored and that many pieces of furniture, a bed, a refrigerator were lacking: 'for now only the social worker has come once, then a worker from the municipality. We do not know what to do. I don't know who to ask for some information. So what do I do? Alexandru waits for work. They brought us groceries, clothes, but we have those'. I asked I. if the social worker had left her a number to call her back, and she said: 'Yes, but she's never in the office.' I was out of town: I was looking for some representatives of the Società della salute Zona Fiorentina Nord-Ovest (Florentine Northwest Zone Healthcare Authority), but I couldn't find anyone. In the municipality of Massa Marittima, after several attempts I managed to talk to someone who knew about the family: 'We are doing what was established in the agreement, we have already activated the services, signor A.S. and his family will have all the necessary support to become integrated'. I returned and in September I went to visit them. 'I'm glad you came', said Iana 'I don't see anyone.' Alexandru squeezed my hand: 'How are you?' The house is still bare. 'You remember at the Luzzi, Sabrina, our house was beautiful, wasn't it?' said Iana while preparing the coffee. 'Here you cannot do anything without permission. But there's still so much missing. But they say it's okay like that'. I asked her if they'd got to know anyone: 'We don't talk to anyone. I am always at home and Alexandru has now started a trial period at work but must go into the woods'. I turned to Alexandru who continued what his wife was saying: 'I have to go cut the wood, but 12–13 hours of work, Sabrina, I'm very tired at night, I can't move my arm'.

...

In the darkness of the room the faces can be glimpsed illuminated by candles. It is cold outside but it is very hot in here, you can hardly breathe: the stove is lit from the morning and the air is saturated with the smell of our bodies and freshly cooked food.

The arrival of the police has been expected for days. The gate is closed with padlocks. The electricity went off in this part of the building, but luckily not in all of the occupation. Tomorrow – if we're still here tomorrow – the men will restore it with the new cables brought by L.

M. and F. also arrive, with the children, but we are not yet complete; A. has yet to arrive back from work (the bus rarely passes and sometimes doesn't come at all). Florence is so close and yet so far from here.

We are ready, we can move to O.'s house. There the space is larger, we can all stay there and there is light!

The children laugh and pretend to be afraid of the darkness ... they run down the stairs even with this little lighting that comes from the street ... 'Is it true Sabrina that they will send us away?', 'But you don't understand', interrupts L., 'Lorenzo said so last night at the assembly: it comes from Maroni [the order]. Now we must see what we can do'.

Meanwhile they put on some music, we eat, we talk, we make fun of each other ... yes because irony always circulates ... it seems a way to ride the fortunes ... The bread is just baked, and M. has even prepared *sarmale* [national dish of the Romanian cuisine], and a dish of pork is never missing from the table. It's starting to rain outside. The children go to and fro between the house and the street, always inside the Luzzi. Never outside the gate.

L. grabs me and starts dancing: 'Brava, brava!' The other women shout at me ... Arms raised to clap their hands. Laughter. Let's do the *hora* [the dance circle].

'Tomorrow we will come to interview the S.', says the social worker.

'Yes, they told me, I'll be there too', I reply.

The family consists of the parents and eleven children, one of whom has returned to Romania and the eldest daughter lives with her partner. The interview involves an evaluation that the association should make about the eligibility of the family for the project that involves the transfer of a certain number of occupying families to apartments managed by various third sector organisations. The accommodation where the S. could go is about 50 minutes by car: the family is worried about the distance from the workplace, but this concern is not comparable to that of being evicted without knowing where to go. The social workers of the association believe that the number of people can 'put at risk' the success of the 'integration' project: the objective is that of 'autonomy'; according to them the number could be a big obstacle 'to [its] achievement'.

On the phone or in person, I speak several times with the operator responsible and explain the situation that, starting from the parameters used for the evaluation, the situation is very good as two entries have employment with permanent contracts. The meeting – the first of those planned – seems to go in the direction that the family hoped for and, in fact, the next day they receive a confirmation phone call: they have been accepted. M. – the mother – immediately begins to prepare the luggage, tidy the clothes and do a laundry wash. G. – the father – now feels relieved of his 'concern for the children'.

A few days pass. I was away for work. On my return I immediately go to visit them. I understand that something has happened. I wait. M. and I sit down. We have a coffee. 'We're not going away anymore, Sabrina', 'Why not?' I reply. 'They called G. while he was at work and told him we're not suitable.' I get angry. 'What can we do: that's life', she says.

We eat. It's nine o'clock in the evening, G. also arrives and starts playing with his two-year-old youngest son. He gives him the keys to the van and they 'drive' together and eat together because L. always wants to wait for his father to come for dinner. We talk. G. is distressed by the situation. His face is serious. His blue eyes are gloomy. The evacuation of the Luzzi is drawing closer and they still do not know where to go. There is the other possibility: find an apartment for rent and take advantage of the 'start-up' that is a public contribution to pay the deposit required at the time of the contract, the first rent and half of the rent for the first six months. G. has already begun to inquire about it, but in the pay cheque – both his and his son's – there is a much lower salary than what they really receive, since a portion is given to them off the books.

The next day I call the operator in charge: 'Have you ever wondered how they live? Because they can manage even without external contributions, you've seen it, but what criteria did you use?! You can't say yes and then no in such a situation!', 'What do you mean?' 'I've been doing this job for ten years' he replies, 'So, you've been doing it wrong for ten years and it would be better if you stop', I countered.

I compare my reaction and that of G. and M. I reflect a lot.

G. dies a few days later due to a cardiac arrest with a haemorrhage. Goodbye G., I wanted to give you the books on the Black Sea that I bought in Bucareşti and that you liked so much, once you settled with your family in your new home.

Chapter 10

SETTLEMENT STRATEGIES AFTER *LA* LUZZI

As we have seen, as a result of the prevalence of the repressive line on the part of the institutions, the families were forced to gradually leave the occupied building. The parallel reading between this part of the text and that of the previous chapter allows us to see from several perspectives the process of forced abandonment of the former Luzzi and to grasp the mismatches, the different logics and the different objectives, between the occupiers, the territory and the institutions, and between the *rudari* families themselves in the elaboration of settlement strategies after the great occupation. Leaving the Luzzi as Roma, our *rudari* later return to the city of Florence as Romanian immigrants, occupiers of buildings or tenants.

In a context of enormous imbalance of power between the actors involved, the Luzzi affair is resolved in favour of the institutions and their neoliberal policies. Nevertheless, and in the midst of unfolding dramas, many families manage to reap some advantages of a different nature. The most obvious are the economic ones, especially for those who choose a (temporary) return to Romania: it is, in fact, money to invest in their own country, in line with their migratory aspirations.

In the medium and long term, however, there are other advantages in terms of knowledge and skills that families acquire, thanks to the relationship established with the Movimento di Lotta per la Casa, most of them fully taking part in it.

The transmission of knowledge with respect to their rights and the enforceability of these (a year after the occupation Romania joined the European Union, albeit with limitations, and it is a far from secondary element in people's lives) did not take place through theoretical and abstract means, but through the sharing of experiences: in taking part in weekly assemblies – that of the occupied building and that of the entire Movement – in demonstrations, and in the anti-eviction marches and pickets in defence of the right to housing. Over the four years – from mid-2006 to mid-2010 – the Thursday assembly at the former Luzzi had become the most numerous, with the highest attendance among the weekly assemblies of the various occupations, even those that are now 'historical'. The awareness of their own life situation in the context of immigration – so often evoked rhetorically by the institutions and social services – and the determination on the ground of rights were won by the *rudari*, through the instruments of political struggle, thanks to the Movement, which immediately acknowledged them as *people*. The Movement has provided people with the opportunity to find agency spaces within a field of forces, which has allowed them to *exercise* their rights, asserting their presence in the urban context: 'you wanted a labour force, people have arrived' ('*volevate braccia, sono arrivate persone*') was the writing on the sheet that waved from the top of the building of the former Donati barracks in Sesto Fiorentino. A highly significant phrase, capable of summing up at the same time both the well-known concept of 'double absence' theorised by Sayad and the very possibility of an active response, first of all through self-assertion as persons and the enforceability of the right to recognition of their dignity.

Without any use of parameters and evaluations, people were immediately considered by the Movement as such and, during the many moments of sharing and discussion, treated as equals. With an attitude far from both the welfare approach and the paternalistic spirit, they have been considered capable of choosing for themselves and as bearers of rights that are denied them, sharing the experience of tools to fight for themselves: they can occupy houses, protest in the streets, in institutional offices, learn to oppose the decisions of the institutions, to negotiate with them or to take positions of firmer resistance if there is no margin for a decent negotiation. This progression of knowledge and skills – different from family to family, and from one member to another – is clearly visible in the choices that families make after the experience of regional projects, having also managed to avoid violent eviction and to represent a novelty in the panorama of policies related to the governance of precarious housing.

Already at the end of 2011 and in 2012, the families who were still at the Luzzi, with their chronic health problems or disabilities, refused the economic contribution offered to them because they demanded a more structural response that would allow them access to a more stable and secure housing resource, at least in the medium term. But it is in the strategies put in place in the return to Italy by those who had left, and with the exit from the housing – of those who had not been able to pay the rent – that it is possible to see how in many families the experience of *la* Luzzi had become a stock of knowledge and practices. This has allowed them to distance themselves from the processes of institutionalisation, choosing in many cases to continue with the Movement or even occupy completely on their own.

The degree of political awareness developed by the people, the interest in this, as well as the skills in the practices related to the protest, differ significantly: for example, the two occupations carried out subsequently by some *rudari* families, in total autonomy from the Movement, denoted significant organisational problems and only some of the people involved asked themselves the question of managing of an occupied environment and its relationship with the surrounding social environment. The occupied building, in fact, ended up attracting people who had nothing to do with family networks, and whose informal economy activities could be very risky for the life of the occupation. Despite the contradictions and suffering, many families have continued in the 'friendship' with that part of the city of Florence, which for decades has been committed to defending the right to housing.

Some families, returning from Romania, opted for the choice of rented housing, sharing the apartment with another related family: each family had its own bedroom; the use of the kitchen was shared, as well as any other spaces. Even in these cases, the link with the occupations was still maintained, both because there were extended family nuclei living there and because the Movement continued to represent a point of reference for bureaucratic aspects or as a resource to be activated in the event of an eviction.

These settlement strategies, although different, denoted some elements of change. First of all, those who were forced to leave the apartments, to which they had access through the 'start-up' programme, or the family nuclei that returned to Italy from Romania, no longer contemplated any living situation represented by makeshift shelters, such as shacks or tents in the urban interstices, as had happened before the occupation of the former Luzzi, during the first years of migration.

The second aspect, closely linked to the previous one, is the 'migration situation' that people were willing to accept. The question of the nature of the accommodation, we have seen, was also connected to the fact that; initially, it was the men alone who departed. The experience of the recon-struction of the family unit in the country of immigration, thanks to the former Luzzi, as well as the skills acquired over time with respect to the migratory environment (in the search for work, in juggling with local asso-ciations to acquire orientation information or benefits, in relating to the health services and the schools attended by the children), have contributed to 'our' *rudari* changing the pre-figuration of their migratory paths. Men no longer departed alone, they tried to settle through a housing situation that had characteristics considered adequate to accommodate all the members of a family nucleus. In their updating, the migrations for these families in the network, following these processes, gradually lost their temporary and transitory character. The 'ferrying' function of the former Luzzi occupation and of the experience with the Movement, have not only supported people in exploring and familiarising themselves with the new environment represented by a foreign city in Western Europe, allowing them to acquire social, cultural and political skills, but in this way, they have contributed to expanding their ability to imagine real possibilities of accessing and/ or building in the country of immigration. We read between the lines the process that Appadurai (2013) talks about – it is not by chance that the field of research is the same: the movements for the right to housing and for access to urban resources. The women of the *rudari* families quickly develop skills to be able to deal, even if not all of them with the same skill and effectiveness, with complex bureaucratic systems, such as those related to the territorial social and health services; they gradually begin to relate to the school institution and to the teachers, sometimes managing to explain to the latter how much the social difficulties to which they are exposed affect the school education of their children. They use the public transport network to reach their relatives, their work, the schools where they accompany and collect their children, and the services. These elements acquire particular importance if we bear in mind the starting conditions of our families. As we know, the context of life in Romania is characterised by great poverty exacerbated by marginalisation mechanisms linked to the categorisation of the *rudari* as *gypsies*. A perspective that moves through time (present-past) and space (here-there) allows us to compare the skills and abilities developed through the possibilities offered by the environment and the migratory experiences.

The reading that is proposed gives greater weight to the loosening of the meshes of the 'impersonal' forces, as Appadurai calls them, operating in the localities, and to the experiences with the multiple events of the former Luzzi as agents of change compared to others, traceable for example, in the field of gender relations.

First of all, in our case, we are not talking about 'female' immigration. With the abandonment of the first strategy, the migrations become in all respects a 'family affair'. This is even clearer if we make a comparison with the families that have remained in Romania, where in the parents' generation (level 3 of the genealogy), there are more women who have the possibility of migratory 'opportunities', since there is, for them, the channel related to care work, replacing a relative for one or two months. As we will see later, this period is often experienced by these women, at least initially, as a break from the physical, emotional and psychological commitments required by a family that constantly has problems finding resources, in a context where it has no protection. In the Romanian context, the social imagination of this community is compressed by the local dimension and, covering its effect on an individual level, which the ethnographic work allows us to see; we note that both women and men are more passive and repetitive in their survival strategies. It doesn't occur to any woman to find out if there are professional courses in nearby Megdia or Constanţa … It doesn't occur to any woman to look for projects aimed at the vulnerable population, in which to participate and acquire new skills … We certainly know that occasions like these are rare in those places, but this is precisely what we are talking about: the negative circularity between the repertoire of conditions of possibility – the local dimension in Appadurai's terms – and the ability itself to imagine other opportunities and develop new strategies.

In the migrations to Florence, the former Luzzi and the Movement also helped to outline the different dimensions of the locality. It is those contexts that have represented the possibility of reducing the negative circularity activated in a migratory context by the repressive forces, which we have seen in place, activating in turn a positive circularity that concerns making imaginable, conceivable and – subsequently – new formative, work and housing paths for oneself and for the other members of the family.

We note that Ionica, who has been living permanently in Florence for some time, despite declared difficulties in understanding the diversity of the social and cultural world in which her children are growing up, advised one of her eldest daughters – who had to return to Romania to look after her grandmother's health and due to the work of the person who would soon become her husband – to make use of her studies in Italy by buying a professional sewing machine and offering her services to the shops of the nearby city, repairing or packaging clothes.

On the other hand, and I oblige the reader to follow me in these 'leaps' of perspectives between contexts and actors, precisely the misunderstanding of this autonomous ability to elaborate responses is one of the problems underlying the relationship with the social services and the so-called 'inclusion' projects in the context of immigration.

In this sense, our families have adopted a double strategy. On the one hand, the pursuit of an 'invisibility' with respect to the engine of social interventions, which allows them both to escape from the institutional powers and to maintain the power to decide on their time and space, without being suffocated by the grip of the 'pacts' with the bodies in charge of the so-called 'inclusion' and 'reception'.

On the other hand, the relationship with social services may become necessary due to the great difficulty that the family nucleus is experiencing (a still difficult housing situation and serious health problems). In this case, which presupposes having registered residence, they will try to access those opportunities that the national and local welfare system provides for all those who are in the same situation of economic hardship, apart from their origins and the stereotypes connected to them.

In both cases, information on the existence of a *benefit* and the procedure to be followed to obtain it circulate from relative to relative, from family to family.

There were certainly episodes of discrimination and misunderstanding: when they decide to turn to social services, the imbalance of power between the latter and the family is tangible, starting from the extremely formal language and the difficult bureaucratic procedures, from the repetition of talks with the various officials, from the creeping logic of the services that tends to blame the 'user' for their difficult situation.

Being inside matters of settlement that unfold between occupations, evacuations, new occupations, rents and evictions, the presence of *rudari* families spreads through several areas of the city: it is an aspect that touches the conformation of the spatial network of family relationships, which are affected both by the distance between homes and the rhythms connected to work activities, making daily socialising more difficult.

In the occupations, an attempt is made to restore proximity, sometimes prevented by evictions that redesign the actual housing possibilities. The network, therefore, tends to make the relational density of the points (which corresponds to the parental network) coincide with the spatial one (the locations of the dwellings), but it must confront external factors that imprint on it an opposite movement, of spatial distancing, which tends toward the territorial pulverisation of their presence: evacuations and the property market hinder the families' desire to live next to each other in a continuous way. From the point of view of spatial segregation – certainly to be understood, beyond the various definitions, as a spatial form of the domain – this housing situation is shaped according to a model that, if it is certainly not that of concentration (rare in Italy), it can hardly be defined as polycentric, since in our case it is not a matter of numerous and specific areas in the city that attract a certain socio-cultural group, but of a forced pulverisation of the presence. Sometimes it approaches a polycentric situation, but with less accentuated characteristics, when, for example, occupations of buildings enable relatives to be reunited or it is possible to find houses nearby. Conversely, at other times, the evictions result in a dispersion, or the offer of truly rentable apartments does not coincide with the desired areas.

Finally, some families, in particular mothers with numerous children or with people in the family nucleus with disabilities or serious illnesses, have sometimes agreed to enter a reception centre for more or less prolonged periods. This is the case, for example, of a widowed lady with seven underage children and others of legal age with their own nuclear families, evicted after two years from the apartment and waiting to be assigned public housing. Or a family whose young mother is paralysed in her lower limbs. In recent years, the prolonged inflexibility of the Florentine municipal administration, supported by new regulations at national level, has contributed to making this solution acceptable also to other family nuclei: they are mostly people who have undergone several evacuations and who, at the time of the last one, were with very young children. In these cases, the families' suffering and fatigue of resistance persist, in addition to fear. And a return to Romania is considered impracticable: the child here enjoys all the health protection he would not have there, and there is financial aid for everything a newborn needs, in addition to the possibility of gain for the mother herself, which are not available there.

Sabina told me about this in Vadrea in July 2015, regarding the announced eviction of the property where she had lived for over two years, the former 'La Querce' boarding school:

> My mum has already received two complaints about the occupations. Sabrina, if they do as for the other occupation, I will go to the centre, I'm frightened, I have a young child … You saw, we can't manage anymore, we took up residence there [at la Querce] because the municipality did not notice [in the registry] that it was the address of the occupation. But then the laws changed and they noticed and they gave me nothing.

The last statement concerns Regional Law no. 45/2013 'Financial support interventions in favour of families and workers in difficulty, for cohesion and to combat social discomfort', in which art. 5 states, among the requirements for access to benefits, they have to be resident in Tuscany, continuously for at least twenty-four months *in buildings that are not illegally occupied.*[1]

Although some families have seen an improvement in their housing conditions over time, precariousness still remains very much a reality, helping to strengthen the intensity of the context of origin in giving a meaning to their life choices and the renegotiation of a physical and social space in Romania, felt by adults as their home.

Note

1. My italics.

Chapter 11

WORK IN THE CONTEXT OF MIGRATION

As regards the job sectors in which families find employment, it is possible to make a first division between those activities that in the context of immigration have full recognition as 'work' and those that do not, with respect to both the job, and the methods of payment. Among the former, there are various types of contract and tax profiles, corresponding to greater or lesser protections. Among the latter, there are, instead, activities that fall within the area defined as the 'informal economy', paid cash-in-hand and therefore not demonstrable; or autonomous activities that are not carried out according to the established procedures and regulations in force, falling into areas of irregularity (in particular, the collection and recycling of metals), which over time have involved a decreasing number of our *rudari* and have been practised more and more marginally.

If we then look at the multiple possibilities of finding useful material resources, we note the importance of the entire circuit of volunteering, in particular linked to organisations of Catholic origin. Through these, a series of goods are obtained, including childhood objects, clothing and food, as well as a series of public benefits, for example the 'purchasing card', the baby bonus, and the contributions provided for large families.

Adopting, therefore, a fuzzy logic that the multifaceted situation suggests we should do, we see the above in more detail, reconstructing the work profile of our families over a decade – starting from the data of September 2009, and comparing them with those collected in May 2015 and October 2019. From a methodological point of view, the data blocks provide a picture of situations that fluctuate over time, that is, three still images of a dynamic situation, which has changed and will change again.

Table 11.1. Occupational status, September 2009. The 'family code' item indicates the ID of the family to which the person belongs. © Sabrina Tosi Cambini.

Family Code	Family Member	Age	Sex	Occupation	Type of Employment Contract
1	Friend		F	*Badante*	Paid off the books
2	Householder	38	M	Bricklayer	Indefinite
2	Spouse	28	F	Housekeeper	Part-Time
4	Householder	22	M	Bricklayer	Paid off the books
5	Spouse		F	*Badante*	Not specified
6	Householder	41	M	Bricklayer, then Courier	Indefinite
6	Second Son	22	M	Courier	Indefinite (but part of the salary paid off the books)
6	First Daughter	21	F	Maid	Indefinite
7	Spouse		F	Baby-sitter	Not specified
8	Householder	40	F	*Badante*	Paid off the books
9	Spouse		F	*Badante*	Not specified
11	Spouse		F	*Badante*	Not specified
11	Householder		M	Bricklayer	Not specified
16	Householder	40	M	Craft Business Owner	Licensed Worker
18	Spouse		F	*Badante*	Paid in the black
23	Householder	43	M	Bulldozer Driver	Licensed Worker
26	Householder	30	M	Bricklayer	Licensed Worker
27	Householder	35	M	Bricklayer	Indefinite
28	Householder	36	M	Bricklayer	Fixed-Term
29	Householder	29	M	Bricklayer	Licensed Worker
32	Householder	30	M	Bricklayer	Indefinite
32	Householder	30	F	*Badante*	Not specified
34	Householder	47	F	*Badante*	Not specified
36	Householder	22	M	Housekeeper	Indefinite
36	Spouse	19	F	Colf	Not specified
37	Householder	40	M	Bricklayer	Licensed Worker
38	Householder	38	M	Bricklayer	Indefinite

38	Householder's Brother	33	M	Driver	Not specified
39	Householder	28	M	Bricklayer	Not specified
41	Householder	48	M	Bricklayer	Not specified
41	Spouse	50	F	Housekeeper	Not specified
44	Householder	42	M	Bricklayer	Licensed Worker
44	Spouse	42	F	*Badante*	Not specified
50	Householder	30	M	Bricklayer	Not specified
50	Spouse	29	F	*Badante*	Indefinite
51	Householder	32	M	Bricklayer	Indefinite
55	Householder	40	M	Bricklayer	Not specified
56	Householder	30	M	Welder	Not specified
56	Spouse	26	F	Colf	Not specified
57	Householder	40	F	Colf	Not specified
59	Householder	47	M	Bricklayer	Licensed Worker
60	Householder	46	M	Bricklayer	Licensed Worker
61	Householder		M	Bricklayer	Indefinite
61	Spouse's Cousin	32	M	Bricklayer	Licensed Worker
61	Householder's Brother	34	M	Bricklayer	Licensed Worker
64	Householder	32	M	House Painter	Licensed Worker
64	Spouse	31	F	Housekeeper	Not specified
65	Householder	30	M	Bricklayer	Licensed Worker
67	Householder	41	M	Bricklayer	Licensed Worker
72	Householder	26	M	Grape Picker	Paid off the books and seasonal
73	Householder	52	M	Bricklayer	Licensed Worker
74	Relative	24	M	Unskilled Worker	Not specified
75	Householder	48	M	Grape Picker	Paid off the books and seasonal
75	Spouse		F	Colf	Not specified

Table 11.2. Occupational status, 2015. © *Sabrina* Tosi Cambini.

Family Code	Family Member	Sex	Occupation	Type of Employment Contract	Notes
1	Friend	F	–	–	In Romania
2	Householder	M	–	–	In Romania
2	Spouse	F	–	–	In Romania
4	Householder	M	–	–	In Prison
5	Spouse	F	*Badante*	Regular Full-Time	
6	Householder	M	–	–	Deceased
6	Second Son	M	Courier	Indefinite (but part of the salary paid in the black)	
6	First Daughter	F	Colf	Part-Time	
7	Spouse	F	*Badante*	Paid off the books	
8	Householder	F	*Badante*	Regular Full-Time	
9	Spouse	F	Colf	2 Part-Time (one regular and one paid in the black)	
11	Spouse	F	–	–	
11	Householder	M	–	–	
16	Householder	M	Bricklayer	Licensed Worker (sometimes paid in the black)	
18	Spouse	F	*Badante*	Regular Full-Time	
23	Householder	M	–	–	In Romania
26	Householder	M	Bricklayer	Licensed Worker (sometimes paid in the black)	
27	Householder	M	–	–	Unemployed (laid off due to lack of work)
28	Householder	M	Bricklayer	–	
29	Householder	M	Bricklayer	Paid off the books	
32	Householder	M	–	–	In Romania
32	Spouse	F	–	–	In Romania
34	Sister-in-Law	F	*Badante*	Regular Full-Time	
36	Householder	M	Housekeeper	Indefinite	
36	Spouse	F	Colf	Regular Full-Time	
37	Householder	M	–	–	Invalid (due to a serious accident at work)

38	Householder	M	Bricklayer	Indefinite	
38	Householder's Brother	M	Driver (from Italy to Romania)	Paid off the books	
39	Householder	M	Bricklayer	–	
41	Householder	M	Bricklayer	–	
41	Spouse	F	Colf	Paid off the books	
44	Householder	M	–	–	
44	Spouse	F	–	–	
50	Householder	M	–	–	Unemployed
50	Spouse	F	–	–	Unemployed
51	Householder	M	Bricklayer	–	
55	Householder	M	Bricklayer	Licensed Worker (sometimes paid in the black)	
56	Householder	M	–	–	Unemployed
56	Spouse	F	Housekeeper	Paid off the books	
57	Householder	F	–	–	In Romania
59	Householder	M	Bricklayer	Paid off the books	
60	Householder	M	–	–	Unemployed
61	Householder	M	–	–	
-	Spouse's Cousin	M	–	–	
-	Householder's Brother	M	–	–	
64	Householder	M	House Painter	Licensed Worker (sometimes paid off the books)	
64	Spouse	F	Housekeeper	Paid off the books	
65	Householder	M	Bricklayer	Paid off the books	
67	Householder	M	Bricklayer	Paid off the books	
72	Householder	M	–	–	In Romania
73	Householder	M	B	Paid off the books	
74	Relative	M	Unskilled Worker	Regular Full-Time	
75	Householder	M	–	–	In Romania
75	Spouse	F	–	–	In Romania

Table 11.3. Occupational status, 2019. © Sabrina Tosi Cambini.

Family Code	Family Member	Sex	Occupation	Type of Employment Contract	Notes
1	Friend	F	–	–	In Romania
2	Householder	M	–	–	In Romania
2	Spouse	F	–	–	In Romania
4	Householder	M	–	–	Unemployed
4	Spouse	F	Housekeeper and Waitress	One Part-Time and one Paid off the books	
5	Spouse	F	*Badante*	Regular Full-Time	
6	Spouse	F	OSA	Regular Full-Time	Wife of deceased householder
6	Second Son	M	Courier	Indefinite	
6	Third Daughter	F	Dress-Maker	Irregular	Currently carries out the activity both in Italy and in Romania. Obtained a high school diploma in Florence
6	Fourth Son	M	Housekeeper	Indefinite	Obtained a high school diploma in Florence
6a	First Daughter Married	F	Colf	Just a few hours per week	Obtained OSA
6b	Spouse	M	Courier	Fixed-Term	
7	Spouse	F	–	–	In Romania
8	Householder	F			He had to quit his job due to serious health problems
9	Spouse	F	Colf	Two Part-Time	In Romania. Her family has opened a shop (magazin) in the new neighbourhood of Sibu Mare
11	Spouse	F	–	–	
11	Householder	M	–	–	
16	Householder	M	–	–	
18	Spouse	F	–	–	In Romania
23	Householder	M	–	–	In Romania
26	Householder	M	Bricklayer	Licensed Worker	

26	Spouse	F	Colf	Regular Full-Time	
27	Householder	M	Employed	Indefinite	
27	Householder	F	Colf	Paid off the books	
27	First Daughter	F	OSA	Fixed-Term	
28	Householder	M	Bricklayer	–	
29	Householder	M	Bricklayer	Regular Full-Time	
32	Householder	M	–	–	In Romania
32	Spouse	F	–	–	In Romania
34	Sister-in-Law	F	*Badante*	Regular Full-Time	
36	Householder	M	Garden Maintenance	Indeterminate	
36	Spouse	F	Colf	Regular Full-Time	Obtained OSS
37	Householder	M	–	–	Invalid (due to a serious accident at work)
38	Householder	M	Bricklayer	Indefinite	
38	Householder's Brother	M	Driver (from Italy to Romania)	Licensed Worker	He bought a van
39	Householder	M	–	–	
41	Householder	M	–	–	
41	Spouse	F	Colf	Regular Full-Time	Obtained OSA
44	Householder	M	–	–	
44	Spouse	F	–	–	
50	Householder	M	–	–	
50	Spouse	F	–	–	
51	Householder	M	Bricklayer	–	
55	Householder	M	Bricklayer	Licensed Worker	
56	Householder	M	–	–	
56	Spouse	F	OSA	Regular Full-Time	
57	Householder	F	–	–	In Romania
59	Householder	M	–	–	
60	Householder	M	Courier	Fixed-Term	
61	Householder	M	Courier	Fixed-Term	
–	Spouse's Cousin	M	–	–	

-	Householder's Brother	M	–	–	
64	Householder	M	House Painter and Bricklayer	Licensed Worker	
64	Spouse	F	Housekeeper	Part-Time	
65	Householder	M	–	–	
67	Householder	M	–	–	
72	Householder	M	–	–	
73	Householder	M	Bricklayer	Paid off the books	
74	Relative	M	Unskilled Worker	Regular Full-Time	
75	Householder	M	–	–	
75	Spouse	F	–	–	

Coming to the data, in 2009, there are 53 people who appear to have a job, with different contractual conditions, ranging from that without any protection (undeclared work), to that with an open-ended contract linked in particular to domestic care work ('*badante*' in Italian[1]), up to the use of a VAT number. On the latter, a clarification must be made for a correct reading of the data. While the previous contract case (care work) concerns women, here it concerns men employed in work related to the construction sector. Obtaining a VAT number, in fact, had represented for many a *stratagem* to circumvent one of the requirements of the civil registry – according to the registry regulations with regard to EU citizens – concerning the production of income. In this way, the holder of the VAT number immediately became employed, but without having to show their payroll (which does not exist for holders of a VAT number) or their tax return (given the registration in the Chamber of Commerce in the same year of the application for residence). This 'circumvention' has allowed family members to obtain residence in the municipality of Florence, with the positive consequence of gaining access to a series of important health and social services.

Following the history of the families over the years, it has been seen that in the medium term this choice has also led to negative side effects, linked to the economic unsustainability of a VAT number. On the one hand, the low earnings, the jobs often subcontracted by other companies off the books, the significant decrease in job opportunities given by the advance of the economic crisis; on the other hand, the lack of knowledge of the regulations, in addition to the priority given to the immediate use of all earnings – survival in Italy and remittances in Romania – have meant that taxes were not paid regularly. This led to freezing VAT numbers, but above all to the initiation of practices by the financial police, which induced those people who preferred to 'regulate' their situation, so as not to incur more serious measures, to pay fines and accountants.

I now provide three summary tables of the 'employed' (i.e. those who carry out an activity capable of producing a secure income with some continuity), for two groups of families. Tables 11.1 to 11.3, which correspond to the years 2009, 2015 and 2019,[2] concern the families who were present at the occupation of the former Luzzi at least since 2008, and the reference universe is that provided by the quantitative table of those present.

Table 11.4. *Rudari* families living in the former Luzzi in November 2011: most arrived after the displacements in 2009; some were there previously but returned later (indicated with previous ID in square brackets). © Sabrina Tosi Cambini.

Family ID	No. Members	No. Adults	No. Minors
n-1	2	2	0
n-2	5	2	3
n-3	3	2	1
n-4	10	2	8
n-8	1	1	0
n-9	7	6	1
n-10	7	6	1
n-11 [79–80]	6	4	2
n-12	3	2	1
n-13	2	2	0
n-14	4	4	0
n-15 [5]	3 (after the arrival of the sixteen-year-old daughter)	2	1
n-16 [22]	2 (after the arrival of the householder)	2	0
n-17	1	1	0
n-18	6	2	4
n-19	5	4	1
n-22	4	4	0
n-23	1	1	0
n-24 [50]	2	2	0
n-25 [56]	4	2	2
Total 22	**78**	**53**	**25**

Table 11.5. Occupational status of the adults in table 11.4, for 2011, 2015 and 2019. The 'family code' item indicates the ID of the family to which the person belongs; previous ID in square brackets. © *Sabrina* Tosi Cambini.

Family Code	Family Member	Age	Sex	Occupation 2011	Type of Employment Contract 2011	Occupation 2015	Type of Employment Contract 2015	Occupation 2019	Type of Employment Contract 2019
n-2	Householder	31	M	Labourer	Indefinite (but part of the salary paid off the books)	–	–	–	–
n-4	Householder	41	M	Employed	–	Bricklayer	Paid off the books	Courier	Fixed-term
n-8	Householder	54	M	Courier	Indefinite	Courier	Indefinite	Courier	Indefinite
n-9	Spouse	43	F	Maid	Part-time	Unemployed		Maid	Regular Full-Time
n-10	Householder	44	M	Bricklayer	Paid off the books	Unemployed		Courier	Fixed-term
n-10	Spouse	49	F	*Badante*	Paid off the books	*Badante*	Regular	OSA	Indefinite
n-10	Son	22	M	Unskilled Worker	Indefinite	Maintenance Services	Indefinite	Driver	–
n-11 [79-80]	Householder	–	M	Employed	–	–	–	–	
n-13	Householder	54	M	Bricklayer	Paid off the books	–	–	In Romania	
n-13	Spouse	51	F	*Badante*	Regular	–	–		
n-15 [5] also in table 11.2	Spouse	50	F	Maid (a few hours per week)	Paid off the books	*Badante*	Regular	*Badante*	Regular Full-Time
n-25 [56] also in table 11.2	Spouse	32	F	Maid	Paid off the books	Maid	Paid off the books	OSA	Regular Full-Time

The data in tables 11.4 and 11.5, on the other hand, refer to those families who arrived or returned to the former Luzzi after the second transfer in 2010, so they are inherent to 2011[3] and, by comparison, to 2015 and 2019. In this case, the reference universe is the one shown in Table 11.4.

Work is surely the concern that afflicts most *rudari*. On the other hand, the possibility of earning, of making a little money, is the main reason why they leave their home in Romania.[4]

In 2009, many people were unemployed and even those who owned their own companies suffered first-hand from the uncertainty linked to the irregular nature of work and the tax burden.

As far as the employed population is concerned, in 2009 the bricklayer/ labourer for men and domestic work – care and assistance to people or domestic helpers – for women are the trades most practised.

P.: So, [in 2009] I was three to four months out of work. Then good fortune came: my wife also started working, and I started working too.

S.: What kinds of work?

P.: I as a bricklayer, she as a caregiver … caregiver in Italian means washing bottoms … [we laugh]

S.: Cash-in-hand or …?

P.: I've worked cash-in-hand. My wife had a contract. Two to three years we worked, my wife and I.: After that, we were out of work. And then again we worked …

S.: How did your wife get a job?

P.: My wife went to a cousin of hers and she got her a job. Then she went to the churches, to the Caritas, to charity, to get food [weekly distribution of food parcels by some parishes].

(Interview, 26 January 2015).

S.: What work were you and your husband doing?

P.: He was a bricklayer and I was a caretaker and a domestic helper for the elderly.

S.: Did your husband have a VAT number? Did he work with papers or not?

P.: Yes, with documents he had regular work – but also off the books.

S.: Good. Who brought you to this occupation [where you are living], how did you find it?

P.: We heard from other *rudari* and we came here. There were many.

S.: Who organised it?

P.: I don't know. You know we meet many people at the Caritas, we heard about this place and we came here, some *rudari* [told me about it].

S.: Are you working now? Your husband? Cash-in-hand?

P.: None [work]. [He] has worked with documents [regular employment contract].

(Interview, Florence, 13 January 2015).

This data on the jobs most practised in those years highlight the interrelationship between the skills of people, the 'gaps' in the Italian job market, and relationships in immigration society, like the urban 'empty' spaces (unused and abandoned), and the meshes of discrimination in access to work. In this sense, the ways in which employment is sought and found are also a sign: jobs, in fact, are mainly informal or linked – especially for women – to the consultation centres of the Caritas or the neighbourhood parishes.

N.: I worked as a *badante* and cleaning lady. To look for work I go to the consultation centres.

S.: Do you go to the consultation centre in Via Faenza, at the Caritas?

N.: Yes, I explain to them that I have children and that I am looking for a job.

(Interview, Florence, 9 January 2015).

There are few unemployed women who have not had a job in the past or who are not looking for one; in fact, temporary insecurity is typical of jobs that concern domestic help and/or care of an elderly person. Almost everyone would like to find a job (for those who are not interested, usually it is because they have very young children, and looking after them does not enable them to work) and, as I said above, the profession to which they have access is almost exclusively that of domestic work and care, often – especially in the last five years – with a contract. Women feel a lot of responsibility for the condition of their family; being able to earn something puts them in a state of calm, which in times of unemployment – especially when prolonged – is replaced by a constant concern, what many have described as 'nervous' (a sort of anxiety).

Work is also an opportunity for women to leave the occupations of buildings where they live or other accommodation. In the case of a concentration like that of the former Luzzi and its location in the outskirts of the city, this aspect was even more evident: going out meant going to the centre of Florence, the possibility to get out and meet other people. Most women, in fact, when unemployed, would go to the city only once a week for shopping and, sometimes, not even that: they had to take turns to look after the children. The women would meet up and talk at someone's house or outside, in front of the buildings, and on those occasions they shared and collectively reworked their anxieties and concerns. This is also the case today in the few, small occupations that remain.

The comparison of the data between 2009, 2015 and 2019, and for the second set of families, between 2011, 2015 and 2019, reveals a situation that over time decreases the number of 'employed' people, but increases the incidence of regular contracts for domestic and care work; 2019 also reveals other processes underway.

The most important aspect, which concerns male labour, between 2009 and 2015, unfortunately, is in line with the effects of the economic downturn and the crisis in the labour market, which ended up also affecting the construction sector. Like many other foreigners, in fact, the *rudari* have encountered difficulties related to the decrease in demand in sectors where, conversely, the supply of labour is high (construction, service cooperatives); and where there is more frequent exposure to discrimination, absence of protection (illegal dismissals, preference of Italians at the time of hiring), and injustices (employment relationship on the fringes of legality, moonlighting, insecure conditions).

With regard to women and work in the domestic and care sectors, a combination of three factors is involved.

The first is represented by the provisions on the emergence and regularisation of undeclared work among Italian families: 'Ministerial Circular no. 10 of 07/08/2009 and INPS Circular no. 101 of 10/08/2009, pursuant to Article 1-ter of Legislative Decree 78/2009, converted with amendments into Law 102/2009 and published in the Official Gazette no. 179 of 4 August 2009, have established provisions aimed at the emergence of irregular work by staff assigned to assistance and support activities for families: domestic helpers and badanti'.[5]

In this sense, the following passage from an interview seems particularly significant:

S.: What was your first job [in Italy]?

R.: I worked as a *badante*.

S.: But what about the children?

R.: While I was working as a *badante*, I went to the park where I met other Romanians, I cried, I missed the children. A *badante* told me that in Campo di Marte [district of Florence] there was a good priest, who could take in me and the children. I spoke to the priest, but when I returned with the children from Romania it was August, and I did not know that there are vacations and therefore I would not find the priest. I had to stay somewhere until he came back and so I bought a tent and put it near the church. I was there for two months, at night, taking them to work, not always, but secretly, the daughter and the lady knew. They went around with my husband all day! The old lady I worked for and her daughter allowed me to bring the children with me to work. We stayed here for a year. The children went to school. In 2005 I met a cousin and she told me about Lorenzo [of the Movimento di Lotta per la Casa] and introduced me to him.

S.: Who is she [this cousin]?

R.: She is called Mariana, she's my cousin. She told Lorenzo about me and he immediately gave me a room in Careggi, in Via Incontri [it was an occupation of a building, which no longer exists]. It was dirty there, but I cleaned everything, painted the room, and brought my children. The neighbours of the lady I worked for saw me there [at the lady's house] with the children and reported us [both me and the lady]. We woke up with the police at the door yelling at me to open; they knew I was working cash-in-hand.

S.: Were all the children with you?

R.: Yes, all of them. It was in the year 2005/2006. I opened up and told them that I didn't have a house in Romania, that I didn't have food, and that I wanted to work to give my children a better future. At that moment they told me to go to the police station, everyone. We went and they told us to go to the Juvenile Court to declare the reason why I was in Italy.

S.: But who sent you there?

R.: The Municipal Police. I told them I was on a trial period at work, and they believed me. They advised me what to say in court, that we were poor, without a home and that we were looking for work and it was the truth, I said just that and at that point the court allowed us to stay with the children and send them to school. I was hired – after the court called the lady where I worked earlier – on a regular full-time contract and in the evening I would go home to my children.

S.: You were lucky.

R.: I know, I was lucky. I worked for a year, so did my husband, and we moved from one job to another. (8 January 2015).[6]

The second factor, consequent to the first, concerns the dissemination to Italian families of the rules regulating the employment relationship of the domestic worker and the obligation to adopt the national collective agreement, with the risk of incurring serious penalties in the event of irregular hiring.

The third concerns the *rudari* women themselves who, for the most part thanks to their experiences with the Movimento di Lotta per la Casa, have become skilled in the management of relations with private employers (Italian families), supported by knowledge of the type of contract, and of the remuneration and protections that it guarantees.

With regard to women's work as caregivers ['*badanti*'], it is useful to bring out some further reflections on what I mentioned earlier. As noted, for our families' network, in fact, there was no female migration connected to the phenomenon of the 'care drain'.[7] In our network this case has been verified from Romania:

- a few experiences of the first women who have migrated, but who after a short time of working as a permanent caregiver (i.e. present day and night), have brought their entire family nucleus to Italy (as in the interview specifically reported above) or have returned home;

- some young women (level 4 of the genealogy) still without children who have joined their parents (level 3 of the genealogy) or the husband who is with his family of origin in Florence: in this case they have worked only a few months or, in any case, less than a year, as permanent caregivers, then changing jobs, working as maids; we have seen young women, not yet married, already inhabitants in Florence, who have had this experience.

- more mature women (level 3 of the genealogy) who have replaced permanent caregivers mostly for one month, who have found this possibility through acquaintances of relatives in Italy, often church sisters.

When already in Italy, therefore with the whole family nucleus, women carry out care work at Italians' homes during the day, with various tasks: they take care of the elderly person, but also clean the house, sometimes also shop for the family of the son/daughter of the assisted person. More often, therefore, they do mixed work, between domestic helper and assistance or they even juggle between several employers. It can happen that a young couple in a difficult period from an economic point of view and with an insecure housing situation, seeks a solution that can meet both needs, and sometimes the husband can stay in the house where the woman is permanently employed.

We will now look at the different points of view about this work.

S.: Do you like working as a *badante*?

L.: Yes, I like it. I put my soul into it.

S.: Why?

L.: If they're good, I live with them, I eat with them, I wash them as if they were children, and when they give you the money you forget all your bad thoughts. I like it even though I don't have a preference. We have debts in our country, the car has broken down, and we are here out of need. Who can help me, my father has many children. He (the husband) has no one, so we fight with all our strength for our family. (Interview 6 January 2015).

M.: Taking care of a person who is alone is not difficult, Sabrina. There are so many problems at home [in Romania], my head is exploding!

A.: I'm happy with this job. It's true that I always have to be with the old lady, but the house is in a nice area, there are shops. I go out, I go shopping, and I buy things for the old lady and things for myself. Then on Sunday I go to greet the relatives and friends who are here. (Conversation, August 2010)

This appreciation of her work in the words of M. is lessened after finding herself in more demanding situations, where the old person to be assisted, for example, has problems related to the loss of mental lucidity.

S.: Do you like working in the Italian family, as a *badante*? What's good? What's more heavy-going?

M.: What's heavier-going and what's better? If you work like this [with families], it would be better to do the house cleaning, it is heavier-going as a *badante*. For cleaning, do what you're told, don't argue about it; you've done it, and you're gone. Instead, as a *badante*, it depends on the person you find, because there are elderly people who are ill, irritable, who have other discomforts, which make your life uncomfortable too. A state of nerves, depression, it makes you ill, because you're with them 24 hours a day. To convince them [to do certain things, like eating etc.], you have to follow them in every movement to be there according to their wishes/needs. Like some kind of slave. Well, not everywhere; I am referring to jobs with elderly people who are sick in the head. Most have characters like that – It's not an easy job to be a *badante*. It's hard because you need your head and a lot of patience. Cleaning is better, more enjoyable, washing dishes in a restaurant or standing around all day and serving people at the table, than being a *badante*. If you need to, you do it.

S.: But is it better to do the cleaning than to be a *badante* also because of the hours?

M.: Yes, cleaning work is good; a few hours a day. And as a *badante*, on the other hand, 24 hours a day. Just two hours off. Thursday 5 hours, Sunday 12 hours. What can you do in two hours off? Relax …? You waste more time out on the road … (Interview, 28 January 2015).

In the words of A., a young woman who found herself working as a caregiver in a village in a province far away from her family, living in a house two kilometres from the suburban bus stop, the memory of that experience, which lasted eight months, is linked to states of loneliness and sadness.

> A.: I was really unhappy, you know. I hardly ever saw anyone at that time, only on an occasional Sunday, not every Sunday because it was far to go [to Florence], there were few buses and I had to do a bit on foot. Every now and then *Şerban* [her older brother] came to see me. But, I think, Dana [her sister] I haven't seen her for a month … and also my mother and the children [her younger sisters and brothers]! (Conversation, April 2011).

The comparison between domestic care worker and domestic helper shows the undoubted advantage of the latter for the timetable: in the long run, almost all women who live with their family and for almost the whole year in Florence try to find this work and are not very willing to have a job without a contract. The latter gives them access to a number of social protections: maternity, unemployment benefit, as well as the very important possibility of taking up residence.

> M.: Then [in 2012] I worked by the hour, for a very good lady, who helped me. She gave me a work contract, because I could not take up residence with my children without a contract; I worked for a year, then, I was only on Thursdays in Scandicci. What could I do? M., my son, helped me a lot. He works at Bartolini's. A., one of my daughters, has [a permanent job, as a carer] in Piazza dei Ciompi: they paid for the apartment [the rent], they bought food, clothes for the children, and they helped me a lot. In 2012–2014, I didn't work. A. got married in May [2013] and I went as a *badante* in her place. In September. I was there for eight months. The old woman has died. Then, I took the sister-in-law to my place [in another family]. I had R. [another of her daughters] ill for three weeks in September 2014. Then, I left work and went in for V. [the other daughter]. Being pregnant, she went on maternity leave and God helped me with my work, He did not leave me. (Interview, 28 January 2015)

In this fragment, the circularity of jobs in the family is highlighted, but they do not have a long duration. If, therefore, initially or at more critical times, women are more willing to work for a few months as caregivers, over time they try to develop other strategies.

This is what the 2019 data show us. Women, both of the third generation and the older ones of the fourth generation, have begun to attend professional courses, in particular for the position of *Operatore socio assistenziale* [Social Welfare Operator] (OSA), recognised by the Tuscany Region and held by associations operating in the social accommodation sector.

This has allowed them to find other types of employment, even in reception centres similar to those where some were guests years ago.

But also for men there is another new sector, already involved in the employment of workers with a migratory background, which is that of transport and logistics for express couriers, where they usually work as drivers, even sometimes carrying out some porterage tasks.

This is a poorly regulated sector, where courier companies rely on cooperatives, lowering protections and the quality of working conditions. In fact, if the worker is hired within the contract of the logistics sector, with regard to rights and working hours, second-level bargaining is involved. Despite these conditions, in this work our *rudari* find advantageous aspects: they cannot be made to work cash-in-hand, unlike the construction sector; they have good and safe remuneration, in addition to a decent autonomy at work. The relationship between supply and demand is not of secondary importance; it also allows workers to be able to leave this job if holidays are not granted for them to return to Romania in the summer months, where work on the new house awaits. So, you can make this choice, and then find yourself a new position on your return fairly easily with another courier.

The decision to quit can also happen because you feel you have reached a threshold of exploitation.

Notwithstanding the importance of structural factors, such as the difficulty of access to the labour market and the widespread discrimination to which they may be subject, there are aspects that have concerned our *rudari*, at least until now,[8] which should not be underestimated. These concern an approach to the labour dimension which – albeit with internal differences – is connected on the one hand to the non-hierarchical organisation of these groups and on the other to the fact that they are not bearers of a capitalist ideology of wage labour.

> Many scholars have pointed out that the 'Gypsies' cultivate flexibility in different contexts, and especially in relationships … mobility, and ability to seize economic opportunities, many of which are absolutely unpredictable. This flexibility is a fundamental theme of Gypsy cultures, with ramifications that go beyond economic aspects. (ni Shuinéar 2005: 334)

And further on, the author adds: 'For the non-Travellers, work determines both a wage and a social status. There is an "objective" pyramid of correlation between status/wage/employment' (ibid.: 335).

These two elements undoubtedly also apply to our *rudari*, above all, we could say, from the point of view of practicality and convenience: as we saw initially for Nico, you can start either with a completely informal job, as a driver for the Roma who go to do business abroad, or through a formal channel, through an agency, as a farm worker in England.

So in Italy, too, the possibilities must be seized, but also weighed up in terms of cost-benefits. Rightly, ni Shuinéar notes that for a non *gypsy* 'it is better to be a poorly paid civil servant than a well-paid plumber' (ibid.). While for both 'her' travellers and 'our' *rudari* the opposite is true and the person who made such an assessment would undoubtedly be considered *prost* (stupid). So Mihai and Liviu, two brothers, after a couple of months as couriers, left work because they were away from home twelve hours a day, while they both took it back, at different times, when they needed money to build their respective houses in Romania. They therefore preferred, for a period, to opt for less regular, but proportionally more remunerative jobs, which, above all, left time to live their lives and for relationships; while in another period, the motivation of the house justified the numerous hours of work stated in the contract.

Non-formal work activities are summarised as opportunities and preferred for some period to jobs that, although they envisage a contract, are affected by exploitative working conditions.

Finally, I report an exchange of wisecracks with Ionica, which took place in a cordial conversation, and this allows me to introduce a theme related to the knowledge of Italian domestic environments, which they compare with their own:

Ionica: The children of Italians pay foreigners to wash their parents' bottoms while they go to work!

Sabrina: And does this seem right to you?

I.: No, they should stay and take care of their parents, to wash their bottoms [everyone laughs].

Women who go to work in the homes of Italians develop knowledge of these families that men are precluded from. It is a localised knowledge (almost always in the city of Florence) and very sectoral: middle-class families, who own properties and often have few children. Intercultural discussion often highlights the difference in the demographic dimension (many old people, few children versus many children and few old people) and the values and priorities of life (the lack of caring for their parents and the primacy of work versus the strong generational respect and the family as a fundamental horizon).

But in this comparison, contradictions and 'crossed' comparisons also emerge between *rudari*, 'Romanian Romanians' and Italians:

S.: For your children [what do you want]?

R.: For them too, but it's hard for me to want in their place if they don't want this! I want them to have a trade so they can live well! Our eldest daughter has found a job and left, our son is engaged and he too has left, he returns only if in need, only for the *rudari* it goes like this! [we laugh]. M. is right when she says that Romanian children go away from their parents' house, they can manage on their own!

S.: M. it's too hard!

M.: But that's how it is, I know them and it has always been like this! The children take advantage of their parents' kindness, I also have children who live together with their in-laws, and this is the immature mentality of the *rudari*! Do you know why? God said: I have created animals, trees, everything on Earth in variety and according to nation, and the same for people! For example, intelligent people have intelligent children, actors have child actors, and teachers have child teachers! [laughs]

S.: Listen M., the *rudari* are intelligent …

M.: Yes, but they don't care so much about the rest of the world, they have many children, not like the Italians! (Interview, Florence, 8 January 2015).

From the words of M., the question of virilocality also emerges and of how it can be subjected to irony from the distance of the migratory context, while continuing, however, to be practised, as well as the same high birth rate (M. herself has many children).

Returning to the discussions, working in these houses, the women discovered a series of comforts, which entered – at first gradually, but then for several families at am increased speed – into the houses in Romania, and also into their own homes in Italy. The way of looking after the home can change, and can generate misunderstandings, as we will see later.

Likewise, the spaces of the house in Romania are modified, enlarged or built from scratch with the remittances; and their use, as well as the inclusion or not of rugs and other objects, changes depending on who lives in the house, configuring a flexibility of these spaces and an original and variable synthesis between elements that come from different histories and cultures.

Notes

1. In spite of myself, I refer to this term for two reasons. The first is that it is used by the women themselves, as it is learned in the context of immigration. The second, because it appears at an official level in the Italian regulations governing this occupation. It is worth remembering, precisely because it is now commonly used throughout Italy, that the indication of domestic care work and assistance to people through the word '*badante*', was introduced by the first leader of the Northern League, Umberto Bossi, with a derogatory value (see Faso 2010: 29-32).
2. The 2009 data were collected by the author and the team coordinated by her within the already mentioned *Housing Frontline* project. Those of 2015 were collected by the

author during the *MigRom* project and those of 2019 by the author in the continuation of field research.

3. The data for 2011, including those in Table 11.1, result from a crossing of data collected by the Medici per i Diritti Umani (MEDU) (Doctors for Human Rights) of Florence and by the author, collected within the framework of the Michelucci Foundation's Observatory on precarious housing.

4. The other reason, as mentioned, is that of health when there are family members with disabilities or serious chronic diseases.

5. INPS – Istituto Nazionale per la Previdenza Sociale Istituto Nazionale per la Previdenza Sociale http://www.inps.it/portale/default.aspx?iMenu=1&itemDir=6372. Obviously these measures were taken in favour of Italian families, who would have run into administrative and criminal justice problems, in the case of non-EU irregular workers without a residence permit (e.g. by incurring the offence of 'aiding and abetting illegal immigration').

6. Interview conducted during the *MigRom* project.

7. A fortunate metaphor coined by Arlie R. Hochschild, in analogy with 'brain drain', to classify the transfer of care skills by women, from their families, and from the elderly, children and sick people of their country, to hospital facilities and homes in the country of immigration. A phenomenon with a global scope, with a flow that goes from economically poor countries to the richest ones, which brings with it consequences at several levels: the personal level, regarding the workers themselves; the family level, with the configuration of transnational families that suffer from the absence of the mother; the local and national level with the loss of knowledge and skills not only in the field of care work, since women employed in migration in these types of jobs, in some contexts of origin may have obtained a medium-high level qualification also in other sectors. In addition to the texts already indicated, reference is also made to Dumitru (2014), which proposes a critical reading of the 'care drain'.

8. We will have to see, in the future, what happens to those who grow up in the country of emigration and go on to higher education.

Chapter 12

ACASĂ/AT HOME

Să facem casa

This chapter focuses on the process of building one's own house in Romania, through an exploration of the interaction between home making (the process of social construction of the domestic sphere) and house building (the material but meaningful construction of a house). Within a *future-homing-oriented*[1] approach – which links home and mobility and impacts a considerable number of issues within the contexts of life – the reflection proposed here moves, connecting those contexts, between the dimension of the domestic nucleus, the networks of kinship and the macro one relative to ('ethnic') social categories and the territory.

The latter becomes not only a map within which to observe the dynamics of exclusion/inclusion of the families considered, but also, and above all, a field in which the subjects build and renegotiate their complex belonging to society at large. The diachronic dimension of this socio-spatial negotiation is offered by combining emic visions of oral memory with the changes over time detected by the ethnographic research, inserting them in the social geography of the village.

If in Italy our network of families 'disappears' ethnically (our *rudari* simply become migrant 'Romanians') – with the exception of precisely the situation we have seen in chapter 8 – and if in Romania we see instead the spatialised imprint in the conformation of the localities, it is possible to reveal the practical and circumstantial dimension of ethnic categorisations and how these assume sometimes explicit roles, sometimes latent and sometimes insignificant in the social practices of the actors.

Returning again to Appadurai's perspective of the 'local dimension as the repertoire of the conditions of the possibilities' (2013), it is possible to highlight how the 'home construction' reveals the conditions of possibility experienced by the subjects and is at the same time an action aimed at the fulfilment of 'thinkable' and 'desirable' futures.

Through the ethnographic narration of scenarios and concrete moments of domestic life, I outline the meanings that circulate among the actors present: the 'family' is thus de-essentialised, reconstructing the processes, between production and reproduction, that generate it and that, at the same time, 'generate' the home.

Let's go back to Valeriu's stories about his grandparents and parents, who during the Second World War would go to the districts of Călăraşi and Tulcea, and then went to Sibu Mare to work in the 1950s and settled there in the mid-1960s (chapter 1).

Before the Crimean War (1877–1878), the village of Sibu Mare*, under the municipality of Alacap (later Poarta Albă), was inhabited by a Turkish population, which lived a few kilometres further north along the road. After those years, some Tatar refugees returned, but from 1884 the village was quickly repopulated by about 90 Romanian families, who came from the area of Vrancea, and some from Oltenia, who settled a little further south and in the following years erected the church (1891) and a small school (1892).

Between 1910 and 1914, the town was under the municipality of the nearby Chiostel (now Castelu), then from 1914 to 1950 it was an independent municipality, then was again administered by Castelu and finally in 2004 it again became a municipality.

During the First World War, the population was forced to take refuge in Brăila, and then return and rebuild the village, now all Romanian.

Perhaps we can understand from this population displacement, the link of acquaintance between the families of *lingurari* and the village of Sibu Mare*, where from the 1950s they began to work, on farms, also staying there to sleep; alternating, therefore, periods in the village with periods in *baltă*. Ionica also told me:

So [my grandparents and parents] heard from [other] *rudari*, that in Sibu Mare* there are many *rudari*, who know each other, because when they went to *baltă* more groups from several parts/villages, they met and got to know each other, and hearing from each other, they came to Sibu Mare* … It was so, every *rudar* went from one village to another, and every *rudar* settled down where it seemed to him that there was work, that it was a village where the Romanians are better [not racists], there was work and there was a nearby forest, water, and according to kinships. For example, if I had a cousin in Sibu Mare*, I would have moved here too, I oriented myself to have a relative here.[2]

In the 1960s, the structure of the population of Sibu Mare* changed considerably: the policy of Ceauşescu, in fact, for the region of Dobruja provided for new inhabitants to be settled and included in the CAPs.

Among these many are *rudari*, originally from Ciucurova (*Juteţul* Tulcea), and Roma defined *nomazi* (*pletoşi, călderări*). In those years, there was also the sedentarisation of our *rudari* families in the municipality of Sibu Mare*. Valeriu explained me that 'the *rromi* arrived after us; we now get along well but there have been big problems in the past'.

Many Romanians have since left the village and, according to municipal data, for several years more than 70% of the population of the *sat* has been inhabited by *ţigani* (*rudari* and *rromi*).

Like the population of the other municipalities of 'our' families, and as often happens in Romania, that of Sibu Mare* is spatially divided, with a distinction between Romanians, Roma (*ţigani rromi*) and *rudari* (*ţigani rudari*).

In the list of voters on 3 March 1963 in the municipality of Sibu Mare* for the elections of the Deputies, the name of the father-in-law of Mamaia Luminiţa,[3] B.I., appears, which corresponds to the reconstruction of the years of arrival made by the daughter Ionica and the son Valeriu.

In October 2010, it was the latter who spoke to me more in depth about their story, starting with an object that Dana found in the attic at her

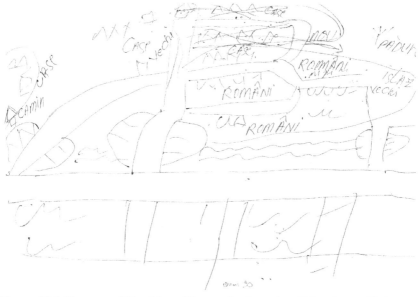

Figure 12.1. The map of Sibu Mare village at the time when Valeriu's grandfather settled there and built the house – designed by 'uncle' Valeriu for me in October 2010. © Sabrina Tosi Cambini.

grandmother's house, while she was looking for something. It is a wooden *covată* or *capeie* made by her grandfather – a sort of tub shaped like a small cradle – where bread was made. The wood is poplar, which is soft and easy to work (the other valued wood was willow).

On the map in figure 12.1, Valeriu inserts the [*Camin cultural*] to provide me with spatial references of the present, in order to orient myself. Where the word *islaz* appears, on the outskirts of the town – Valeriu explains to me – the first *rudari* lived there and subsequently the poorest ones remained, with mainly small houses, dry-built with *adobe* (mud brick), and even in 2010 it continued to be so. Although a few were better cared for, most of the houses showed severe structural and maintenance deficiencies. Valeriu adds that when the *rudari* came to Sibu Mare, including his grandparents, before settling permanently, though he was not yet born, they stopped in the *islaz*. The *rudari* then began to buy the land and build better houses than the first ones, but always with *adobe* and less important than those of the Romanians, in the other area of the country corresponding to the words *case vechi* (old house).

In August 2011, Luminiţa tells me that, initially, she and her husband had built a small two-room house: 'We had nothing, we slept on the floor … Then I went to work for a [Romanian] lady who gave me many things, the bed, the carpet … That day, when he came home [the husband] he found everything!' Then the lady had gone to see Luminiţa to see how she had arranged, at home, what she had given her. In addition, seeing that she did not have it, she had returned the next day to bring her a blanket, which – together with the rug – Luminiţa still has.

The area beyond the river and the main road – where, in the drawing, I noted 'the '90s' – is that of the third 'expansion' of the *rudari*, where there are the houses of the sons of Luminiţa, that is, of Valeriu himself, Ionica and Alexandru, built starting from those years, some from scratch, others enlarged with new rooms, thanks to the first remittances coming from the work abroad.

These elements of socio-spatial configuration are important to understand today the different aspects that contribute to configuring the construction of the house – in the double sense of house-building and home-making – as one of the central factors in migratory processes.

In this sense, Valeriu explains to me[4] that the *rromi* call them *caştali* (i.e. 'woodworkers' in a derogatory sense), and that the 'Romanian Romanians' call them ţigani: 'Even the "Romanian Romanians" work as drivers for the *rromi*', says Valeriu, 'there are beautiful Romanians who speak ţiganeşte [*romanes*] and then they call us ţigani, even if we don't speak the ţiganeşte language'.

Figure 12.2. The author with an elderly *rudari* woman and her old home behind them (2011). © Sabrina Tosi Cambini.

We have seen that there is sometimes the possibility for the *rudari* to fluctuate between different categorisations: certainly considered *ţigani* in Romania, in their own land they can choose whether to weave a conjunctural alliance with the Roma or not; while in foreign emigration countries, depending on the migratory 'channels' which they manage to enter, they can instead declare themselves 'only' Romanians. Although the latter are, in any case, the subject of discriminatory discourses and practices, there is no doubt that the possibility of not being associated with the Roma opens up greater opportunities for them to settle and work.[5]

This position 'between the borders' is also reflected in the spatial position occupied in the villages, between the 'Romanian Romanians' and the *rromi*, but with the latter undoubtedly united by an unequal treatment (at the level of civil society or at the institutional level) by the Romanians (even racist treatment) and by a housing situation which – with the cessation of itinerant crafts and the beginning of sedentarisation – placed their homes in an unequal comparison with the homes of the Romanian peasants.

Now, with remittances – which in the history of migration, it is known, have always played an important role not only for people but also for the development of their countries of origin – the houses of many *rudari* have gradually taken on forms of construction that increasingly have characteristics defined by (all) the inhabitants as 'modern', considered in that context not only as better than the previous *rudari* houses, but also than *Romanians'* peasant houses. As in cases of other groups with which, as noted above, they share a treatment of marginalisation by the majority population, even for the *rudari* their homes are considered a sign of 'civilisation'.[6] Ionica says: 'we are modernised, we have cars, and we have beautiful houses'.

This 'modernisation' takes shape and becomes visible in their country of origin both for other *rudari* and for 'Romanian Romanians'. Compared with the latter, this has made it possible to open a continuous process of socio-spatial 'renegotiation', with multiple nuances and discrepancies, which – in particular with respect to the theme we are discussing – can be read in the configuration of the new portion of the village parcelled out by the municipality, where new houses have been built by both *rudari* and 'Romanian Romanians' (figure 12.3).

With respect to the internal equilibrium of 'our' *rudari*, mutual views and positioning emerge among the 'localised groups' based on acquired lifestyles and assets.

Speaking one evening in the garden of his house in Romania, with Mihai, uncle Valeriu and his neighbour Stefan, the latter asserts that 'the *rudari* of Sibu Mare are the ones who are better off'. 'You see', he continues, turning to me, 'we have more beautiful houses, cars ... this is because we started to emigrate earlier, we went all over Europe, to Italy, Germany, France,

England'. Then he looks at Mihai, remembering that he is from Vadrea and tells him: 'I'm sorry, but that's it, don't you think?' Mihai, initially hesitant, replies 'Yes, but here you have the *țigani* [*pletoși, călderări*], that also counted, you can't say that it didn't'. Stefan can only confirm. So I ask him: 'But in your opinion, Stefan, is it also because communism took place here, the *rudari* from here, from Sibu Mare, worked more in the CAPs than the others in Vadrea, Sibust …?' 'Well, that can be so', he replies, but it does not seem to be a topic that convinces him, as he shows little interest in it.

Stefan returns to migration and the improvement of the material conditions that it has made possible: 'Have you seen how they are doing in Badra?' Along the same lines are the telephone messages that Constantine, while visiting his wife's parents in Badra, sends to his cousin Dana, when he is in Vadrea.

The competition that emerges between people from different places is rarely made explicit between them, that is, intergroup (Stefan forgets for a moment that Mihai is from Vadrea), while it is more likely that it is intragroup, as in the case of the aforementioned cousins. On both occasions, the game of competition also passes through the search for a common

Figure 12.3. Street in the new part of Sibu Mare and in Vadrea, 2015; panorama of the new part of Sibu Mare, 2015. © Sabrina Tosi Cambini.

understanding, in the tones of irony, as in messages such as: 'Help ... there are mice here! I can't wait to go home [to Sibu Mare], believe me'.

To interpret it adequately, this competition must be correlated with the family structure of these groups discussed in the first part of the volume. They are spatially localised groups, whose territorial location is the result of the intertwining of internal and external factors: of historical-political dynamics, of their different forms of mobility, of the residence model of the new couple based on viri-patrilocality; of the circulation, within parental networks, of information on work-economic opportunities (element of continuity in the social organisation of the *rudari* who we know, from the times when they went to *baltă* up to the new emigration contexts).

So these groups correspond to genealogical 'clusters' placed spatially, among whom there is, it was said, a marriage alliance, possible thanks also to the absence of differences in power levels and therefore of a formal political hierarchy between these groups, as well as between families.

'In this anti-hierarchical society, internally fragmented but at the same time interrelated and densely intricate' (ni Shuinéar 2005: 343), in our case, every adult person, both man and woman, can say 'something good' about their family or network of families, which brings with it, in turn, an affirmation of (temporary) superiority.

Now, in 'that something good', there are references to multiple areas of life, for example, the behaviour of one's children, but in particular – returning to migration – the skill demonstrated in achieving the objectives of economic improvement that have allowed the purchase of vehicles, the investment of remittances in activities such as the opening of a shop or the purchase of a van to begin the local transport of goods or the international transport of goods and people, and – above all – the building of a new home: 'And what did we leave for, then!', exclaims Dana.

What in the literature is defined as migratory 'success' is therefore replayed in the context of origin both internally and externally, making the social and spatial arrangements fluctuate toward new balances, where the house seems to be the cornerstone.

How to Build a House: A Family Matter

We will now tell how was built, from August 2015 to the summer 2020, the home of Mihai and Dana, who – third cousins, one from Vadrea, the other from Sibu Mare – eloped[7] together in 2009 while they were in Florence.

Mihai and Dana have three children: Dorina, now (2022) ten years old, Marco, eight years old and Rachele, almost two years old.

Their union, sanctioned by the acceptance of the respective families, followed the practice (in its many variants) of this wide *rudari* network: the frequently occurring elopement and the following 'pardon' (as one of the possibilities), and the tendency to maintain the unity of genealogical space through endogamous marriages between relatively distanced kin.

There is, however, an element that slowly emerges in the story of the couple, after the birth of their children, of the new family. It is the tendency to not respect virilocality, which is completely set aside with the decision to build their home in the village of the bride.

Let's see the temporal succession, in 2015, of the phases that led to the beginning of the construction works and how the man's family compensated for this will, from a symbolic-cultural point of view, in order to avoid a fracture between the families involved and to allow the new nucleus to build a house: the last act which materially sanctions the completeness of adulthood and the start of the family.

The land was finally purchased by an acquaintance of the village, he too a *rudar*. It is located in the new part of Sibu Mare, the fourth *rudari* 'expansion' in the territory of the country, this time, as mentioned, the space of new houses also of Romanians. It is located near the house under construction of Dana's brother, that of her cousins – at the time, almost finished – and the one of a couple of uncles.

Already in the spaces and times of migration to Italy, since the couple went to live together and, therefore, with the consequent collective recognition of their union, Mihai is – we could say – incorporated into his wife's family, an aspect that was the source of strong disagreements that have lasted for years between the latter and her mother-in-law, and that only in the last two years seems to have subsided a little. In fact, with the passage of time and especially the birth of the grandchildren, the mother-in-law gradually gave in, also after having talked repeatedly with Dana's mother.

An important role for the family approval for the construction of the house in 2015 was also played by Liviu, Mihai's elder brother, who also emigrated to Florence with his family and who also ended up accepting Dana's choice of country:

Sabrina: What did Liviu say to Mihai?

Dana: He said he's sorry they're not close, but if we have made up our minds, that's fine with him.

This passage represents the final approval by Mihai's family, certainly not with enthusiasm, which in fact made it possible to complete the purchase of the land and for the decision to start work on the house. The works will be done in the way they always are, that is, as we will see shortly, through the activation of the close parental network of both spouses.

The plot measures 500 square metres and 2,000 euros have been paid for it. The deed will be registered with the municipality in a subsequent period in order not to spend on bureaucracy the resources needed for its implementation.

While Dana, in July 2015, tells me all this, we are still in Vadrea, in the home of Mihai's parents. Indeed, to compensate for the imbalance due to the breach of the principle of virilocality, the following steps have been undertaken in Vadrea: the making of 'documents' of the union of Mihai and Dana (what externally would be perceived as the wedding in the municipality), the following *grătar* (barbecue) at home with kin and the closest 'brothers and sisters in Christ' (the *masa*, the table, is laid), and the (Pentecostal) baptism of little Marco on the evening of the following day.

'Sabri', Dana tells me, 'we left in a rush, with not even the time to prepare our luggage: Mihai's mother with his [older] brother arrived in Sibu Mare and we had to leave immediately … I have nothing to wear to go to the municipality. Mihai's mother wants me to buy a dress, but I have no money, and at home I have plenty of clothes!'

Once order is re-established through the different above-mentioned passages, one can start to speak about how the home should look: what shape (not the purely external one, it is indeed a 'vision of the home'), how many floors, how many bedrooms.

In this sense, Mihai – like the other man who I have had the opportunity to hear on the subject – indulges the woman's wishes, especially with respect to the location of the kitchen and other features (for example the built-in wardrobes in the bedroom), often absent or transformed compared to the traditional *rudari* houses. Although this aspect is connected to the close relationship between the domestic space and the activities/skills related to gender, it has in itself novelties arising from the work activities of women in Italian homes, which men have less to do with. The homes of Italians, in fact, represent one of the main models of inspiration in imagining the interiors and from which objects and furniture often come. With an original mix between this model, a little bit of *kitsch* and the *rudari domisticité*, the walls are coloured, the windows enriched with chiffon curtains of various colours, the kitchen is equipped with all the household appliances, but then often the bed is added to it, a living room is set up with sofas, knick-knacks and decorative objects, where initially we tend not to let the children go and use only for guests, but then it is invaded by the TV, bags and anything else that comes from Italy, all while waiting to be placed elsewhere (in the house itself or, more often, in that of relatives).

Figure 12.4. Interior of a new house: living room with various objects and furniture from Italy, some of which are destined for relatives' houses. © Sabrina Tosi Cambini.

Figure 12.5. Traditional stove in the new house. The emigrant woman's mother is seated beside it on a low stool, a traditionally used type of seat. © Sabrina Tosi Cambini.

In Vadrea, using the wi-fi network of a shop, Mihai and I connect with my computer (their tablet, bought in Italy, in the hurry of the departure, was forgotten in Sibu Mare) and we browse a Romanian site where they sell projects to build houses. Obviously, it is not Mihai's intention to buy one, but only to take inspiration from the pictures of the houses and the measurements of the areas indicated, and also to get an idea of how much building material is needed and how much it may cost.

We see one house in particular, with one floor, which has the entrance as Dana would like it – so Mihai tells me – and also the kitchen and living room spaces. Even the bedrooms, three in number, correspond to their wishes, while the bathrooms – which in the image are two – will be reduced to one, which to them is obvious. Happy with the choice, we save the web page and, a little later, in the evening, Mihai shows it to his parents, who like it.

Now we can leave and return to Sibu Mare: Dana's mother-in-law, who had insisted on coming too, will not be able to do so because her eldest daughter, in Florence, has found her a job for two months, so in a few days' time she will have to join her.[8]

It is possible to retrace the stages of those busy days in July 2015 spent in Vadrea:

- Wednesday 22: recognition of paternity, by Mihai, of the two children (who will now bear their father's surname and no longer that of their mother), in a notary's office for the public administration, in the city near Vadrea, Peteşi.
- Saturday 25, morning: marriage 'documents' in the municipality to which the town of Vadrea belongs. From here on, Dana will also bear Mihai's surname, which completely replaces her own.
- Saturday 25, evening: the grătar is held.
- Sunday 26, evening: baptism of Mihai's son, Marco and of his little cousin, son of his elder brother, Liviu. To celebrate the baptism, the arrival of Mihai's mother's brother from England was expected. The ceremony is held during the *adunare* (the Pentecostal meeting), next to the home of Mihai's parents, since it was they, about fifteen years earlier, who gave the land for the construction of the 'church'.
- On Monday 27 we are therefore ready to return to Sibu Mare and after a few days, on 3 August, construction of the house begins.

How to Build a House: A Family Building Site

In the week between the return and the start of the actual work, Mihai draws the floor plan of the house in a notebook, and discusses it with a *rudar* peer of his age from Sibu Mare who works as a bricklayer and is involved in the early stages of the work.

In the evening, this guy joins us at Dana's family home. The men talk about measurements, the material needed, how to spend as little as possible; we women serve them but we also listen, we look after the children and then, when the conversation lightens, we too are involved. Unlike the others, I remain silent and listen, so every now and then they make fun of me, especially Mihai and uncle Valeriu, who has seen me go to their house for years: 'Don't you have anything to say? Are you dumb?' But everyone is happy with my progress in the language and it is an aspect that is greatly appreciated.

The picture just outlined is an example of how the whole process of building the house is incorporated into the genealogical space from the beginning, and also inherent in the filiation, as it is linked to the fact of the formation of the new family nucleus, a segment that detaches from the parents' home, but remains close to it (although in this exceptional, but not unique case, the close housing proximity is recreated in the wife's parental network).

Figure 12.6. Plans of the house designed by Mihai with some modifications made by bricklayer, and foundations. © Sabrina Tosi Cambini.

The close scanning of the times makes it clear that, when the conditions are met for the fulfilment of something that is expected to happen in any case (whether it is in the near future – for example, a departure – or in a less definable time), you do it immediately. Especially when this fulfilment is linked to economic resources: as they exist, they must be used immediately.

Finally, the technical aspects of the construction of the house are also dealt with in the same context of family relationships: the only person who is not in the parental network, the bricklayer from Sibu Mare, however is a *rudar* and has been known for many years, and is invited home, in the evening, when the family reunites.

The bureaucratic aspects – the registration of the joint project and the planning permission – can wait, but will still be done before departure for Italy.

Mihai, Valeriu, the son of the latter, Iuli, and Dana's younger brother clean the land together with the mason, and on 2 August everything is ready. The food for the week is purchased, and in the morning of the following day the men arrive from Vadrea: Mihai's father and the brothers (from the oldest to the youngest teenager). As soon as they arrive, they start to work.

The women, after serving coffee and breakfast (bread, cheese, bacon, etc.), rearrange the house and start cooking.

There is a bit of excitement – the grandmother and Dana don't get along very well. I lend a hand, above all by looking after the children. This time, it is not a question of cooking for the grandmother or for the cousin Nicolae – as happened in March and April – but for *the men who were working*. And the men have clear roles: they are the father-in-law, the husband, the husband's brothers ... And even the men of the house, like Valeriu and Costantin, demand greater respect in that situation.

I must, therefore, adapt the relations to the new context: Mihai is no longer Mihai, but a man to whom things must be asked at the right moment, or not asked at all; Ioan, the teenage brother of Dana, whom I knew already as a child, is not the boy I reproach when he is in Italy or with whom I make jokes about his 'girlfriends', but a young man to whom food must be served when he is back from work.

Even among women there are hierarchies, and I come last, since I cannot prepare food as men like (one must be sure that the food is made in the proper way, and as they expect), nor do I have a husband to serve.[9]

This means that in this specific situation I do things that are very similar to those that teenagers would do, if they were at home: I prepare the table, cut bread, I quickly buy it in the shop if it runs out (and this is bad), I serve water and beer, clean the table, help to wash the dishes. Sometimes, if needed, I bring the dishes: a task which I do increasingly frequently when *mamaia* (the grandmother) notes that I can actually do it (even when they are boiling and exceedingly full of *ciorbă*, soup). To measure myself the respect and the changes of attitude that this situation involved has been fundamental to understanding the internal mechanisms.

While men eat, the women stay in the kitchen or at the side of the table, listen to the conversations of the men (and later on, with great precision and subtle rhetoric, circulate, making 'assessments' and preparing 'strategies' if need be, or simply preparing for something that will happen), and staying ready to immediately bring them what they ask for (more food, something else to drink …).

My presence is 'reshaped' even by men, particularly by those who know me less (even if I have been with them as a guest twice, staying for several days each time) and the use of humour. For instance, Mihai's father, when Dana is asking me to bring some soup also for little Marco (and I do it wrong twice, since I bring it with too much fat) says, laughing: 'Our women are *badanti*[10] in your country and you do it with us'.

When the lunch comes close to the end, the women become less nervous: everything has gone well, the men (and the father-in-law in the first place) are satisfied, and they drink coffee in the shadow in the *grădină* (garden), some of them together with a cigarette.

We can eat too. Dana and Grandma are always worried that I do not eat enough. Mamaia sometimes invites Dana's father-in-law to rest for a while, but he regularly and politely refuses, and goes back to work with the others.

The solidarity between relatives, which in living nearby also involves production and reproduction, here remodelled according to the needs of the case, is the basis on which the construction of the house can take place. All the men in the parental network, who are present in Romania and who are not already working elsewhere, participate. The tenacity of parental ties and their persistence even on a symbolic level make the construction of the house a social and cultural fact in which the kinship (ascending and descending, by consanguinity and affinity) is 'deposited'.

Also for Mihai and Dana's house, once the foundations, the external walls and the roof have been made, the work stops, as happens in all the many cases we know. And it is not certain that it will be resumed in August of the following year: the time of construction of the house follows the state of the resources that families are able to put away, and these – in turn – are linked to the vicissitudes in the immigration country.[11]

Mihai and Dana's home remains essentially in the same state for three consecutive years. Finally we start to put in the windows and the front door, then the internal doors. At this point, the house – four years have now passed – is ready to accommodate the first pieces of furniture and the first objects. Next year it is hoped that it can be plastered externally and painted internally, 'So, Sabri', Dana tells me with her eyes shining, 'when I go home, I won't go to my mother's anymore, I'll go to my house'.

The Washing Machine – or On Respect

It happens that sometimes mistakes are made during the development of ethnography, in the heart of the relationships. There is a feeling of shame, a sort of modesty that envelops the experience in the field: therefore not only the fundamental question of what the scholar will be able to say about the others – not failing their trust and 'confidentiality' – but also, what he or she will be able to say about themselves, where this saying is connected with the formation of knowledge. In other words, how far does (or can) the anthropologist go in reporting to the scientific community the steps of the ethnographic process that led to the 'forming' of that knowledge that is systematised in writing?

Below, therefore, I will venture to relate one of my mistakes, which also represented a point of momentary rupture, transformed for me into a dense episode, an opportunity for 'incorporation' of the understanding of cultural elements: and in this lies its importance and that of narrating it.

This episode concerns family relationships, the rhetoric of the construction of family roles, the new elements arising from the migratory experience that change people's points of view and that, in those family relationships, whose meaning must be renewed, the inter-generational respect. And an object brought by migration: the washing machine.

The analysis of that moment provides the opportunity to see, under a magnifying glass, cultural mechanisms linked to family relationships, which serve to manage what we can call 'every-day' conflicts, that is, those tensions, those disagreements that are inevitably created when living in close contact every day, within a context in which the roles are culturally and socially well defined. They are roles that undergo changes, shifts, in the moments in which those who have emigrated return home to spend the summer holidays or other periods.

Of this broad theme, here I take into consideration the imbalances and the consequent attempts at re-balancing that the relationships between the women of the family go through due to the novelties brought by migration in the organisation of the domestic sphere (objects, places and practices), always, however, within key elements – that is, of continuity – structuring these relationships (such as generational respect).

So let's start the narrative. It is 15 August 2015, this year we never go to the beach in Constanța, as used to happen for a few days in past years, because Mihai and Dana's house is being built, so resources must be dedicated to this: time, effort and money, in particular. The men leave very early, after breakfast. I feel the house come alive, but I usually wait for their departure before getting up.

One morning, Dana asks me if I want to go with her, Mihai and little Dorina to town to buy meat to make the *grătar*. I understand that it is better to give a negative answer, so I say no; at home remains little Marco, the other son of the couple, the two sisters of Mihai (therefore Dana's sisters-in-law and aunts of the child) and *mamaia*. While the two girls take care of the newborn and Grandma is busy in the *grădină*, I do a quick wash with my clothes in the washing machine, which Dana had forgotten to put with the others in the previous wash, and after a few minutes I go out to hang out those of the first wash. As I return, Grandma comes to me angry, telling me that the washing machine is running without water and if it breaks … 'Haven't you noticed that there is no water in the house?' she exclaims. And she adds that Ionica, her daughter, paid a lot for it, and that I don't understand anything and so on.

I tell Grandma that it is not a problem, that the washing machine has only just been turned on and that nothing has happened to the machine. While I am stopping it, kneeling in front of the buttons, Grandma, following me and stopping a step away from me, continues to reproach me out loud. Caught in the physical and emotional space, I reply. Falling into error.

I answer, with the same altered tone as Grandma, that I was born with a washing machine, that I always had one at home and therefore I know very well how it works. I take out my clothes and close the window with a firm movement. I get up and go to the kitchen. Grandma remains silent. The girls look out of their room to go back almost immediately.

Dana and Mihai return with the groceries; he immediately leaves, to work on the construction site of the new house. I help put away the items bought, then I start doing some chores. After a while, I notice that Dana is particularly silent with me, and she answers me in monosyllables.

'Has something happened?' I ask her; 'Mh, no, no', she replies. I try again: 'Did something happen with Mihai? Are you angry?' Silence. Then she turns around and says to me: 'I'm cross with you.'

With Dana, I could ask. And she explains to me: 'You got angry with Grandma. You treated Grandma badly. Sorry, but that's not the way to behave'. She also tells me what her sisters-in-law told her and I notice a certain aggravation in their narration of what happened, with the addition of elements, such as the child crying, woken up by my voice.

I know that's not what you do. And I know just as well why these narratives were added.

'See', continues Dana, 'I too, Sabri, when Grandma treats me badly and tells me all those bad words, you see, I keep quiet, I don't say anything to her'. I apologise profoundly. Dana adds: 'I've never seen you angry, you're the only person I know who has more patience than me ... I understand that Grandma made you tense ... but you didn't have to answer her like that'.

I know it's going to take some time to get over this. I don't know how long. And apart from the time, the silence.

Let's take a step back. A month had already passed since my arrival: a week spent in Vadrea, with Dana's in-laws, and three in Sibu Mare. As we have seen previously, Dana and I had talked a lot – or rather she talked and I listened – about her mother-in-law, about all the problems ... She had updated me on things that I knew in part, or she told me about the new ones, so I knew all the facts to be able to understand. And accept her point of view, and keep quiet.

Arriving at her *sat*, in another way and for other reasons, it is her grandmother and other relatives who are the recipients of Dana's 'indiscretions'. I am, however, also an interlocutor of the grandmother, who concerning her granddaughter Dana, her daughter, her daughters-in-law and so on, does not spare 'chatter' and 'gossip'. In short, there is a reworking of the internal conflicts that involves a fine art of rhetoric, the construction of a dramatisation in which the actors know how to move.[12]

I am a part of that dramatisation in a 'special' way: depending on how much the person considers me capable of being part of it, and therefore becoming or not their interlocutor, and assuming a passive role, that is, I limit myself to listening. For example, the grandmother treats me like a granddaughter; she has known me for several years, I have been alone with her for several weeks, she has seen that I behave appropriately with her and with her relatives, she trusts me and – a very important aspect – having never been to Italy and above all having never worked in the homes of Italians in Florence – unlike, for example, her daughter and granddaughters – she does not know how family relationships are managed in my context of origin. The attitude of the grandmother toward me is, therefore, a mixture in which, for several relational areas, the 'taken for granted' prevails, that is, that I should know. Knowing how to behave, what to say and how. Also knowing how to kill and pluck a chicken. However, for other areas, this does not apply: these are contexts that involve other people and involve, we could say, different 'levels' of respect and relationships, for example between genders, as we have seen previously in the preparation of food for the men and in serving them.

Grandma, therefore, makes me part of that dramatisation.

Dana, too, for our long-term friendship and mutual trust and because, over time, I have given reason not to fail her in this emotional-relational investment in me.

Ionica, sometimes yes and sometimes no, depending on the context (whether we are in Romania or Italy) and who we are talking about.

On the other side, Dana's cousins, who know how to move in the Italian context and know the friendly relationship that exists between her and me, do not participate in that dramatisation because they believe that I would not be able to adopt their way of managing relationships, but only the assessments and behaviours of the cultural environment of where I come from.

With respect to the passive role I play in this 'dramatisation', it is linked to my position in the field as an ethnographer: it is an actual strategy, which allows me not to enter into the circulation of 'gossip'.[13]

Being able to stay inside this relational theatre also means having knowledge of the context and the relational skills to measure the gravity of what you are being told. The very fact of being the object of 'gossip', a behaviour or an event, in itself, indicates that it is not perceived, however, either as so serious or so unexpected as to put in real danger the social relationship between whoever is narrating the gossip and the protagonist.

There is little talk on the contrary, of what would entail a risk for the maintenance of the relationship itself, and in a completely different way.

Returning to the episode of the washing machine, we understand, then, that I had made a double mistake. From an emic point of view, I had not respected the grandmother, leaving my role as a granddaughter; from an ethical point of view, relating to the research methodology, I had taken on an inappropriate, active role.

After what had happened, during the day Grandma keeps me apart from the preparations of the *grătar*, she does not call me to pass a glass or a plate, she does not let me take part in tidying up the kitchen with her.

I am, therefore, very saddened. I wait. In the afternoon, while we are both in the kitchen, I venture an 'I'm very sorry, forgive me' and *mamaia* answers me: 'It's nothing. I respect you'. With those words, which represent a real relational gift, she means that I must always respect her, and that, at the same time – despite what has happened – she continues to respect me.

Finally, the next day, in the evening, she asks me to give her a glass of water; and the next day, she makes me stand next to her while she cooks: I understand that she has completely forgiven me.

The house and those who, present or absent, are part of that house, represent a protected and respectful cultural entity. The rhetoric of 'gossip' seems to be a counterweight to a moral discipline that requires strong respect for older brothers and generations (grandparents, parents and in-laws). They are one of the ways in which the possible conflict is controlled.

Even the disagreements, the misunderstandings, which are not uncommon, and the silences that follow – not talking to each other for a while – enter into a constant elaboration of the latent conflict, allowing people to (almost) never reach breaking point. As also, if the issue is serious, is the fact of avoiding meeting the person who is directly involved in the matter or not dealing with the topic in daily talk with others.

On the opposite side, irony, used in public and with the person present, has the same function, but through the mechanism of reversal: the wife can make fun of her husband; younger brothers the older ones; a woman, men. One episode, in this sense, is exemplary.

The men had been fishing all day, leaving the women at home alone and unhappy, especially the young ones. They come back in the evening with a bucket full of water and few fish, and small too, inside. While we are outside talking, in the backyard, Grandma looks out of the kitchen window with the fish we had bought at the market and, shaking it in front of us, exclaims: 'Hey, men, this is my fish from the garden' and she repeats again, the gesture and the phrase, in the midst of everyone's laughter.

Now, in a context of respect between family roles such as the one outlined above, it is no coincidence that grandmother and granddaughter have had several episodes of misunderstanding over the course of a few months and that, as far as I am concerned, the relational short-circuit has occurred around an object of migration.

What, in fact, had Grandma scolded Dana for? The way she brought up the children: the behaviour of Dorina, who is three years old, was not good (her grandmother says, while adoring her, that she is *nebună*, crazy/stupid) and not being with her children all the time. Mihai's behaviour toward Uncle Valeriu, Grandma's son: Mihai was disrespectful and should not have been like that just because he owns a car and has more economic resources at his disposal. Finally, *mamaia* was irritated at the way her niece Dana ran the house, which was not her way.

These elements are all related to migration. Dorina has an upbringing that in part does not coincide with how she would have been brought up in Romania, being in the extended family, nor with that given by her mother in Florence, in a more restricted family context, given that in Italy Dorina goes to nursery school. How much this attendance at nursery has an influence is seen in a difference in education that emerges in Dorina's interactions with her *rudari* peers: the child, for example, has a strong sense of possession of objects, which other children do not have; jealousy for the attention that her parents give to other children, which others do not have; she is not used to the extended family, but to being together with only some relatives: her grandmother Ionica and her teenage aunts. She had little to do with the other aunt, the married one, and her family, or with the older uncle. While the other grandparents, her father's parents, living in Romania she has almost forgotten, also her father's younger sisters, her aunts; every now and then she sees the older aunt, who lives in Florence with her partner, and the older uncle, who also lives in the Tuscan capital with his family. But these family ties are not part of her daily life. And then, Dorina loves to eat the foods they give her at the nursery school: the baby soup and the spaghetti with lots of Parmesan cheese, and she doesn't adapt to anything else.

The second point, the relationship between Mihai and Uncle Valeriu, concerns the kinship between a young man and an older man, uncle of the wife of the former, who, however, plays an even stronger role, because the granddaughter has lost her father. He has never emigrated[14] – his knowledge is restricted to the world in which he has always belonged and he has ways of talking with the young man that reflect his role, therefore he demands respect, especially in the decisions to be made (what is to be done and when it must be done). This creates a latent friction with the young man, who often has more knowledge in certain fields because he has had the opportunity to learn in the migratory context in formalised learning paths – for example, the course at the construction school that he attended during the period of the former Luzzi's occupation – or, in any case, because he has shared more varied experiences. In addition, Mihai was becoming more and more intolerant, feeling 'commanded' by his uncle Valeriu: 'he always tells me: "let's go there", "where are you?", "come and get me"', Mihai complains, addressing Dana. As a result, the irony Mihai uses with his uncle is not always adequately controlled, and sometimes overflows into a lack of respect, breaking into dissent.

The third point – the different way of running the house between grandmother and granddaughter Dana – approaches and intersects with what happened between Grandma and me. And it lies first of all in a crucial point: the house for the grandmother and the house for Dana do not coincide, *they are not the same house.*

Ruba Salih writes in this regard:

> they push us toward a reflection on what truly constitutes a 'home' for Moroccan women. If analyzed through the goods that women acquire, consume, exhibit and exchange in their transnational movements, the relationship with the country of origin emerges significantly as very complex. To feel 'at home' in Morocco, women need to take with them those goods that represent the other 'home' that they have built in Italy. Through these goods, Moroccan women express their change, simultaneously asserting their difference from those they have left behind in Morocco. Nevertheless, building a 'house' in Italy means surrounding oneself with objects that mark Moroccan and Muslim belonging. The 'house' becomes for these women a space built through the interaction and combination of goods and objects that symbolise their dual belonging. (2008: 107)

Now, the difference that we find with this statement lies only in the objects of the country of origin in a migratory context, which in our case are not actually artefacts, but the very use of things, which takes place in a different way; food, with its smells and flavours, and the television always tuned to Romanian channels. The *rudari* families do not come from a world of objects, and they begin to be part of their daily life, in fact, with migratory experiences; perhaps also for this reason they bring many into their home in *Țara* (homeland), signs of interpenetrating worlds. Romania enters Italy and Italy enters Romania.

Dana, Marieta, Ionica and other women told me: 'We've got used to it by now: we're there and we're here', 'Problems here and problems there: before you had problems in one place, now in two!'

The new houses have bedrooms like in Italy, the kitchen equipped as in Italy, the living room to receive guests, the appliances, the tiles ...; the rugs are removed and then for a while they are put back, and the living room at the end is used, if necessary, also as a bedroom: a use simultaneously remodelled, but which has as a reference the structural model of the flats in Florence, where the women work.

When, in March, a van arrived from Italy and there was only me at home waiting for it, after unloading the packages, once I returned, Grandma said to me: 'Let's put it here, then when Dana comes, she'll sort it out.' Those packages, in fact, contain objects that are foreign to the grandmother, sometimes useless or meaningless, superfluous, like some for the children. Other times, however, she senses their preciousness and is afraid to break them because she does not understand how they work, which creates some upset for her. The washing machine is one of these: being elderly she feels that she has lost some seniority, that recognition of knowledge and wisdom to which her status should be connected. Even in her house – but strictly speaking, it is her daughter's house, as she makes a point of saying and occasionally even threatening to return to her own – there are too many things that she would not know how to mend if they were broken, that she does not know how to use, that she would prefer not to be there.

The house in winter, inhabited only by her, is reduced to only the kitchen. The only heated room and finally again to her size: the AGA cooker and the bed; the toilet outside in the *grădină*, the body is washed in a basin by heating water on the stove, and also the few dishes that get dirty, but strictly in another container (never mix the two basins).

And so I was with her, between March and April 2015, and without a moment of tension ever occurring.

The transformation of the habitat, with the coming of those who live elsewhere every day and for a prolonged period, created a widespread and latent relational imbalance, in which everyone participated – including me – both in outlining it and in the consequent strategies to contain it, which I too have learned.

The *Magazin* and the Food

We are in Sibu Mare, August 2011. Ionica tells me that she would like to save enough money to open a shop (*magazin*) in the new area of the country, where many *rudari* are building houses, and where also – after a few years – two of her children will build one.

'Sabrina, there's nothing there, you see, you have to walk a long way to get to the first shop, you go round behind, and you get to where my mother's sister is, remember?' She continues – 'So I can go back and have a job here, even for the children when they grow up …but it takes a lot of money'.

'Does it cost a lot, Ionica?' I ask. 'Yes, it costs a lot', she answers. 'Its like building another house, then you have to buy all the products, at first, otherwise what do you sell? You have to have everything: food, drinks, beer, detergents, bread every day… then you have to buy the fridge for ice cream, the coffee machine like there is with you.'

Four years later, in 2015, a shop really does open in the new area, which gradually begins to be populated, not by Ionica, but by the family of her daughter-in-law's sister, whose husband in Norway manages to earn a lot of money. After having built his own home, where his wife lives permanently, and the one for his daughter's nuclear family, he also built the shop, which is run by her together with her (second) husband.

'See', Dana tells me, they were smart. 'Now they have to earn money here, they don't have to do as we did'. She adds – 'have you seen what a big house she [the young woman] has?', 'Yes' I reply, 'I went in March to visit her with Nico, they had invited us'. 'Is that so? I didn't know', says Dana.

The shop located almost opposite Ionica's house belongs to the neighbour – who was the witness for one of his grandchildren, the son of one of his brothers – in partnership with his brother. The neighbour, Stefan, has been in Florence for a dozen years. He works as a general care nurse at a facility of the local health service, and has had access to public housing also for the fact of having a child with a serious disability. When I went to Romania in March 2015, he too was there with the whole family, having taken a period of leave from work.

Alone, the grandmother and I, in that period still with a winter climate and with the snow that covers the country, we went to their shop to get the bread – when Grandma did not want to make it – and other small things. In August, on the other hand, when people return from their places of emigration, the family, like the others in the neighbourhood, goes there several times a day to buy soft drinks, ice cream, chewing gum and sweets for the children.

The *rudari* shops have all been opened with the money obtained with the migrations and their own earnings and also the supplies continue to be tied to them; these, in fact, follow the periods of the returns (often annual, linked to the summer holidays) and the arrival times of the monetary remittances (money that is transferred from the countries of immigration or that arrives with the people who have emigrated only for a few months). There is a bit of everything, even single items removed from the packaging: per unit, in fact, you can buy cigarettes, babies' nappies, sanitary towels for women, and so on; washing machine detergent can be bought by weight. They are all expensive products in relation to the economy of the place and people do not always have enough money to buy them, nor is it so simple to go to the nearby city to get them at a lower price since the bus ticket costs 3.5 lei per ride, so seven lei there and back,[15] corresponding to almost two euros: a figure that seems disproportionate in the context.

The people who remain are used to getting food supplies by using products that come from their own kitchen gardens or from the fields owned by neighbours, especially, in this second case, for tomato preserves. Some of the jars of these preserves are not for their own consumption, but are used in other ways: as a gift, when visiting relatives who do not have the same possibilities, for example, because of illness; as a 'means of exchange' when they go to ask a favour of families with whom they do not have a close relationship; or these jars are among the few objects that go from Romania to the emigration contexts.

The latter aspect, the circulation of food in the opposite direction, a traceable *leitmotif* of these families' migrations, has an important role and a special meaning. There are three types of food that is sent from the Romanian *sat* to the foreign city. Food that is prepared at home with vegetables and fruit from the home garden or – the second type – the one represented by the products purchased. The latter can be particularly loved and consumed, such as sunflower seeds; or linked to traditional dishes, such as cabbage leaves that are used to prepare *sarmale*; or, again, pieces of pork. All are products, however, that cannot be found outside Romania, except in specialised stores and very expensive for our families, therefore of no use to them. The third type is food parcels as humanitarian aid from European funds.

The first type of food, and also the second, most common in transnational stories, have a strong symbolic meaning. Referring to the domestic sphere of origin, they bring it here, together with the family ties that are there. It is one of those actions – sending from there and consuming here – that contribute to cancelling the spatial distance between the contexts of life, and to establishing a material, symbolic and affective co-presence, *through* the bodies.

The third type, on the other hand, seems to be more linked to the family strategies of this network and concerns the maximisation of resources that can be activated. In the country of origin, in fact, we try to maintain those possible benefits to which we can have access. When the bureaucratic procedures allow it, in the sense that you can find stratagems useful for the continuation of the disbursement of a social bonus,[16] the families remain formally present in the *sat*. This is the case, for example, for food supplied by the European Community, which is distributed according to the number of family members, adults and minors. It can happen, therefore, that in the country of origin – even after an internal redistribution between the nuclei – an amount of these foodstuffs is set aside for family members living abroad, as it is known that the work situation is fluctuating, that there are many children and there are many expenses to face for daily survival. There is, therefore, a counter-flow of aid, which arises from the knowledge of those who remain – often the elderly of the family – of the sacrifices and precariousness to which their loved ones are exposed. All these types of food are sent through relatives, friends or acquaintances, always *rudari*, who carry out transport between Italy and Romania.

Food is one of the few items that come directly from relatives in Romania, sometimes together with some handmade clothes (I myself brought Ionica two waistcoats from her mother). It is easier, however, and usual, for those who go home to the *sat* for the summer holidays, to then return to Italy with various things bought at home, where prices are considerably lower: rugs, shoes, sweaters, trousers and do on – even with objects that are not found in Italy, such as the round electric oven that is used in Dobruja and is Turkish, very popular among our families.

The flow of food from Italy to Romania – unlike other situations described in ethnographic works – in our case does not take place: at home money is sent – with money transfer services or by giving it to very trusted relatives; or objects, even large, such as furniture, mainly through acquaintances who carry out transport operations.

Stocks of consumer goods are brought from Florence to the *sat*, when they go there for the whole month of August. These are products that are not to be found or that cost the same or not much less (therefore very expensive for Romania), and whose purchase could give rise to some discontent, since the money is used for other things: for work on the house, to offer drinks, have a baptism, give to relatives, buy gifts and go to parties, buy new clothes for the children for important occasions, and so on. Spending three euros at the Italian supermarket and spending the equivalent in the Romanian one is not the same thing, and it seems inappropriate to do so. This is especially true for women's products, such as body creams, bubble baths, nail varnish and other beauty products.

Dana: You know about Mălina, don't you?

Sabri: What?

Dana: They opened a *magazin*!

Sabri: When?

Dana: A few months ago. They put everything up, like a bar, a shop that has a bar.

Sabri: Are they okay? Are they happy?

Dana: Yes, Sabri. It was their dream. They built their house, they sold the other one, they're helping Ariana with her house.

Notes

1. For the concept of *homing* (thinking, feeling and making home), see the work developed by Boccagni (2017); Boccagni and Duyvendak (2020). See also Nieto et al. (2022); Bonfanti and Pérez Murcia (2023) about home-mobility nexus.
2. From an interview collected during the *MigRom* project, February 2015.
3. National Archive of Constanța, Dosar 2, /341 'Lista de alegători Regiunea Dobrogea, Raionul Medgidia 3 martie 1963'.
4. Sibu Mare*, Romania, 2010.
5. Similarly, Slavkova reports the same thing about the *Rudari* of Bulgarian nationality, who in Spain and Greece claim to be Bulgarian and have nothing to do with the 'Romanian Gypsies, whom the Rudari perceive as beggars and nomads, and with whom they do not want to deal' (2017: 62). Another case, rare at the moment in the literature, is that reported by Teodorescu (2020) in Uppsala (Sweden) where the *rudari* from the province of Vâlcea in Romania use begging every day.
6. See Tesăr (2016); Toma, Tesăr and Fosztó (2017).
7. Elopement, as a 'form' of marriage, is widespread among the *Rudari*, as we saw.
8. Leaving by bus, which in such a short space of time, costs much less than the plane, does not require a reservation and, giving the possibility of making any changes in departure dates, allows for much more luggage to be carried.
9. Also in the presence of Dana and her husband's female cousin, who in the second week also contributed to the construction, the grandmother, who saw me slightly worried when having to serve lunch, tells me 'let it go, they (the two women who are her grandchildren, Dana and Maricla) will serve their men'.
10. This precise word was used when speaking in Romanian.
11. Teodorescu also notes that 'the investments made by the *Rudari* are gradual and often interrupted by insufficient funds' (2020: 103).

12. 'In a society without a formal infrastructure, detailed, perpetual, reciprocal observation, evaluation, commentary and conjecture – in a word, gossip – constitute the most important form of social control and determination of your relative status' (ni Shuinéar 2005: 338).
13. Saletti Salza notes the same thing in another context (2010).
14. Unlike his wife and children.
15. In 2016.
16. Like, for example, the renewal of the necessary documentation every time you return to the country of origin, even once a year.

Chapter 13

Ethnographic *Morceau*

Feeling Lonely

Grandma

August 2011. Last night it rained all the time, a long storm, the thunder broke my sleep and the lightning ripped through the darkness. Last night I was very tired, I felt a little heartache, some worries about the news that came to me from Florence, in this strange August. The families were under threat of new evictions from the occupations; we exchanged messages on our mobile phones. Lorenzo had called me to keep me up to date. I was happy to be in Romania, but I felt I was not where I would be most useful; I felt I was divided. Was the same happening – with the opposite directionality – also to my *rudari*?

I got up early, but Grandma was already up and active from the first light of dawn. When I entered the kitchen, the words she spoke to me contained a world: 'You left me alone last night.' You don't sleep alone, and you don't leave someone to sleep alone during a storm like the one that just happened.

Then, she told me to sit down and, on the bed, we ate together (breakfast for me, the second course for her), *ciorbă de pui*, soup with pieces of vegetables and chicken.

10 October 2010. Grandma was very angry because her nephew Viorel (son of one of her sisters) went to her to change the door, which had broken. The nephew took the new one to be assembled from Grandma's sister-in-law, but then he wanted it back (although he didn't have to use it elsewhere). So, Grandma, who was very disappointed, went to her sister-in-law to reproach

her, telling her that she had given her the land to build her house, that she had helped her build it, and that when they got married she paid for the wedding. 'She never comes to greet me [visit me]' – said Grandma – and added: 'When you're left alone, everyone turns on you'. She explained to me that she had dreamed of eggs breaking that night, and that meant she was going to quarrel with someone, and in fact she did.

9 August 2011. Luminiţa was worried; Ionica, her daughter, had gone to work in Italy for two months. 'You don't leave seven children at home alone!' she exclaimed. It was very tiring for her, alone, to take care of her grandchildren; she had diabetes and had undergone two operations. Estera, Sorina and Pauna, three of the granddaughters, were ill a while ago and Grandma didn't know what to do. 'Angelica [one of the daughters-in-law] is in Spain, Nico is never around. Alone it is hard [*greu*]'.

Ionut and Mariana

'Sabrina, you know – Mariana told me – Ionut has been like this for a long time, he is not working, he stays at home. He's depressed. It's very difficult. I thank God that we have the house from the municipality ... But the children go to school, there is never enough of anything'.[1]

The thoughts and words go back to when Ionut, years ago, had worked as a bricklayer and as a courier, in both cases with a good monthly salary. Living at the former Luzzi, the family had managed to save some money. 'Remember? We were fine [financially] and wanted to go home' ... Ionut's parents were there and also his brothers'.

The two, at that time, therefore decided to return home. Ionut quit and they returned to Vadrea, his father's guests, while they were building their house. But the accumulated money soon ran out between the costs of the house, helping relatives and everyday life. Ionut hoped to find work in Romania, but he soon had to surrender to the fact that the context had remained the same as when he left a few years before: the jobs that could be done were linked to a very poor economy, salaries were very low.

Ionut and Stefania decided to return to Italy.

'When his father died, it was winter, we were not at home. I remember that very well. Ionut got a call from his brother, then another one. He wanted to leave right away, but we couldn't because the van was from the company and his car was no good for the trip. He had returned home and immediately went to see if anyone, a church brother, could lend him one.

He'd left his mobile phone somewhere. It couldn't be found. Then [when he found it], he saw other calls. Then his brother told him that his father was dead.'

'He' – continues Mariana – 'felt ill with grief. I swear … I didn't know what to do, he started crying like a child. Perhaps he felt guilty because he was not at home, because he left his father alone, when he was old and needed him; perhaps it is for this reason, Sabrina, that he is always sad, that he is depressed'.

Note

1. Florence, 2014.

Chapter 14

SHIFTING SENSE

We have seen how in migrations the space of kinship represents the horizon of meaning, that is, the reference that allows our *rudari* to move in a protected way in a foreign environment.

In a purely ethnographic article, Saletti Salza (2009) uses an object, a fragment of Romania in the shack, as a metaphor to describe the sense of family and home: the rug.

The *rudari* old houses, and often those of the Romanian peasants, were (and are, where they remain inhabited), full of rugs, spread out on the ground or hanging on the walls in the rooms. Ionica, in the summer of 2014, gave me one of theirs – she made me choose it, she no longer hangs it: now her home is different, it is new, it has many rooms, tiles that cover the floors, and those in the kitchen. Her rug is now hanging on my bedroom wall. Grandma, while we were choosing the rug for me, pulled out hers: 'my man bought this one'. Her old house, made of *adobe*, gradually enlarged, where she no longer lives, is now bare. The rugs were removed, washed, and stored in the wardrobe of her daughter's new house.

But even before, in the *bordeie,*[1] which were much more unadorned, the *rudari* had practically only a bed, which in the present we see appearing everywhere – in homes in other countries, in the kitchens of the new houses built with the money of the migrations, in the 'old' houses and so on. On the bed they talk, they watch television, they take care of the children, they change the babies, they sing lullabies, they squeeze up together, and when it is cold even more, they make others feel their warmth. In our *rudari* families the *pat* (the bed) is their rug: 'get into the bed!'

While watching television, the feet of one on the feet of the other: you do not move, it is nice to feel one another. To feel your bodies close, to family members, to people with whom you live. I remember that, in the early days, to make me sit down, they offered me a chair, then they noticed that I liked to be there, on the bed, everyone together. At first, if I found myself too close to someone, I apologised, then I got used to this mode of contact. Obviously the proxemic rules to follow are there and I certainly cannot approach a man in this way, but the blankets are divided anyway.

They also eat, on the bed: 'in the manner of the *rudari*', as Nico told me. A piece of cloth – like a kitchen towel – resting on the bed like a tablecloth, or a small table or a stool, placed in front of the person sitting on the bed.

And, then, in the end, you sleep on the bed, better not alone, especially if it is winter or bad weather. I remember Grandma who after a storm, told me: 'you left me to sleep alone' (see chapter 13). Or, when, in Sibu Mare, in the weeks spent with her, she was happy that I was there, that I slept with her. And again, in the autumn of 2010 when the children had returned to Romania, we all slept together, in two beds in the kitchen: how cold it was in the other rooms!

In Italy in occupied houses, you set up the kitchen, with a table and chairs, sometimes a sofa, but then, when you do not have to cook or do other chores, you are on the bed. Even in the apartments for rent you can recreate the intimate and comfortable place represented by a bed or a large sofa, where you take a breath from your problems and the tiring days, perhaps by telephoning relatives at home, in Romania.

The children grow up, some go to high school, they start asking for their own furniture, unheard of for *rudari* domestic spaces: a desk, shelves for their books, drawers to store notebooks and other objects.

I will now try to grasp some intricate and interdependent elements, which are given in those concrete and localised possibilities, which enable our *rudari* to feel less like *foreigners* and more *at home* (and also, on the other hand, so that they are perceived as less *different* and *closer*). These are processes through which the immigration context can gradually take on new meanings, becoming a place 'that makes sense'. I will try to frame this question using a double phrase: the sense of leaving and the shifting of the sense.[2] From this point of view, the main question is when and how the place of emigration begins, over time, to acquire (but certainly not in a linear way, by sum, as if it were a trajectory) an autonomous sense or a sense of presence anchored to that same place and not to the motives that made them leave their country of origin. What are the symbolic and material factors of this 'shift in the sense of presence'? When, in other words, does being in Florence acquire a motivation for our people that is detached from that of achieving something in Romania? When is *home* no longer only the *sat* in Romania, but also the city to which they emigrated in Italy?

The word [migrate] implies a locative abandonment: *ex-migrare* [from Latin], go away from a certain place … A migrant ceases to be a migrant as soon as he leaves the limits of his village, after which he is an immigrant. The distinction directly concerns the process through which a human being outside his own culture may or may not obtain the status of 'person'. (Salza 1997: 316–17)

The possibility of shifting the sense of presence is strongly linked to the recognition of the status of 'person': 'You wanted arms, people came', so the writing that I remembered earlier on a large cloth formed of sheets sewn together, which waved from the terraces of the upper floors of one of the occupations related to the story of the former Luzzi. Women, men, children, desires, dreams, affections have arrived …[3]

If the adjective 'transnational' does have any specific meaning in referring to migrants, I suggest that it should lie in problematising the 'attachment' to places of origin among deterritorialised persons who are not only denied full membership of the 'society' in which they mainly live and work but even a full personhood. (Gledhill 1998: 4, quoted in Grillo 2015)

This aspect of 'attachment' is fundamental in my reasoning, together with the complementary aspect of developing a sense of belonging toward the place of immigration.

If, as we have seen, the element of housing insecurity can negatively affect the relationship with the territory and slow down the formation of a feeling of being at home (an eviction can disrupt what had been built, the trace of our material presence and its meaning), now I would like to reflect directly on those 'non-material' elements that have to do with a slow and profound process of 'signification'.[4] The sense of migration that moves, in time and space, which marks internal *décalages* within my reference families, 'molecular' changes,[5] those changes that ethnography allows us to feel and understand, and that continuously interface with the social, cultural and political environment of arrival.

With respect to the living space, the reference is no longer only the accommodation and the place of this accommodation, but the entire city; and at the same time, the living space in Romania, the *sat* and the neighbourhood and, again, the space between the *here* and the *there* – how thousands of kilometres are filled, the void that is crossed creating contemporaneity with the television satellite, the mobile phone and the Internet. The space that is cancelled – through technologies, discourse (what we talk about), behaviours (what we do), the priorities we give and the decisions we make, and the objects that move with or without people – contributes to creating a continuous contemporaneity: being here and there, always. Because if you work here, you do it to survive (here) and fulfil your wishes (there).

This picture, however, must be interpreted depending on the families and challenged according to the generations – since in the shades of meanings we find new dense areas that concern those children and adolescents who are growing up in Italy – and with respect to that which a family nucleus and its members gradually manage to acquire in the place of emigration.

The main reason why the adults of our network emigrated was to be able to have and do in Romania what they considered important for their lives: to have a job that would allow them to marry and build their house next to that of their parents and siblings, to take care of themselves and send their children to school, and help them build their future. The new house, thanks to the money earned in a foreign land, will be bigger and more beautiful: these desires have, in fact, changed with migration; they have taken different forms, due to both increased financial resources and to their encounter with the housing cultures of Italian families.

In this moving, transfer, leaving, the meaning is all contained in what they want to achieve at home, in Romania, and what the economic and social situation of their country does not allow them to do.

'And why did we leave, then?!' says Dana. And this is a phrase that, with multiple variations, has recurred with some frequency. You can also decide to leave 'intermittently', as we have seen, that is, only a few months, for a seasonal job several times a year, now one (the husband) now the other and more often (the woman), or both together (young couples). The comparison between those who emigrate in this way and, therefore, with the intention of not remaining in the context of immigration and those, instead, who, although starting with temporal uncertainties, are willing to remain in the new context for much or even all of the year, allows us to see some of those shifts of meaning on which we are reflecting.

'Here with you it's sad', Nico tells me. 'What's sad?' I answer. 'You stay all day in the house, there is no music, you can't do anything', he replies.

Nico is the cousin of Mihai and Dana (son of Dana's mother's brother). As we have seen previously, he has emigrated several times: to Spain, Germany, England and Italy, always for short periods. In Florence, he remained at the occupation of the former Luzzi for a couple of months, and in 2014 another two months, one at a distance from the other, hosted by his cousins in the occupation of the former hotel in Via Gori.

Nico and Mihai, and their uncle Lucian, often went to another occupation, carried out in total autonomy, that is, without even the support of the Movimento di Lotta per la Casa. When I went there for the first time, I said to myself: 'here is Romania!', certainly exaggerating in my exclamation, but there were, however, some features: the *grătar*, the music, the men outside playing, the women on the other side of the street sitting and talking.

There was a sociality, undoubtedly restricted, suffocated in a minimal portion of the city, but that came out of the building, took over the front courtyard and the street. Anyone passing, for those 50 metres was forced to cross a lively, almost domestic space, which referred to something else. Another place. It was not a good housing situation: a very old building, small rooms, electricity and water present but not safe and so on. And Ionica did not like it because, being a Pentecostal, she does not like to see men drink – so she told me; but when we went together, she immediately recognised one of her classmates in elementary school, and immediately started talking to her, involving me too, and staying with her for a long time.

We are, however, far from Romania: that place is too small, it is a grain within the city; and it could be evacuated at any moment (as happened in 2015). But it is the forms of sociality that attract us, and above all the sociality that is linked to a space where the reference persons are either relatives or neighbours or otherwise known, belonging to a broader *we* defined (in the double meaning: we define ourselves and are defined) as *rudari*.

The districts of the localities from which they come, as we have seen, are inhabited by *rudari* family networks; thinking of the 'spatialisation of social relations' that I was discussing, these 'social worlds' appear clear to us. Beyond the complex relationship with the 'Romanian-Romanians', the space of everyday life for the *rudari* is equivalent to that of the houses and streets where the relatives and the neighbours live (among whom, however, if one goes in depth, common kin is often found). The daily living space, therefore, corresponds largely to the genealogical space, and between the position in the kinship and the social role there is correspondence: we are what we are – that is, we think of ourselves and are recognised as – being the son of, grandson of, and so on and so forth.

This correspondence with migration breaks down: that microcosm is no longer there, the outside becomes huge and is incarnated in the people we meet and who move away as we approach, in the police who control the documents and evacuate the building, in the television programmes. The process of marginalisation and racialisation actually takes them over. Their bodies swell, they get fat.[6]

Families and their members in the migration undergo a repositioning in the social topology that erodes a certain perception of themselves within a collective context, which is no longer the *sat*, but – to be precise – a foreign city.

We would say, then, that a sort of 'compression' happens in the family sphere. The territory and social space of signification and signifier are everything in internal relations, familial but – unlike the *sat* – of a kinship reduced numerically, and more difficult to reach because it is scattered throughout the city and because it is often no longer aligned with the times of daily life, which have *décalages* between families connected to work activities, especially of the women, who travel mainly by public transport. Paola Sacchi (2010), albeit in a context doubly different from ours, that of the Palestinian situation and of 'Arab familism', refers to an essay entitled 'Living Together in a Nation in Fragments. Dynamics Of kin, Place and Nation' by Penny Johnson,[7] in which the theory is that marriage practices and the importance of parental ties are not:

> the remnant of an archaic tradition that is slow to die (in a society that is still undergoing modernisation) but is a 'new' choice made to respond to new circumstances and life scenarios. In a highly insecure world, marrying close to you, with those who are closest to you, is a strategy that men and women adopt – not everywhere in a uniform way – to deal with the precariousness of daily life and the risk of the disintegration of the family and the community. Marriage between first cousins[8] ... and family solidarity ... constitute a symbolic capital that becomes an instrument of resistance to colonial domination, they are fundamental articles in an economy of symbolic (but also material) goods that makes it possible ... to obtain security and collective survival and to achieve objectives of social improvement. (2010: 73)

It is precisely these aspects that are of interest: in an explicitly adverse context, such as that of the immigration to which I have referred (from the experiences of daily encounters in which people suffer continuous direct and indirect discrimination, to the constraints of material life, to the public discourse of which they are the subject, which paint their group as a constant threat, up to the paternalistic relationships that they are forced to suffer), the family and its ethos constitute a multiple resource, which not only coagulates in relationships of reciprocity (an element often underlined in the description of the internal dynamics of the 'communities'[9]), but become the possibility of 'resistance', 'security' and 'collective survival'. In this sense, we can then affirm that the 'identity power' of the family and its ethos is put to work, together reinvigorated and renewed in the migratory context, since only in the family network are they recognised as a *person*. The family becomes capable of supporting its members in the face of pressure from external society, to which they are continually exposed, either by sending them a 'positive' image of themselves (linked, in fact, to their own family role and relationships, duties, expectations connected to it, such as family ethos, internal feeling), or by supporting the sense of being there, in the place of emigration, and not in their own *sat*, and therefore also the ability itself to accept and endure certain situations, very difficult materially, cognitively and emotionally, since the sacrifices that are being made serve to fulfil their own desires (as fathers, mothers, etc.).

The last aspect reported in the quotation above – the achievement of social and, I would say, economic improvement objectives – also supports the 'sense of guilt' that can arise from the fact of having gone away: toward their loved ones who remain there – sometimes leaving them in a condition of solitude, so feared by the *rudari*[10] – and toward those who cannot leave. In this sense, a circularity is established between marriage practices and family relationships, and migration: the second adds material and new possibilities to the first, with a view to continuity; the second legitimates it (legitimation of the departure from the *sat*, that is, of the migratory choice), specifically for its achieved and visible objectives, and among these, first of all the construction of the new house in Romania: a social and cultural fact, as analysed, in which the kinship is 'deposited'.

On the other hand, however, as noted above, it also sets in motion another, complementary mechanism, that of compression, which seems to me to be twofold.

In migration, the power of everyday places to generate meaning appears reduced because they are 'restricted': the reference places are closed, delimited contexts, occupied or rented housing, to which you connect with public transport or, when you own one, by car, for example when you go with the entire nuclear family to visit a relative. The city in its entirety, therefore, disappears to reappear pulverised into discrete units: the apartment where you work as a caregiver or the consultation centre where you go to look for work or, again, the parish where you go to collect your food parcel. With what kind of symbolic resources do the latter places provide us?

The construction of meaning, which we are dealing with, also envisages a possible shift of the imagination, of the basin from which to draw the symbolic resources of positive structuring of our own presence. And this also implies being able to access new 'territories', understood as a metaphor and as real, contextual landscapes. The city, as such, Florence, then seems to remain outside its 'thinkability': the city to which they have access often has to do with subordinate positions and obtaining residence, with the important rights connected to it, and does not materialise in the full recognition of being a citizen. They, therefore, can come within the framework of formal law, but remain, however, outside the area of citizenship.[11]

The duality of the compression, then, is due to the fact that the domestic group increasingly corresponds to the nuclear one (parents and children), therefore the family space is also 'reduced'; a reduction that increases even more because often these family branches are not close as in Romania, but located in various parts of the city and therefore not easy for them to reach each other. The 'compression', then, at times, can press on several members or even just one woman.

Time

The question of the places in the life of our families often intersects with a particular configuration of time, which we could define as 'emergency'. This is linked in a double thread with the size of the emergency: the emergence of things (situations, circumstances, opportunities) with a certain speed of succession, on the one hand; and if these represent elements of fracture of the normal development of life, they become 'emergencies', that is, problems to deal with. The latter, if frequent, can contribute to constituting a sort of fundamental uncertainty, which becomes difficult to counteract in the experience of daily migration.

One of the threads by which the 'emergency' is represented is undoubtedly the political macro-factor (in its double meaning of *policy and politics*), which thinks of and treats the immigrant as a problem and whose emergency approach does not only concern a set of practices, but is a strategy of control and at the same time of exclusion from access to material and symbolic rights and goods, helping to outline the meshes of the migratory possibilities and opportunities, within which people are allowed to move. As we have seen, 'allying' themselves with a movement that fights for the right to housing, the *rudari* have developed strategies to avoid institutionalisation, which have progressively allowed them to break away from welfare projects, entering and leaving where it was considered useful to do so for their contextual life situation.

In this sense, the use of social service resources (envisaged by the ordinary instruments of assistance or by specific projects, activated when the Authorities proceed with an eviction) is a possibility that families put in place, starting from their internal evaluations with respect to needs and necessities, in emergencies to be precise, which must be addressed in that specific situation.

With the expression 'emergency time', however, I want to indicate, rather, the time that accompanies a migration of the type I have outlined and that contributes to the construction of the sense I am talking about. It is a migration in which people's lives undergo changes even with respect to their close material conditions: the work that you do (e.g. a bricklayer for three weeks, then you remain unemployed and you look for another source of income), the place where you live (an occupation, a rental apartment, which almost always ends up with an eviction). The uncertainty of life in the place of immigration reinforces the certainty of the reasons for which we started. On the other hand, however, a definite uncertainty is also part of life in Romania, connected with work: there, worse than here, we 'invent' how to get by, and the gain is incomparable. It counteracts this multiple uncertainty, the deep built-in certainty of the family dimension, being within a dense family network, and of the cultural *desid-erata* connected to it: getting married, definitively becoming an adult with the birth of children, and fulfilling this last step through the construction of the house, which can be achieved, in this historical period, only by emigrating.

An elastic and multi-faceted time, then, emerges: between an uncertain present and a future supported by the very reasons for which they left, but characterised by a remarkable unpredictability.

The present is represented by everyday life. The future, in a narrower sense, can be the programming of things that will be done, shaping future daily lives: from having a *grătar* for Easter, to when we leave to go to Romania. This dimension has to do with a plurality of factors, over each of which people have different margins of manoeuvrability and which refer to different levels: from that of material resources (there is the money to buy meat or to leave) to that of family reciprocity (can activate the help of some family member; the level of the hierarchy between generations and between genders) – who can make the final decision; and, lastly, the order of priori-ties – what is more important to achieve.

As long as the framework of the elements that can contribute to the decision has not been clearly outlined, nothing can be said. But it is not a passive waiting, especially for men (who in many areas have greater deci-sion-making authority), it is only a putting in brackets of the decision, and the decision does not lose them in conjecture, but they try to remove the obstacles or – better – they try to *circumvent* the obstacles. The *rudari* know how to wait and if necessary, also how to weasel out of situations.

This future is nourished by daily movement and its fundamental moments of conviviality, which give rise to those of solidarity. Supported by kinship, understood as an element of social cohesion, time is lived in a 'relational' way, in which people and their relationships are at the centre. This connotation remains, even if the changes in migration often impose a reorganisation of daily life, especially for women if they work, but when they return to the context of origin for an even more limited period, this time is immediately resumed: in the morning they do the chores, they work, then they rest and then they go to visit or they receive visitors. They usually spend their evenings together. And the early morning (when they have coffee before starting their activities) and the evenings are the times when information and decisions circulate most.

If we observe what is happening in Romania, we can see that the approach to that near future, with all the decision-making circumstances I have outlined above, is the same. Could we, then, conjecture that the way of living, feeling and conceiving time, intimately connected to their socio-cul-tural architecture and to the material world, has produced in the long run a *culturally original* way of facing uncertainty? And that the migration is put in place as a *resource*? A resource in the sense that, with and in the migrations, the uncertainties multiply, since the context of arrival, to outline a new daily life, is objectively much more complex than that of departure and subjectively little known.

What they would propose is a very different approach from the one developed in the Western urban contexts of their arrival, where *programming-prevention* is, instead, a key element through which we approach the future. Appadurai calls it 'trajectorism', which has trapped the relationship between knowledge, imagination and the construction of the world, that is, 'the idea that time's arrow inevitably has a telos, and in that telos are to be found all the significant patterns of change, process, and history' (2013: 196), represented by the white West (Europe and the United States) and by the modernisation imposed worldwide. A clear example in this sense are the analyses of demographic behaviour, which are approached only by the Euro-Western model of the so-called second demographic transition, without attempting an understanding of the existence or otherwise of other avenues. And this, like so many other external gazes, scientific or political, that do not commit to 'discovering alternative sources of the always evolving European self, sources that might be more congenial to dialogue rather than dominion as a world strategy' (ibid.: 199), nor to understand, examine and be compared with other ideas of the good life.

And for 'a good life', in reference to a broader future, what do the members of our reference network foresee? As we were saying: to form a family, that is, to get married, to have children, to build a house. A future, therefore, that is anchored to an intimate cultural dimension, achieved through a series of constants that lend themselves to considerable flexibility; they are – we could say – 'flexible constants'. This future, which is difficult for external actors to understand, is not visible in the eyes of the services, as it is obscured by their own procedures, bureaucracy, parameters, and so on. Faced with uncertain migratory paths, social workers mix the logic of the services with the 'preventive' approach, ending up confronting people through a very distant category, that of the 'migration project', very unsuitable, and clashing with their way – not without difficulties – of 'celebrating' life.

> Decisions about where to 'invest', from a material and symbolic point of view, can become an area of negotiation or discussion in a situation characterised by scarce economic possibilities and precariousness. For many women in this situation, it becomes a priority to be able to build the basis for their own future and that of their children, to acquire something more than the economic capital represented by material objects, that is, a long-term symbolic capital.

Analysed from this point of view, virtual or physical movements between Morocco and Italy are not able to reconcile fractures, but seem, on the contrary, to exacerbate anxiety about the future and exacerbate the sense of insecurity and precariousness. Paradoxically, along with the desire to maintain intense relations with their country of origin, Moroccan women emphasise the need for territorialisation and stability. (Salih 2008: 107–108)

In interpreting the impact of transnationalism on people's lives we should therefore be careful not to emphasise a quantitative dimension, focusing on the number of times, frequency or speed with which migrants visit their country ..., at the expense of an analysis of the qualitative endeavour that every single visit involves in terms of negotiation of cultural and symbolic resources and, therefore, of repercussions that these connections have on the their lives ... For many of them [women], transnationalism means struggling to distribute resources evenly between Italy and Morocco, satisfying children's needs in Italy and relatives' expectations in Morocco, operating a balance between the desire to display their success in Morocco and the concrete requirements of everyday life in Italy. (Salih 2000: 69)

These words of Ruba Salih express with effective synthesis the position that many of the *rudari* women in our network experience. The more that the sense moves to the country of arrival, involving more and more areas of everyday life through which we trace our presence here, the more the contradictions increase. In this regard, Salih writes of paradoxes of transnationalism.

The thought of giving their children real possibilities for the future, starting from a longer school education, is an element that in some families is gaining weight. In these cases, the shift in meaning is remarkable because not only the resources but also the fulfilment of their own aspirations is in the country of immigration (the children live, grow up and study there).[12] However, this does not affect the adults' attachment to their country of origin or the possible development of a sense of belonging to the territory of immigration.

In the scheme proposed by Grillo (2008), built on the issue of attachment, as posed by Gledhill and reported above, many of our *rudari* families, settling in Florence, seem to fall within the 'scenario' of 'being in the middle' according to the 'reason' 'here *and* there', according to a stable double orientation in which transnational links are extremely important and maintained.

With respect to this scheme, with reference to the same family network and the same local context, interesting changes are recorded in some young people in their twenties, but especially in older children and adolescents (let's say from an age of ten) who have had all, or almost all, their school education in the migrant country. Changes that make us see investments differently from the adults toward their country of origin and the city where they live and have grown up. Their main relationships, including those with their peers, are located, at least for now, within the network of *rudari* families, but with a strong enlargement: through school, *in primis*, they experience other possible relationships, sometimes difficult and which suffer because they are influenced by widespread discrimination present both among the staff and among their classmates. The latter, at times, can lead to explicit attitudes of expulsion toward them. Girls and boys – like their peers who immigrate from other countries – experience the weight of the *difference* every day.

But in addition to these experiences of suffering, there are others of discovery, of amazement, of new encouragements. They, children and adolescents, are growing up in an environment outside the home that is strongly different from the *sat* in Romania. And even the domestic environment itself, although immersed in the dimension of the family network, it goes without saying, presents new, changed features.

Raluca has decided to marry Ionathan, from a Pentecostal family. Although her mother advised her against it, the girl – little more than twenty years old – stops attending the study course she had undertaken because it is her/their intention to have their first child immediately after the marriage.

However, Raluca and Ionathan introduce a significant novelty: the *nuntă* – the celebration and the wedding feast – for the first time takes place in Italy. We must ask ourselves, therefore, why the two young people decide to marry in Florence, when the *rudari* of their family network attend their marriage, the same ones who would have been present in Romania if it had been celebrated there.[13]

It wouldn't have been so much the guests who changed, as the venue. Therefore it is the place as such, and the practices connected to it, that have prevailed for the newlyweds, also receiving their parents' consent. As for all spouses, therefore, also for Raluca and Ionathan the photos were taken in front of the Cathedral of Santa Maria del Fiore and at the Piazzale Michelangelo.

Among the differences that the new generations begin to experience and that have to do with the development of the sense of belonging to the territory in which one lives and grows up, there is a specific one that concerns the perception of the *beauty* of the places. Detected in different ways by the young and the very young *rudari*, and felt as an added value, it also enters into the shift of meaning. We could ask ourselves about the passage from the perception of this beauty, to that of experiencing it until we feel it is our own. How to make it accessible to these *new* inhabitants, what possible basin from which to draw symbolic resources. The process of expulsion from the city centres, from the artistic heritage, and therefore from *beauty*, does not only affect the bodies, but also – to be precise – the sense: it is the constant attempt to leave or make the constitutive beauty of that heritage foreign, unreachable, 'non-thinkable', something that does not belong to *them*, to the *others*, which they cannot and must not access.[14]

Notes

1. Huts or pit-houses fully or semi recessed into the earth (see also Part I, chapters 1 and 2).
2. 'The question of meaning, that is, of the means by which human beings who inhabit a social space agree on the way to represent it and act within it, constitutes the horizon of the anthropological process' (Augé and Colleyn 2004: 17–18).
3. The inscription affixed by the occupiers – most of whom are represented by the *rudari* I have referred to (see chapter 8) – seems to me to be a dense synthesis, elaborated from within, that is, from the experience of immigrants and with an immediate language – of the difference between the 'double absence' (Sayad 1999) and what, by opposition, has been defined as the potential 'double presence' (see Riccio 2008).
4. One could imagine this process through a slow, difficult and contradictory construction of a new bell tower of Marcellinara. The latter is a famous metaphor among *Italian Studies*, used by Ernesto de Martino – from an experience of his own during his fieldwork in 1950's Calabria – to indicate the *existential homeland* (2002: 480–81): 'Surely our presence becomes at risk when it touches the limit of its existential homeland, when it loses its "bell tower of Marcellinara"'(ibid.: 481). See also the two recent translations of de Martino's works: *Magic: A Theory from the South*, translated and annotated by D.L. Zinn (2015) and *La fin du monde. Essai sur les apocalypses culturelles*, translated and annotated by G. Charuty, D. Fabre and M. Massenzio (2016).
5. Reference is made to Gramsci's notion of 'molecular', for which see Debenedetti 1972 (and previously 'Gramsci, uomo classico', *L'Unità*, 22 May 1947) and, among the numerous and most recent references, the entry 'Molecolare' of the Gramscian Dictionary edited by Forenza. In Pizza we find an interpretation of the notion starting from an anthropological approach, emphasising that: 'Gramsci looks at the term "molecular" for the possibility it offers of referring to the minimum unit of life experience, to the immediate detail drawn from daily life. It is a word-bridge between politics and the body' (2012: 98).
6. Obesity – in our case, in a migratory context – is a phenomenon closely related to social inequalities, as public health scholars have long demonstrated. Obesity and tobacco smoking are the two risk factors on which chronic diseases (cardiovascular diseases, cancer, chronic respiratory diseases and diabetes) are based: 'This is the substance: when it came to tackling the prevention of infectious diseases, the public health system had at its side several "friendly" sectors such as education, housing, nutrition, water and hygiene; local administrations and national governments intervened, planned, issued rules and laws. Faced with chronic diseases, there are few, if any, "friendly" sectors around, while the global scene is occupied by actors who derive enormous profits from the trade in tobacco and unhealthy food products, in the silence and inertia often complicit with governments' (Maciocco and Santamauro,

2014, chap. 5). When, in Sibu Mare, I spoke with some *rudari*, who had been to Italy (Florence) and England (Birmingham): on two occasions they gave me the same explanation as to why they gain weight abroad: 'It's the air. Here there's the sea, the air is dry. There [abroad, where they have been] it is different'.

7. In Taraki, ed. (2006).

8. In our case we have seen other matrimonial 'rules' (see chapter 1).

9. Economically, too. As Karl Polanyi wrote in *The Economy as Instituted Process* (2011), behaviours of reciprocity between individuals integrate the economy only if symmetrically organised structures exist, such as symmetrical systems formed by groups of relatives.

10. E.g. Dana turning to me, a few years ago: 'but how can you be [live] alone? I really can't imagine … *mamma mia!*'; or Ionica about my mum: 'what is she doing at home alone?' A passage from Martin Block comes to mind: 'They fear only two things: being alone and falling ill' (1936: 181).

11. The issue of health is a partial exception, linked to the possibility of treatments that in Romania are precluded both for economic reasons and due to the racism to which they may be subjected; that can become the main reason for the decision to emigrate, where the health problem is very serious, such as the presence of disabilities or degenerative diseases. As political philosophers have noted (e.g. Balibar), in a complex relationship between law and territory, nationality completely replaces territoriality.

12. This parental aspiration not only gives a new meaning to their presence in the country of immigration, but can also affect changes with respect to other dimensions of the children's life, such as reproduction, with an increase in the age of marriage and of having the first child.

13. To whom still others would be added. Also, as an Italian, I was the only one at the dinner; and during the day, besides me, there was only one other person present.

14. The historical-artistic heritage, understood as a living work of art, present in its historical generating power, is also weakened, deprived of its transforming force (it therefore becomes more and more a form and less a content; when emptied it becomes the aesthetic satisfaction of the hegemonic classes and at the same time a commodity).

Chapter 15

ETHNOGRAPHIC *MORCEAU*

Seven Sisters

Dana, Raluca, Iuliana, Izabela, Estera, Pauna and Sorina are seven sisters. They live in Florence and are the great-granddaughters of the *rudari lingurari* 'nine sisters'.

Dana, the eldest, is thirty-three years old; Sorina, the youngest, sixteen.

Her hair tied, busy from morning to night looking after the house and family, Dana takes care of everything and everyone. Her first two children have gone to pre-school and, soon, the third will also begin. 'As a child, I went with my grandmother to the market, to sell the geese and other animals', she tells me. 'I helped my grandmother, I helped my mother, I cleaned, I fed the children [her younger sisters and brothers]. As soon as I turned eighteen, my father took me to Italy.' Her Romanian has the specific sound of the *rudar* dialect.

'I met Mihai at the pool, but do you know I thought he was Moldovan?' Dana ran away with Mihai, but he had to return to the construction site; his parents were not in Florence, the families could not meet, the couple did not ask for forgiveness as would have been expected: Dana returned to her parents' house alone and her mother accused her of being a bad girl – there and then she did not even want to let her in. It would take a little time to put all this right.

Crossing worlds, Dana has become increasingly competent in dealing with life in an urban context. Once she left her first job, which lasted a few years and which placed her in a situation of greater isolation, she began to use the family grapevine concerning possible resources and the indications of the consultation centres scattered around the city; she quickly learned to travel on the urban transport network, to deal with the territorial services and it is was she who enrolled her sisters in school.

Dana attended evening classes and took her secondary school diploma; She took the driving licence test, mastered more and more Italian and local expressions, until she became very competent. After the birth of her children, she no longer accepted jobs that occupied her all day. 'You see, I learned, I do like my aunt who works for many families', she explained. She built relationships with some Italian ladies who called her for household chores; and together with relatives followed a course for Social Welfare Operators. 'Ah, Sabrina, problems here [in Florence], problems at home [in Romania]: my grandmother is ill, my uncle has hepatitis', she tells me. 'We took out a loan for the house [built in Romania]; we have to pay the bills for that, the bills here, all the expenses, Sara's school … Now that Rachel can start at pre-school, I want to find work in some facility, otherwise how can I manage?! I have to work!'

Raluca got married, leaving her studies. Her mother did not agree with this: 'She wanted it this way', commented Ionica, 'now it does not concern me'. The couple spoke to both of their parents, got engaged and shortly afterwards celebrated their marriage with the Pentecostal rite. Raluca went to live with her in-laws and after a few months she was expecting her first child. Catalin finished high school in Florence and started working. Raluca, on the other hand, stayed at home, helping her mother-in-law with her younger children. With the first money put aside, they immediately thought of building a house in Badra, the Romanian village where Catalin comes from. The latter, over the years, managed to get an excellent job; Raluca always stayed at home with her children and her Italian got a little worse. The family nucleus rented a house on its own. Raluca followed the children's education, all the health aspects, becoming good at the digital technology required to access services and so on. 'We have to move house, this one is too small, it's damp, and it's bad for the children. We are looking; however, we want it in another municipality, closer to where Catalin works', she explained. 'I tell you the truth, we are thinking of buying a house, if they give us a mortgage. The rents are expensive; if they give us a mortgage we will buy a four-bedroom house'.

Iuliana was a child when she was brought to Italy. She had started school in Romania and, except for a brief interlude, continued her schooling in Florence, where she graduated. She started working, but after some experiences in cleaning cooperatives, she resolutely decided not to accept other jobs of that type. She has been engaged for a few years and has temporarily returned to Romania to help her grandmother who has gone through a period of very poor health. There she began to sew clothes and is thinking about how to put her aptitudes and studies between Italy and Romania to good use. She was not the main child in the family who was involved in the chores and care of younger brothers and sisters, which allowed her to have more time for herself than her other sisters.

I look at her drawings that she had done for me when, as a child, she was at the occupation of the former Luzzi. I look at the photographs of the little sisters with their younger brother in the snow. Many years had gone by. 'Yes, I'm getting married, maybe in Romania, I don't know yet. Maybe in Florence. Ionel has his parents and a house in Sibu Mare'.

I take Izabela and Estera to see the preview of the film 'Fuori campo', at the circle of San Bartolo in Cintoia. At the end of the film, Eli comments that it should be shown in the schools; she said: 'they [her classmates, teachers] do not realise', and she added: 'It is not enough to hear it, they must see'. At the time, five years ago, the two girls were in middle school. In their expressions there was all the weight of living in a reception facility, of perceiving the differences that, thin as pins, slip into the fabric of their daily lives. Estera told me that for her mother it was not a problem if she could not buy things for school: 'she only says: "I don't have money, I can't", she doesn't make it a problem because she doesn't have money'. Izabela went even further by asserting that her mother did not understand. I rebuked them both, drawing their attention to the diversity of the context in which their parents grew up and lived for a long time. It is a question that will return often, this of the inter-generational relationship, with moments of anger on the part of the girls, of increased misunderstandings.

When older, they managed to pay attention to my words, to see more that their mother stayed in Italy to give them chances that they would not have had in Romania. Izabela went through difficult years: one year she managed to catch up at school, the next she did not. She went out in the evening secretly, established her first romantic relationships with boys who were not *rudari* and not Romanian, of whom she said nothing, only some remarks to Estera; I helped her with her studies, but I was not quite part of her daily life. I found out many things later.

Estera was more reflective, although sometimes she came up with exclamations like: 'I hate Italians.' At the high school she found professors who valued her a lot and she was committed and thought about what she would do 'when she grew up': 'I want to work a bit, I have kept in touch with the restaurants and bars where I did the internships and where I have done many evenings [of work]. I put some money away and then I will enrol in an institute to specialise in my field'. Sweatshirt, long gathered hair darting out from her hood, she sat in the sun with me nearby. She was very beautiful, but she'd put on weight: 'I know, I eat badly, and then I put my head into this too!' When I accompanied her home, she told me about the boyfriend she had recently left, disappointed by his 'superficial' behaviour. And I thought of Dana's words a few days earlier: 'I told Estera, "think about studying, you don't want to find yourself with a child to raise and without a job?!"' The girl hugged me and told me that next time we would go for a walk in the Cascine. I answered that I would wait for her at home, where she knew that in a few months she could come to prepare for her high school exam.

Pauna and Sorina were already teenagers; I had seen very little of them in recent years and still their image for me was that of two little girls, but they were two tall girls, who were becoming women. They shyly greeted me when they looked into the kitchen, where I was having lunch and chatting with their mother, Dana, and a relative of theirs who had stopped by. I congratulated Ionica on her progress in Italian, which had improved considerably since she began work in a canteen. We started laughing and remembered that everyone in the family always made fun of her for this: 'They [Pauna and Sorina]', Ionica informed me, 'when we go to the doctor they tell me, "don't say anything, I'll do the talking", understand what they say to me!?'

Pauna had just taken a shower and let her hair air-dry as she sat with a book at the edge of the condominium garden. She told me that there are too many people in the house and that she often got headaches because she had a hard time concentrating, so when it was nice weather, she started studying outside. Sorina, who had heard, teased her, but then turned to me and told me that she was right and that there was little room for everyone. They often came back from school, helped their mother, stopped for groceries or cleaned the house. Sometimes they went to the library. 'Do you like it here?' I asked. They shrugged a little, for a moment their gaze and breaths were suspended. They both smiled at me. Dana came out with little Rachel, Sorina went up to her and took her in her arms; Pauna started playing with them. The young aunts and granddaughter had fun in the garden: 'It's nice here, this is a home', the girls told me.

Conclusion

AN OPEN FIELD

The *Rudari* and Brâncuşi

A few days ago (December 2020), I came to see Dana, who was home alone with the youngest child. Like every time, she presented me with the coffee cups already on the table: mine with a saucer and hers without. And I, as always, took it off. A small ritual for which we laughed, intertwining words and now familiar gestures.

On her mobile phone, she showed me her Facebook account, with wedding photos of her cousin Alina, uncle Valeriu's daughter. 'But it's wonderful!' I exclaimed. 'Yes', said Dana, 'and she is very well, she works at the McDonald's that they opened in Medgidia'.

'The party', she told me, 'was wonderful … See?' Dana scrolled through the photos, gave me the phone, magnified the images, while she showed me all the people I haven't seen in a few years, the children who have grown up and the newborns. Then she updated me on the health of her relatives and repeated to me how lucky they were to be here: the pandemic has affected the country a lot and three *rudari* aged between 40 and 50 years, who I also knew at the time, died from health complications caused by Covid-19.

Then I asked her how her mother's cousin, Sandra, was and her husband, Florentin. A few years ago, he had said to me: 'Sabrina, go to Romania, you need to know. *Rudari* and Romanians are another race. *Rudari* if they have something, they give it to you from their heart; it has always been like this: for my father, my grandfather, my grandfather's father; they give it to you from their heart, understand? [A *rudar*] looks at how you are inside, not how you are outside. Romanians, on the other hand, look at you outside. If you are darker, then they call you 'ugly', [for example]: me, Ionica, they

212 • Other Borders

see [that] we are brown, so …' And then he added straight after: 'You were lucky, you entered Romania with Ionica'.

Florentin is very proud to be *rudar* and – as Aurel had already told me a few years before: 'See, even Brâncuși, Costantin Brâncuși, the greatest sculptor, was *rudar*. Brâncuși made wood carvings that were alive.'

Florentin's words echo in my mind, and marry those of Stelu and Aurel, who many times have brought my attention to the origin of Brâncuși; they became confused in the morning light at Târgu Jiu, when I walked from *Coloana fără sfârșit* (Infinite Column), along *Calea Eroilor* (Heroes' Way), to get to *Poarta sărutului* (Kissing Gate), past it and reach *Masa tăcerii* (Table of Silence).[1]

I mention it to Dana, who is now preparing lunch. She looks at me and says: 'You have to go back to Romania! As soon as possible, come with us this summer.'

'Yes, it's been four years now', I tell her. 'I have to come to Sibu Mare, Vadrea, and Burdu … And I have to go back to Brâncuși. Estera could come with me!' I had left Ionica's house in Sibu Mare to go to Craiova and from there, then to Târgu Jiu. Upon my return, I immediately wrote a research project that explored the oral sources of the sculptor's *rudari* origin, analysing his writings and works through interdisciplinary methods. 'Wait!' I say to Dana. I open the computer and go through the files as if they were notes: 'There it is! Look: the case of Brancusi is a demonstration of the blurred line of the socio-cultural boundaries and how these are the result of a relationship process. (The very name Brancusi: his name was Brâncuși [briŋ'kuʃi] – "Je suis Brâncuși", David Lewis recalled from his first encounter with the artist – but all over the world he is known as Brancusi). Brancusi offers to cross all kinds of borders, not only geographical, historical or formal, but also cultural and what is called "ethnic"'. I say it with such emphasis and satisfaction that Dana turns around, leaves the spoon, looks at me and starts laughing: 'Did you write it?' 'Oh, yes, of course', I answer. 'Afterwards you must explain it to me because you write too difficult, but, sorry, I have to tell you: *esti nebună*! (you are crazy)'.

Note

1. This is the monumental complex of Târgu Jiu created by Brâncuși and inaugurated in October 1938.

REFERENCES

Achim, Viorel. 2004a. *Documente privind deportarea țiganilor în Transnistria*. Bucharest: Editura Enciclopedică.

———. 2004b. 'The Gypsies in the Romanian Principalities: The Emancipation Law, 1831–1856'. *Historical Yearbook* I: 93–120.

———. 2007. 'Romanian Public Reaction to the Deportation of Gypsies to Transnistria'. In *The Roma: A Minority in Europe: Historical, Political and Social Perspectives*, 89–102. Budapest: Central European University Press.

Achim, Viorel and Constantin Iordachi. 2004. *România și Transnistria. Problema holocaustului*. Bucharest: Curtea Veche.

Alexa-Morcov, Florin. 2013. 'Stratégies identitaires d'une minorité au statut ambigu. Les Rudari d'Islaz, Roumanie'. In *Endoétrangers. Exclusion, reconnaissance et expérience des Rroms et gens du voyage en Europe*, ed. Kàtia Lurbe i Puerto and Frédéric Le Marcis, 223–42. Louvain-la-Neuve: L'Harmattan-Academia.

American Journal of Comparative Law. 1997. 45 (2), 'Symposium on Gypsy Law'.

Anghel, Remus Gabriel. 2013. *Romanians in Western Europe: Migration, Status Dilemmas, and Transnational Connections*, Plymouth (UK): Lexington Books.

Antolini, Paola. 1989. *Los agotes. Historia de una exclusión*. Madrid: Istmo.

Appadurai, Arjun. 2013. *The Future as Cultural Fact: Essays on the Global Condition*. London: Verso.

Asséo, Henriette, Petre Petcuț and Leonardo Piasere. 2017. 'Romania's Roma. A Socio-Historical Overview'. In *Open Borders, Unlocked Cultures*, ed. Yaron Matras and Daniel Victor Leggio, 26–56. London-New York: Routledge.

Augé, Marc and Jean-Paul Colleyn. 2004. *L'antropologie*. Paris: PUF.

Basciani, Antonio. 2001. *Un conflitto balcanico. La contesa fra Bulgaria e Romania in Dobrugia del Sud. 1918–1940*. Cosenza: Periferia.

———. 2009. 'Il trattato di Craiova del 7 settembre 1940 e gli scambi di popolazione tra la Romania e la Bulgaria (1940–1943)'. *Geschichte und Region/Storia e regione; Spostamenti forzati di popolazioni in Europa 1939–1955*, XVIII (2): 155–76.

Benarrosh-Orsoni, Norah. 2019. *La maison double. Lieux, routes et objets d'une migration*. Nanterre: Société d'ethnologie.

Bengelstorf, Jens. 2009. *Die 'anderen Zigeuner'. Zur Ethnizität des Rudari und Bajeschi in Südosteuropa*. Leipzig: Eudora-Verlag.

Block, Martin. 1936. *Moeurs et coutumes des tziganes*. Paris: Payot.

————. 1991 (original edn 1923). *Die materielle Kultur der rumänischen Zigeuner*. Frankfurt am Main: Peter Lang.

Boccagni, Paolo. 2017. *Migration and the Search for Home: Mapping Domestic Space in Migrants' Everyday Lives*. London: Palgrave Macmillan.

Boccagni Paolo and Jan Willem Duyvendak. 2020. 'Making Home'. In *Pragmatic Inquiry: Critical Concepts for Social Sciences*, ed. John R. Bowen, Nicolas Dodier, Jan Willem Duyvendak and Anita Hardon. London: Routledge.

Bonfanti, Sara and Luis Eduardo Pérez Murcia, eds. 2023. *Finding Home in Europe: Chronicles of Global Migrants*. New York-London: Berghahn.

Bouras, Alain. 2018. *La civilisation des clairières. Enquête sur la civilisation de l'arbre en Roumanie. Ethnoécologie, technique et symbolique dans les forêts des Carpates*, avant-propos de P.-H. Stahl. Besançon: Presses universitaires de Franche-Comté.

Buchowski, Michal. 2001. *Rethinking Transformation: An Anthropological Perspective on Post-Socialism*. Poznań: Humaniora.

Burawoy, Michael and Katherine Verdery. 1999. *Uncertain Transition: Ethnographies of Change in the Postsocialist World*. Washington, DC: Rowman & Littlefield.

Çaglar, Ayse and Nina Glick Schiller. 2018. *Migrants and City-Making: Dispossession, Displacement, and Urban Regeneration*. Durham, NC: Duke University Press.

Calotă, Ion. 1974. *Graiul rudarilor din Oltenia. Rezumatul tezei de doctorat*. Craiova: Sectorul de reprografie al Centrului de științe sociale.

————. 1995. *Rudarii din Oltenia. Studiu din dialectologie și de geografie lingvistica româneasca*. Craiova: Sibila.

————. 1996. 'Elemente sud-dunărene în graiul rudarilor din Oltenia', *Dacoromania*, serie nouă, II: 47–51.

Cartwright Andrew L. 2001. *The Return of the Peasant: Land Reform in Post-Communist Romania*. Dartmouth: Ashgate.

Chelcea, Ion. 1943. 'Les Rudari de Muscel. Contribution à l'étude des Tziganes'. *Archives pour la science et la réforme sociales*, 16 (1–4): 81–130.

————. 1944a. *Țiganii din România: monografie etnografică*. Bucharest: Institutul Central de Statistică.

————. 1944b. *Contribuție la o 'enigmă' etnografică*. Bucharest: Casa Școalelor.

————. 1969. 'Rudarii de pe Valea Dunării (între cursul inferior al Oltului și Mostiștei)'. *Comunicări. Seria Etnografică*, III: 3–37.

Cherata, Lucian. 2015 (original edn 2008). 'Cine sunt rudari'. *Arhivă Linguistică*, 4. https://limbaromana.org/revista/cine-sunt-rudarii/#.

Citzer, Laura Diana. 2012. *Toponimia județului Tulcea. Considerații sincronice și diacronice*. Bucharest: Editura Lumen.

Coleman, Simon, and Rosalind I.J. Hackett. 2015. *The Anthropology of Global Pentecostalism and Evangelicalism*. New York: New York University Press.

Constantin, Marin. 2016. 'Arta cioplirii lemnului la rudarii din Băbeni (județul Vâlcea)'. In *Antropologie și spiritualitate*, ed. Andrei Kozma, Cristiana Glavce and Costantin Bălăceanu-Stolnici, 186–201. Bucharest: Editura Academiei Române.

Costescu Angela. 2013. 'Marginalizare socială în cazul unei comunități de rudari din județul Gorj, România, in *Terra Sebus. Acta Musei Sabesiensis*, 5: 547–59.

————. 2015. *Autoidentificare și heteroidentificare etnică în cazul rudarilor și băieșilor, Teză de Doctorat*. Cluj-Napoca: Universitatea 'Babeș-Bolyai'.

Cvajner, Martina. 2018. *Sociologia delle migrazioni femminili. L'esperienza delle donne post-sovietiche*. Bologna: Il Mulino.

Dalakoglou, Dimitris. 2010. 'Migrating-Remitting-Building'-Dwelling: House-Making as "Proxy" Presence in Postsocialist Albania'. *Journal of the Royal Anthropological Institute*, 16 (4): 761–77.

Davis, Chris R. 2019. 'The Moldavian Csangos as Subculture: A Case of Ethnic, Linguistic and Cultural Hybridity'. In *Identities In-Between in East-Central Europe*, ed. Jan Fellerer, Robert Pyrah and Marius Turda, 110–29. London: Routledge.

Debenedetti, Giacomo. 1972. 'Il metodo di Antonio Gramsci'. In *Rinascita-Il contemporaneo*, 39, 6 ottobre 1972: 15–19.

Deleuze, Gilles. 1989. 'Qu'est-ce qu'un dispositif?' In *Michel Foucault philosophe*, Rencontre internationale Paris 9, 10, 11 Janvier 1988. Paris: Éditions du Seuil.

de Martino, Ernesto. 2002. *La fine del mondo*, 2nd edn (original edn 1977). Torino: Einaudi.

———. 2016 (original edn 1977). *La fin du monde. Essai sur les apocalypses culturelles*, translated and annotated by G. Charuty, D. Fabre and M. Massenzio. Paris: *Éditions EHESS*.

———. 2015 (original edn 1959). *Magic: A Theory from the South*, translated and annotated by D.L. Zinn. Chicago: HAU Books.

Diminescu, Dana. 2003. *Visibles mais peu nombreux. Les circulations migratoires roumaines*. Paris: Éditions de la Maison des sciences de l'homme.

Dorondel, Ştefan. 2007. 'Ethnicity, State and Access to Natural Resources in Southeastern Europe: The Rudari Case'. In *Transborder Identities. The Romanian-Speaking Population in Bulgaria*, ed. Stelu Şerban, 215–39. Bucharest: Paideia.

———. 2008. '"They Should Be Killed": Forest Restitution, Ethnic Groups and Patronage in Postsocialist Romania'. In *The Rights and Wrongs of Land Restitution*, ed. Derrick Fay and Deborah James, 43–65. New York: Routledge-Cavendish.

———. 2016. *Disrupted Landscapes: State, Peasants and the Politics of Land in Postsocialist Romania*. New York-London: Berghahn.

Dumitru, Speranta. 2014. 'From "Brain Drain" to "Care Drain": Women's Labor Migration and Methodological Sexism'. *Women's Studies International Forum*, 47: 203–12.

Études Tsiganes; L'esclavage des Rroms, 29, 2007.

Faso, Giuseppe. 2010. *Lessico del razzismo democratico*, 2nd edn. Rome: Derive Approdi.

Favell, Adrian. 2015. *Immigration, Integration and Mobility: New Agendas in Migration Studies. Essays 1998–2014*. Colchester: ECPR Press.

Fay, Derick and Deborah James, eds. 2008. *The Rights and Wrongs of Land Restitution*. New York: Routledge-Cavendish.

Filipescu, Teodor. 1906. *Coloniile române din Bosnia. Studio etnografic şi antropogeografic*. Bucharest: Ediţiunea Academiei Române.

Fondazione Michelucci. 2010. *L'abitare di Rom e Sinti in Toscana. Rapporto 2010*, ed. S. Tosi Cambini, research supervisor N. Solimano, Fondazione Michelucci, Regione Toscana, www.michelucci.it.

———. 2014. *Case e non case. Povertà abitative in toscana*. Firenze: Seid.

Forenza, Eleonora. 2009. 'Molecolare'. In *Dizionario gramsciano, 1926–1937*, ed. Guido Liguori and Pasquale Voza. Rome: Carocci.

Foszto, László. 2009. *Ritual Revitalisation after Socialism: Community, Personhood, and Conversion among Roma in a Transylvanian Village*. Berlin: LIT-Verlag.

Fosztó, László and Dénes Kiss. 2012. 'Pentecostalism in Romania: The Impact of Pentecostal Communities on the Life-Style of the Members'. *Erreffe La Ricerca Folklorica*, 65: 51–64.

Fotino, Dionisie. 1859. *Istoria generala a Daciei*. Bucharest: Imprimeria naţională a lui Iosef Romanov et Companie.

Foucault, Michel. 1982. 'Space, Knowledge, and Power', interview with Paul Rabinow. *Skyline* March 1982: 16–20; republished in *The Foucault Reader*, ed. Paul Rabinow, 1984. New York: Pantheon.

———. 2002. *Spazi Altri. I luoghi delle eterotopie*, ed. Salvo Vaccaro, Milan: Mimesis (from M. Foucault, *Dits et écrits*, ed. D. Defert, F. Ewald. Paris, Gallimard, 1994, vol. I: 407–12; vol. IV: 752–62; vol. II: 447–56; vol. IV: 270–85).

Ghodsee, Kristen. 2010. *Muslim Lives in Eastern Europe: Gender, Ethnicity, and the Transformation of Islam in Postsocialist Bulgaria*. Princeton, NJ: Princeton University Press.

Glick Schiller, Nina, Linda Basch and Cristina Blanc-Szanton, eds. 1992. 'Towards a Transnational Perspective on Migration: Race, Class, Ethnicity and Nationalism Reconsidered'. Annals of the New York Academy of Science, 645 (1): 1–258.

Grillo, Ralph. 2008. 'Riflessioni sull'approccio transnazionale alle migrazioni'. In *Migrazioni transnazionali dall'Africa. Etnografie a confronto*, ed. Bruno Riccio. Turin: UTET.

———. 2015. *Living with Difference: Essays on Transnationalism and Multiculturalism*. University of Sussex, CDE.

Gunder Frank, Andre. 1991. 'Transitional Ideological Modes: Feudalism, Capitalism, Socialism'. *Critique of Anthropology*, 11 (2): 171–88.

Holsapple, Christiana. 2022. 'Bordering and Strategic Belonging in Gagauzia', *Journal of Borderlands Studies*, 37 (5): 935–53.

IOM (International Organization for Migration). 2007. *German Forced Labour Compensation Programme (GFLCP)*, document, https://www.iom.int/files/live/sites/iom/files/What-We-Do/docs/German-Forced-Labour-Compensation-Programme-GFLCP.pdf.

Iordachi, Costantin and Dorin Dobrincu, eds. 2009. *Transforming Peasants, Property and Power: The Collectivization of Agriculture in Romania, 1949–1962*. Budapest: Central European Press.

Kahl, Thede. 2002. 'The Ethnicity of Aromanians after 1990: The Identity of a Minority that Behaves like a Majority', *Ethnologia balkanica*, 6: 145–69.

Kahl, Thede and Ioana Nechiti. 2019. *The Boyash in Hungary: A Comparative Study among the Arğeleni and Munćeni Communities*. Vienna: Austrian Academy of Sciences.

Kligman, Gail and Katherine Verdery. 2011. *Peasants under Siege: The Collectivization of Romanian Agriculture, 1949–1962*. Princeton: Princeton University Press.

Kogălniceanu, Mihail. 1976 (1837), *Esquisse sur l'histoire, le moeurs et la langue des cigains*. In *Opere*, ediție critică publicată sub îngrijirea lui Dan Simonescu. Bucharest: Editura Academiei Republicii Socialiste România.

Kürti, László and Peter Skalník, eds. 2009. *Postsocialist Europe: Anthropological Perspectives from Home*. New York-London: Berghahn.

Maciocco, Gavino and Francesca Santamauro. 2014. *La salute globale. Determinanti sociali e disuguaglianze*. Rome: Carocci.

Magris, Claudio. *Danubio*. Milano: Garzanti.

Marcetti, Corrado and Sabrina Tosi Cambini. 2013. 'Urban Places and Public Space: The Luzzi Case Study'. *Planum. The Journal of Urbanism*; *Living Landscapes (Landscapes for Living) Policies, Practice*, 27 (2).

Marcetti, Corrado, Giancarlo Paba, Annalisa Pecoriello and Sabrina Tosi Cambini. 2011. 'L'ex-sanatorio Luzzi nel comune di Sesto Fiorentino. Racconto di un'esperienza, tra emergenza abitativa, progettualità sociale e impotenza delle politiche istituzionali'. In *Housing Frontline. Inclusione sociale e processi di autocostruzione e autorecupero*, ed. Corrado Marcetti, Giancarlo Paba, Anna Lisa Pecoriello and Nicola Solimano, 169–209. Florence: Firenze University Press.

Marshall, Ruth. 2009. *Political Spiritualities: The Pentecostal Revolution in Nigeria*. Chicago: University of Chicago Press.

Marushiakova, Elena and Veselin Popov. 1997. *Gypsies (Roma) in Bulgaria*. Frankfurt am Main: Peter Lang.

———. 2013. '"Gypsy" Groups in Eastern Europe: Ethnonyms vs. Professionyms'. *Romani Studies*, 23 (1): 61–82.

———. 2016. 'Identity and Language of the Roma (Gypsies) in Central and Eastern Europe'. In *The Palgrave Handbook of Slavic Languages, Identities and Borders*, ed. Tomasz Kamusella, Motoki Nomachi and Catherine Gibson, 26–54. Basingstoke-New York: Palgrave Macmillan.

———. 2021. 'Who Are "Oamenii Noştri" (Our People)? Rudari, Lingurari, Boyash and their Identities'. In *Boyash Studies: Researching 'Our People'*, ed. Annemarie Sorescu-Marinković, Thede Kahl and Biljana Sikimić, 37–74. Berlin: Frank & Timme Verlag für wissenschaftliche Literatur.

Mladenov, Maxim. 1993. *Bulgarskite govori v Rumunija*, Izdatelstvo na. Sofija: BAN.

———. 2007. 'Vlach Population in Bulgaria: Distribution, Origins and Toponymy'. In *Transborder Identities. The Romanian Speaking Population in Bulgaria*, ed. Stelu Şerban, 13–56. Bucharest: Paideia.

Nieto, Alejandro Miranda, Aurora Massa and Sara Bonfanti. 2022, *Ethnographies of Home and Mobility in Europe: A Theoretical Approach to Shifting Roofs*, 2nd edn. London: Routledge.

Neagota, Ileana and Bogdan Benga. 2016. 'The Healing Gurban: On the Trace of the Rudari from Southern Romania'. *Transylvanian Review*, 25 (1): 74–94.

Nicolăescu-Plopşor, Costantin S. 1922. 'Gurbanele'. *Arhivele Olteniei*, I (1): 35–40.

ni Shuinéar, Sinéad. 2005. 'Viaggatori irlandesi. Una cultura anti-gerarchia'. In *La dipendenza. Antropologia delle relazioni di dominio*, ed. Pier Giorgio Solinas, 335–43. Lecce: Argo.

Petcuţ, Petre. 2015. *Rromii. Sclavie şi libertate*. Bucharest: Centrul Naţional de Cultură a Romilor.

Pétonnet, Colette. 2002. *On est tout dans le brouillard*, Réédition *établie* et présentée par C. Choron-Baix. Paris: *Éd.* du CTHS.

Petrovici, Emil. 1938. '"Românii" din Serbia Occidentală. In *Dacoromania*, IX: 224–36.

Piasere, Leonardo. 1995. *Comunità girovaghe, comunità zingare*. Napoli: Liguori.

———. 2005. 'La schiavitù dei rom in Moldavia'. In *La dipendenza. Antropologia delle relazioni di dominio*, ed. Pier Giorgio Solinas, 289–331. Lecce: Argo.

———. 2015. *Mariages romanès. Une esquisse comparative*. Seid: Firenze.

Piasere, Leonardo, Nicola Solimano and Sabrina Tosi Cambini, eds. 2014. *Wor(l)ds Which Exclude: The Housing Issue of Roma, Gypsies and Travellers in the Language of the Acts and the Administrative Documents in Europe*. Fiesole: Fondazione Michelucci Press.

Pizza, Giovanni. 2012. 'Second Nature: On Gramsci's Anthropology'. *Anthropology and Medicine*, 19 (1): 95–106.

Polanyi, Karl. 2011. 'The Economy as Instituted Process'. *In The Sociology of Economic Life*, ed. Mark Granovetter and Richard Svedberg, 3rd edn, 3–21. New York-London: Routledge.

Poli, Roberto. 2014. 'Anticipation: A New Thread for the Human and Social Sciences?' *CADMUS*, 2 (3), part 1: 23–36.

Popp Serboianu, Calinic J. 1930. Les Tsiganes. Histoire - Ethnographie - Linguistique - Grammaire - Dictionnaire. Paris: Payot.

Promitzer, C. 2009. 'Small is Beautiful: The Issue of Hidden Minorities in Central Europe and the Balkans'. In *(Hidden) Minorities: Language and Ethnic Identity between Central Europe and the Balkans*, ed. C. Promitzer, K.-J. Hermanik and E. Staudinger, 80–88. Berlin: LIT.

Raţ, Cristina. 2018. 'Social Citizenship at the Margins'. In *Racialized Labour in Romania: Spaces of Marginality at the Periphery of Global Capitalism*, ed. Enikő Vincze, Norbert Petrovici, Cristina Raţ and Giovanni Picker, 97–121. Cham: Palgrave Macmillan.

Riccio, Bruno, ed. 2008. *Migrazioni transnazionali dall'Africa. Etnografie a confronto*. Turin: UTET.

———, ed. 2019. *Mobilità. Incursioni etnografiche*. Milano: Mondadori.

Robbins, Joel. 2004. *Becoming Sinners: Christianity and Moral Torment in a Papua New Guinea Society*. Berkeley: University of California Press.

Rubiolo, Cecilia. 2016. 'The Ambivalent Autonomy of Mobile "Pocăiți" between Vicovu De Sus, Romania and Turin, Italy After 1989'. *Studia UBB Sociologia*, 61 (2): 71–96.

Rotaru, Julieta. 2018. 'Mapping the Roma Communities in 19th Century Wallachia'. *Baltic Worlds*, 2–3: 34–50.

Rotaru, Julieta and David Gaunt. 2023. *The Wallachian Gold-Washers: Unlocking the Golden Past of the Rudari Woodworkers*. Brill, E-book (PDF).

Sacchi, Paola. 2010. '"Vivere insieme". Persistenze e metamorfosi dei legami di parentela sullo sponde del mediterraneo'. In *Scelte di famiglia. Tendenze della parentela nell'Italia contemporanea*, ed. Simonetta Grilli and Francesco Zanotelli, 65–77. Pisa: ETS.

Saletti Salza, Carlotta. 2009'Migrare nel tempo. Sulla migrazione delle comunità Rom romene a Torino'. *DiPAV Quaderni*, 24: 105–18.

———. 2010. *Evocare. Toccare i morti*. Rome: CISU.

Salih, Ruba. 2000. 'Moroccan Migrant Women: Transnationalism, Plurinationalism and Gender'. In *Here or There? Contrasting Experiences of Transnationalism: Moroccans and Senegalese in Italy*, ed. Ralph Grillo, Bruno Riccio and Ruba Salih, 655–71. University of Sussex, CDE.

———. 2008. 'Identità, modelli di consumo e costruzione di sé tra il Marocco e l'Italia'. In *Migrazioni transnazionali dall'Africa. Etnografie multi locali a confronto*, ed. Bruno Riccio. Turin: UTET.

Salo, Sheila. 2021. 'The Ludar of Huerfano County (Colorado)'. In *Boyash Studies: Researching 'Our People'*, ed. Annemarie Sorescu-Marinković, Thede Kahl and Biljana Sikimić, 425–42. Berlin: Frank & Timme Verlag für wissenschaftliche Literatur.

Salza, Alberto. 1997. *Atlante delle popolazioni*. Turin: UTET.

Sayad, Abdelmalek. 1999. *La double absence. Des illusions de l'émigré aux souffrances de l'immigré*. Paris: Seuil.

Schirripa, Pino. 2012. *Terapie religiose. Neoliberismo, cura, cittadinanza nel pentecostalismo contemporaneo*. Rome: CISU.

Șerban, Constantin. 1959. 'Contribuții la istoria meșteșugurilor din Țara Romîneasca. Țigani Rudari în secolele XVII–XVIII'. *Studii. Revista de Istorie*, 12 (2): 131–47.

Șerban, Stelu. 2007. 'Politics Against Ethnicity: The Case of Rudari from Varna District'. In *Transborder Identities: The Romanian-Speaking Population in Bulgaria*, ed. Stelu Șerban, 241–76. Bucharest: Paideia.

Sheller, Mimi and John Urry. 2006. 'The New Mobilities Paradigm', *Environment and Planning A*, 38: 207–26.

Sikimić, Biljana (ed.). 2005. *Banjaši na Balkanu. Identitet etničke zajednice*. Beograd: Balkanološki institut SANU.

Slavkova, Magdalena. 2010a. 'Challenging Boundaries: Contemporary Migratory Patterns of Bulgarian Rudari'. In *Balkan and Baltic States in United Europe: Histories, Religions and Cultures*, ed. E. Anastasova and M. Koiva, 188–97. Sofia: Paradigma.

———. 2010b. 'Schimbarea reprezentărilor despre viața emigranților: migrația la muncă a rudarilor din Bulgaria în țările mediteraneene'. In *Teme în antropologia socială din Europa de sud-est. Volum dedicate memoriei Profesorului Paul Stahl*, ed. Stelu Șerban, 283–308. București: Paideia.

———. 2017. 'Social Ties of Bulgarians and Rudari in the Mediterranean Countries', *Sator*, 18, *Balkan and Balticum: Current Studies in the Postsocialist Space*: 42–69.

————. 2019. Slavkova, M. 'Everyday Pentecostalism in a Rudari Family'. In *Boyash Studies: Researching 'Our People'*, ed. Annemarie Sorescu-Marinković, Thede Kahl and Biljana Sikimić, 161–78. Berlin: Frank & Timme Verlag für wissenschaftliche Literatur.

Solinas, Pier Giorgio. 1998. 'L'esogamia perfetta. Lo spazio genealogico dell'affinità'. In *Le ideologie della parentela e l'esogamia perfetta*, ed. Leonardo Piasere and Pier Giorgio Solinas. Rome: CISU.

Sorescu-Marinković, Annemarie. 2007. 'The Gurban Displaced: Bayash Guest Workers in Paris'. In *Kurban in the Balkans*, ed. Biljana Sikimić and Petko Hristov, 137–51. Belgrade: Institute for Balkan Studies.

————. 2008. 'The Boyash in Croatia: Romanian Vernaculars in Baranja and Medjimurje'. In *The Romance Balkans*, ed. Biljana Sikimić and Tijana Ašić, 173–225. Belgrade: Institute for Balkan Studies.

————. 2018. 'Rudarii și patrimoniul cultural imaterial'. In *Patrimoniu și patrimonializare*, ed. Elena Rodica Colta, 174–94. Bucharest: Editura Etnologică.

————. 2021. "What Language Do We Speak?" The Bayash in the Balkans and Mother Tongue Education'. In *The Romance-Speaking Balkans: Language and the Politics of Identity*, ed. Annemarie Sorescu-Marinković, Mihai Dragnea, Thede Kahl, Blagovest Njagulov, Donald L. Dyer and Angelo Costanzo, 207–32. Leiden-Boston: Brill.

Sorescu-Marinković, Annemarie, Thede Kahl, Biljana Sikimić. 2021. 'Boyash Studies: Towards a New Paradigm. Editors' Introduction'. In *Boyash Studies: Researching 'Our People'*, ed. Annemarie Sorescu-Marinković, Thede Kahl and Biljana Sikimić, 9–36. Berlin: Frank & Timme Verlag für wissenschaftliche Literatur.

Spittler, Russell P. 1988. 'Implicit Values in Pentecostal Missions'. *Missiology: An International Review*, 16 (4): 409–24.

Stahl, Paul-Henri. 1972. 'L'Habitation enterrée dans la région orientale du Danube (XIXe et XXe siècles)'. *L'Homme*, 12 (4): 37–61.

————. 1986. *Household, Village and Village Confederation in Southeastern Europe*. New York: Columbia University Press.

————. 1991. 'Tre insediamenti di Rudari in Romania'. *La ricerca folklorica*, 22: 55–66.

————. 1992. 'Les règles de vie des anciennes communautés villageoises', *Études et documents balkaniques et méditerranéens*, 16.

————. 2007. 'The Frontier That Separates. The Frontier That Brings Together. The Political Frontiers and Peasant Civilizations'. In *Transborder Identities: The Romanian-Speaking Population in Bulgaria*, ed. Stelu Șerban, 163–87. Bucharest: Paideia.

Taraki, L., ed., 2006. *Living Palestine: Family Survival, Resistance and Mobility under Occupation*. Syracuse: Syracuse University Press.

Teodorescu, Dominic. 2020. 'Homeownership, Mobility, and Home: A Relational Housing Study of Argentine Ludar and Romanian Rudari'. *Geoforum*, 116: 98–109.

Tesăr, Cătălina. 2016. 'Houses under Construction: Conspicous Consumption and the Values of the Youth among Romanian Cortorari Gypsies. In *Gypsy Economy: Romani Livelihoods and Notions of Worth in the 21st Century*, ed. Micol Brazzabeni, Manuela Ivone Cunha and Martin Fotta, 181–200. New York-London: Berghahn.

Țichindeleanu, Ovidiu. 2010. 'Towards a Critical Theory of Postcommunism'. *Radical Philosophy*, 159: 26–32.

Toma, Stefánia, Cătălina Tesăr and Fosztó Fosztó. 2017. 'Romanian Roma at Home: Mobility Patterns, Migration Experiences, Networks, and Remittances'. In *Open Borders, Unlocked Cultures: Romanian Roma Migrants in Western Europe*, ed. Yaron Matras and Daniele Viktor Leggio, 57–82. London: Routledge.

Tosi Cambini, Sabrina. 2010. *Luoghi e persone: Casa Luzzi*, research report, Fondazione Giovanni Michelucci.

———. 2015. 'Lo spazio del razzismo. Il trattamento del corpo (degli) *altri* nel governo della città'. In Gaia Giuliani (a cura di), *Il colore della nazione*, Milano: Le Monnier-Mondadori Education.

———. 2016. 'Par. 2. Ethnography in Florence' and 'Par. 3. Local Policies in Florence'. In *Report on the Follow up Survey, MigRom* project, University of Verona.

———. 2020. 'Acasă, în România: Ongoing Housing Improvement in Homeland'. *Visual Ethnography, Dwelling. An Ethnographic Approach* 9 (2): 93–123.

———. 2021. *Altri confini. Storia, mobilità e migrazioni di una rete di famiglie* rudari *tra la Romania e l'Italia*. Milano: Mimesis.

Tosi Cambini, Sabrina and Giuseppe Beluschi Fabeni, eds. 2017. 'Thematic Section. Antiziganisms: Ethnographic Engagements in European Cities'. *ANUAC*, 6 (1): 99–232.

Vaccaro, Salvo. 2002. 'Introduzione'. In Michel Foucault, *Spazi Altri. I luoghi delle eterotopie*, ed. Salvo Vaccaro, Milan: Mimesis.

Vietti, Francesco. 2019. *Il Paese delle badandi*, 2nd edn. Milan: Meltemi.

Williams, Patrick. 1984. *Mariage tsigane. Une cérémonie de fiançailles chez les Rom de Paris*. Paris: L'Harmattan and SELAF.

———. 2011. 'Une ethnologie des Tsiganes est-elle possible?' [En ligne], 197, http://journals.openedition.org/.

West, Harry G. and Parvathi Raman, eds. 2009. *Enduring Socialism: Explorations of Revolution and Transformation, Restoration and Continuation*. New York-London: Berghahn.

INDEX

wood itinerancy, 21
woodlands/woods, 17, 24, 38–39, 40,
    42–43, 51, 57, 77, 106
wood workers, 19, 23, 50–51, 165
woodworking, 23, 51, 63, 90
work, 141, 148–60, *149, 150*
    badante, 148, 153, 156, 157, 160n1
    gender and, 151–53
    for men, 158
    non-formal, 159
    occupational status, 142–48

private agencies, 102–3
undeclared, 148
VAT number, 148, 149
by women, 152–53, 155–56, 159–60
work-economic opportunities, 32
World War I, 16, 22
World War II, 17, 32, 65, 163

Y
Yugoslavia, xiii

Milton Keynes UK
Ingram Content Group UK Ltd.
UKHW022252151123
432643UK00006B/119